The Environmental Impact of
Later Mesolithic Cultures

The Environmental Impact of Later Mesolithic Cultures

The Creation of
Moorland Landscape
in England and Wales

I. G. Simmons

EDINBURGH UNIVERSITY PRESS
for the University of Durham

© I. G. Simmons, 1996

Edinburgh University Press
22 George Square, Edinburgh

Typeset in Palatino
by Bibliocraft, Dundee, and
printed and bound in Great Britain
by Redwood Books, Trowbridge, Wiltshire

A CIP record for this book is available from the British Library

ISBN 0 7486 0842 7

Contents

List of Tables

List of Figures

List of Plates

Preface

Ever since I sat with Geoffrey Dimbleby in his room in Oxford in 1960 and he said that it looked as if there was good evidence of Mesolithic forest clearance in the pollen diagram from Dartmoor that I was showing him, I have been interested in the possible impacts of these last hunter-gatherers in Britain. The fascination of those uplands which were to become moorlands, and of the relations between those people, their scanty remains and the environments in which they lived, has remained and has provided a focus for empirical research over these years, although I have to admit to being distracted by other matters from time to time.

This book tries to pull together in one framework all the work for which I have been responsible (mostly on Dartmoor and the North York Moors, but also on Bodmin Moor and parts of the northern Pennines), and tries to expand upon those parts which I think have been undervalued (for example, Squires on Upper Teesdale) or which have not been published, like Dr Ann GreatRex's pollen diagrams from Malham. But all of this is set in the context of an immense amount of published and thesis work by other people over perhaps forty years. Some of this was undertaken for other purposes, and other investigations would not now measure up to the standards currently set (I include my own early papers in that category); but I have tried to use whatever is available without stretching its findings too far. The palaeoecological data are then used to model the environmental relations of the later Mesolithic, using a variety of analogical material gathered from an eclectic set of sources. The object in all this is to tell one story which can then be taken on by others: I regard this as my last substantive contribution to the upland Mesolithic.

Over all these years, I have incurred debts to many people and organisations. Without Geoffrey Dimbleby's encouragement, I doubt that I would have had the courage to say out loud 'this is probably Mesolithic', since that was not then a very utterable thing in certain quarters. Later, I was also given a boost by discussions under the auspices of Harry Godwin at Cambridge. Behind this was the tolerance of Frank Oldfield in teaching me pollen analysis and the guidance of Palmer Newbould in teaching me some ecology. The University of Durham has been a generous provider of time and equipment; more than that, my department has been an excellent place in which to work, with colleagues who have been both stimulating and enjoyable individuals with whom to work. Our teams of technicians and cartographers have always been great assets, and the quality of the latter is especially obvious in the linework in this book. In other departments, Brian Huntley (Biological Sciences) and Bob Layton (Anthropology) have always been generous of their time and knowledge. The University of Bristol was in 1977–81 a very good base from which to validate some of the early Dartmoor work (I find it curious that people will still cite the 1960s papers but ignore the much better 1983 paper which showed that I was basically right) and to look, if only frustratingly, at Bodmin Moor. Many people provided sources of stimulus and assistance, as research students and research assistants, and I am grateful to all of them. More than anybody else, much of the hard work on the North York Moors sites was done by Jim Innes, whose dedication to the long hours of palaeoecological grind is unsurpassed by anybody I have ever known. Our many joint papers reflect his involvement in that phase of the work. Later discussion with Peter Rowley-Conwy and Tim Schadla-Hall has always been fruitful, as has been that with Paul Mellars.

Finance has been provided from time to time by a number of bodies. The NERC gave a grant for work on the North York Moors in the 1960s, as did the University of Durham in the 1980s. The SBAC of SERC underwrote work on Dartmoor, Bodmin and the Pennines; the North York Moors National Park Planning Committee has helped with radiocarbon dating; various bodies have awarded research students sufficient grants to keep them going through Ph.D. research.

For discussion of the work at various stages, the list of people seems endless; but let me single out two of them. At Durham, Judy Turner has been not only a co-worker but always a source of new ideas, penetrative thinking and above all intellectual generosity. The 1993 paper of which she is the senior author sets, to my mind, new standards of interpretation of complex palaeoecological databases, and much of the credit for it is hers. In North Yorkshire generally, I always benefited enormously from going into the field with the late Don Spratt; I know that I am not the only person who in that context misses his knowledge, his commitment and his sense of enjoyment in what we were doing.

University staff these days need, above all, time to write up work at this length. This book was facilitated by the award in 1992–3 of a Sir James Knott fellowship by the University of Durham, which gave me a year free of teaching and administration and thus allowed me to gather in all the material I have used; both then and in 1996, the library of the Society of Antiquaries of London has been a valuable resource. The publication of the book has been made possible by the Publications Board of the University of Durham in association with the publishers, and I am very grateful to the Board for their support. The attention paid to the production process by Edinburgh University Press has been absolutely exemplary in its thoroughness.

I suppose that my whole academic career has been set against the study of human-caused changes in the natural environment. What this book shows is that such changes have a very long history indeed, and that change is a normal accompaniment of the human condition. This affords no comfort to ultra-greens who would find in hunter-gatherers some kind of Golden Age, even an Eden. Neither does it remove from us today the challenge of constructing creative rather than destructive relations with the non-human world. The way to do that is probably through greater understanding of the social knowledge that we have of our world; but inputs from science are never irrelevant, since we are products of our past. I hope that, over these nearly forty years, I have contributed to that necessary history.

I. G. Simmons
Durham, February 1996

Note on Dating

When gathering together work from the last forty-odd years, it is very frustrating to read the results of radiocarbon dating only in 'calibrated' form, when of course that particular calibration has long since been consigned to the historic past of that technique. Therefore, all radiocarbon dates in this book are expressed in conventional radiocarbon years BP. The laboratory numbers will be found in the original sources as cited, but I have deliberately avoided fragmenting the text still further with them; the few who will find this a problem will, I hope, be outweighed by the many who will not need such detail in a synthesis of this kind.

List of Abbreviations and Symbols

The abbreviations in this list are used extensively in the text, tables and figures; other abbreviations are explained as they occur, or are inferable from the context of the discussion.

~	approximately
Σ	total
AP	tree (arboreal) pollen
ASL	above sea level
BAT	Boreal–Atlantic Transition
BM	Bodmin Moor
CHE	Cheviots
CP	Central Pennines
EW	England and Wales
Fl	Flandrian. Fl I = 10,250–7500 BP; Fl II = 7500–5000 BP; Fl III = 5000 BP to present
kya	thousand years ago
LA	large charcoal
LM	logistical mobility
LP	land pollen
MI	microscopic charcoal
MT	Malham Tarn
NAP	non-arboreal pollen
NG	North Gill
NNR	National Nature Reserve
NP	North Pennines
NW	North Wales
NYM	North York Moors
OD	Ordnance Datum
PAZ	pollen assemblage zone
RM	residential mobility
SM	small charcoal
SM	Soyland Moor
SP	South Pennines

SP	shrub pollen
spp	species
SW	South Wales
TM	Tarn Moss
WFF	Waun Fignen Felen
yr^{-1}	per year

CHAPTER ONE

Environment and Archaeology in the Uplands

The moorlands of upland Britain exert an endless fascination. They present a wildness which is unexpected in so densely-settled a country with so few extremes of climate or topography. Hence, the scientists have long wondered about their special features of geology, landform and ecology; the poets and novelists have explored their influence upon individuals and communities. Rural economists wonder what is to become of them, and the National Farmers' Union threatens a return to wilderness if sheep-rearing is not subsidised. All acknowledge that human activity today is a powerful influence on ecology and landscape, yet there is often an underlying assumption that the basic lineaments of the landscape in terms of its openness, treelessness except for recent planting, and partial coverage with peat, are of natural origin. The environmental historian and the ecological historian have a rather different story to tell, and this book represents a detailed investigation of just one episode in the post-glacial history of the uplands; it looks at the extent to which the last hunter-gatherers present in these upland regions may have influenced the development of those elements of landscape which now so powerfully characterise 'the moorlands'.

The main purpose of this chapter is to set the scene for the reviews in the later chapters. The regions to be considered are given, along with some background in terms of physical geography; and the limits of the time period considered and its internal chronology are given, as are some of the changes in climate, vegetation and human culture which are relevant strands in the story which will eventually be woven together.

1. THE MOORLANDS OF ENGLAND AND WALES

This book's focus is upon early prehistoric human–environment relations in those uplands of England and Wales which have become moorlands. Uplands which are obviously mountainous, such as the Lake District and Snowdonia, are omitted as parts of

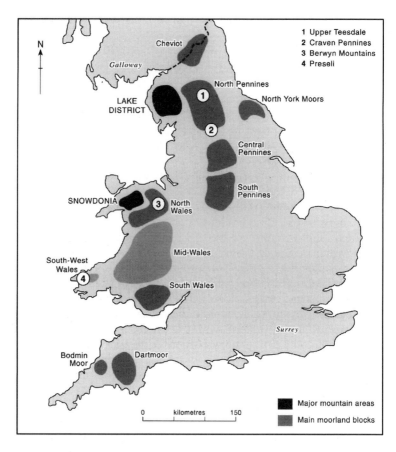

Figure 1.1   Location map showing the major areas discussed in
the text. Note that the mountain areas (Lake District
and Snowdonia) are not part of the discussion; neither
is Scotland, though there are some comparative
references to Galloway.

the main history, as are the lower ground of the South and North
Downs, the Cotswolds and the Chilterns, for example. Hence
the uplands of south-west England, of south and central Wales,
the Pennines from Cheviot to Peak, and the North York Moors
provide the core of the material. No attempt is made to describe
the history of each region in turn: the examination is thematic
rather than area-by-area. Material from southern Scotland is
introduced occasionally, but that from the Highlands is generally
reckoned to originate in too different a set of circumstances to be

germane, as is that from Ireland. Figure 1.1 specifies those areas whose evidence has contributed most to the discussion herein. In Chapter 2 in particular, there is an emphasis on the author's own studies (carried out jointly with, especially, J. B. Innes and J. Turner) on the North York Moors, since these, together with the investigations of A. G. Smith in South Wales and J. H. Tallis in the Pennines, form the most detailed palaeoecological data-sets available. Other studies are, however, used when appropriate, including some unpublished material from theses.

The common denominator of these uplands is that of moorland landscape today. In such regions, the areas are mostly over 300 m, and are characterised by flat or gently sloping interfluves. The presence of steep-sided valleys is common but not ubiquitous. The vegetation is described below, and, except where recent afforestation has taken place, it is low and treeless (see Plate 1). A major point to make now is that the public perception of this state is that of 'natural beauty', with the inference that it was basically the upland climate which had produced the lack of trees. One aim of this discussion will be to reinforce the newer perception that most if not all these areas were covered with trees at some stage during the post-glacial period, and that human societies were implicated in some phases of the removal (Atherden 1992). One of the tasks of this book will be to look for the origins of the recession of forest and to weigh up the relative roles of natural forces and those of human societies.

In England and Wales, a number of rock types have proved sufficiently resistant to erosion to form the basis of upland terrains; these are summarised in Table 1.1. Their ages are not strictly relevant to this book, but it may be noted that the youngest are of Jurassic age (North York Moors) and the oldest Ordovician (parts of Wales). More germane is the variety of lithologies, for while some of these strata are of limestone and thus predispose to soils with a high base status (e.g. the Carboniferous Limestones of the Pennines), others are highly siliceous and easily develop soils with a tendency to acidity. The granites of the south-west peninsula are of this type.

The lithology of any of these rocks might, however, have been affected by the glaciations of the Pleistocene. Among a number of glaciations of the British Isles, there have been two major episodes. In the Wolstonian (~250–165 kya), most of upland Britain was subjected to glaciation, though the highest areas may have been sufficiently upstanding to divert ice-flow round them. In the context of this book, only the south-west peninsula was

Plate 1   The landscape of Dartmoor. The only woodland is from recent
          planting (on hill in distance) and the rest of the landscape is a mixture of
          bracken, grasses and open moor. The skyline is broken by granite tors
          but has the characteristic low slopes upon which peat can accumulate.

outside the ice limit. The Devensian glaciation was at its height
at 18 kya, and the southern limits stretched from East Anglia to
South Wales. Parts of the Pennines and the North York Moors
projected above this ice sheet, and again the south-west uplands
were not directly affected. Around 10,000 BP, there was a further
cold period which resulted in some valley glaciations and ice-cap
formations in mountainous areas of Britain. The landforms of the
moorlands were affected in three main ways by such episodes:

- The formation of erosional features such as corries (not as
  spectacular in e.g. the Brecon Beacons as in Snowdonia,
  but present nevertheless) and over-deepened valleys,
  incised glacial meltwater channels and other sub-glacial
  drainage features.

TABLE 1.1 Rock types of moorland England and Wales.

Period	Region	Lithology	Summit heights (metres)
Jurassic	North York Moors	Limestones, Sandstones, Shales,	454
Carboniferous	Dartmoor and Bodmin	Granite	619 (DM) 572 (BM)
	Pennines, South Wales	Whin Sill, Coal Measures, Millstone Grit, Yoredales, Carboniferous Limestones	893 (NP) 724 (CP) 637 (SP)
Devonian	Cheviot	Granite	816
	South Wales	Red Sandstone	886
Silurian	Wales	Shales and Volcanics	705 (CW)
Ordovician	Wales	Slates, Shales, Volcanics	811

Regional abbreviations: BM = Bodmin Moor; DM = Dartmoor; SW = South Wales; CW = Central Wales; NW = North Wales; SP = South Pennines; CP = Central Pennines; NP = North Pennines; NYM = North York Moors. For locations, see Figure 1.1.

- The deposition of material picked up by ice as many kinds of valley deposit, like moraines, kames and outwash fans. Lakes were formed which may have been temporary or which (as in kettle-holes) persisted through into the Holocene, filling up only slowly.
- There was periglacial activity marginal to the ice, resulting in solifluction on slopes and the formation of patterned ground. In limestone areas, drainage may have been on the surface at these times, since the rocks were subject to permafrost.

Hence, any of the rock types in Table 1.1 may be obscured by deposits of glacial or periglacial origin: the more basic types may be plastered with patches of till of a lower nutrient content; equally, the most siliceous areas may be diversified with sheets of drift which locally provide more fertile soils. The outcome of these interactions, together with 10,000 years of post-glacial weathering, is a fairly standard type of upland topography. There are flat summits with accordant high points; long interfluves with large areas of slow slope are common, as are sudden breaks of slope falling to steep valley sides with broad dales. Interruptions may be caused by volcanic intrusions like the Whin Sill in Upper Teesdale, and the south-western granites have their special boulder-strewn slopes or 'clitter'. Granites and sandstones alike form tors. Transitions between moorland regions and the surrounding lowlands are of interest: the North York Moors present both a steep scarp on the north and west, and an almost imperceptible (to the motorist at any rate) slope up from the Vale of Pickering. The Black Mountains seem almost like an island surrounded by lower terrain, as does Mynydd Preseli.

The diversity of soil types reflects the variety of combinations of substrate, slope, climate and vegetation. The very thickness of the soil profile may vary from the few centimetres of organic material and quartz overlying Carboniferous Limestone, which may easily be washed into the joints of the rock leaving a bare pavement, to a metre or more of colluvial material washed down a valley side to become the basis of a deep brown earth profile. Under woodland and on gentle to moderate slopes with grassland at the present day, brown earths (acid or calcareous according to subsoil type) are the commonest soil type, and it may be presumed that all these were once woodland soils. Underneath most types of moorland vegetation there are now podsolic soils, and these may be gleyed where the drainage is slow. Where water accumulated in the past, and on the high area of low slope, peat has accumulated. Much of the blanket peat in watershedding sites at high altitudes started to grow in the mid-Holocene, and its history will be considered in more detail later. Although the present diversity of soil types is a valuable ecological indicator, it must be recalled that soils and vegetation form an interactive system, and if the vegetation has been different in the past then the soil too may have possessed different characteristics. The fossil soils beneath Bronze Age barrows on moorlands, which often suggest the former presence of brown earths in a zone now dominated by podsols, are a clue to such dynamic processes. So, care is needed when retrodicting soil types back to the mid-Flandrian.

Clearly, today's vegetation can only be an imperfect guide to past conditions. Some areas of ancient woodland exist in upland valleys, but they are probably not very like their prehistoric forebears (Rodwell 1991a). Their isolation makes them more open to the weather, for example. It seems likely, too, that many if not all of them were heavily managed during historic times, for fuel or bark for instance. This may account for single-species stands, such as the Pennine ash-woods or the Dartmoor oak copses, in places where it is known that the prehistoric woods consisted of mixed stands. The non-woody vegetation has also been subject to recent use practices which have changed its composition: shifts from cattle to sheep by moorland graziers, or the moorburn procedures that accompany grouse-moor management, have produced species' dominance configurations which are of quite recent date. The normally unwanted spread of bracken on so many hillsides is also quite recent.

All these patterns have developed within the framework of the highly seasonal climate of upland Britain. Where this varies from the lowlands is in features such as an altitudinal lapse rate for temperature of about 1°C for every 150 m above sea level: British lapse rates are among the steepest in the world. One result is a plant growing season that decreases by about 13 days for every 100 metres gained in elevation. In winter, the main temperature gradient is from west to east, whereas in summer it is north to south. The winter gradient is echoed in the rainfall, so that a valley in mid-Wales may average 1130 mm yr^{-1} whereas only the highest part of the North York Moors receive over 1000 mm yr^{-1}. Eastern slopes generally have a rainshadow effect. Most of the rain is precipitated as air rises over high ground, and so totals rise with altitude. Snow is commonest in the north and east of Britain, with the Cheviots topping the moorland league at 30–40 days yr^{-1} of snow and sleet; the south-western uplands rarely exceed 10 days. Climate, though, consists of extremes as well as averages. For example, heavy rainfall may often precipitate flooding in river valleys (Exmoor in 1952 for instance); long periods of drought dry out peat and vegetation alike, rendering them vulnerable to fire, as on Glaisdale Moor (NYM) in 1976. These events must however be seen in the context of today's land use and cover: neither would have been so severe in a largely forested landscape. But a period of low temperatures might well have affected the ecology by preventing the flowering of a species of tree, or a high one encouraged the immigration of a new parasite. In either case, the effect is likely to be lagged, as would have been the case with vegetational response to climatic change, though less so that of insects.

Though the basic lineaments of the physical geography of the moorlands show much continuity between past and present in the last 10,000 years, what you see is in many respects not what you got. Climate has changed, the biota have changed, the soils have undergone some degree of transformation, and many slope profiles have altered quite sharply. Stream courses on the uplands have altered as peat blankets grew and were eroded, and stream regimes and alluviation have altered with the density of vegetation cover. So, use of all available palaeoecological data is necessary (as well as a critical imagination) in thinking about the landscapes during prehistory.

2. CHRONOLOGICAL AND ENVIRONMENTAL CONTEXT OF THIS BOOK

This section will deal with the climatic history of the post-glacial period in Britain, and then go on to discuss the types of vegetation which came to occupy the uplands. Because some of them (e.g. Exmoor and the North York Moors) abut the sea, and none is far from it, the coastline of the post-glacial period will also be considered.

Chronological Context

It is generally accepted that Palaeolithic cultures were super-seded in the British Isles by those of Mesolithic type at roughly the same time as the final disappearance of the ice. That is, the transition from the period of late-glacial climate and ecology to that of post-glacial also saw the replacement of Palaeolithic cultures by those labelled Mesolithic. The horizon of 10,000 yr BP will be accurate enough for this present purpose, although it is scarcely possible to imagine that the change was sudden. In biostratigraphic terminology, the change is from the Devensian (in older sources sometimes called Late-glacial) to the Flandrian (an accepted term for the Post-glacial; Holocene will also be commonly found in the literature). The end of the Mesolithic came with the introduction and adoption of agriculture, which, as E. Williams (1989) has demonstrated, is diachronic within the British Isles but appears to hinge around 5300–5200 BP on the mainland (Rowley-Conwy 1995). So, within the years 10,000–5000 BP, the British Isles were occupied by these cultures designated as Mesolithic. Neither culture nor environment was unchanging in this time: the main cultural division of the Mesolithic is

TABLE 1.2 Lithics and chronology of the British Mesolithic.

Period	Lithics	Dates BP	Cal 2.BC
Upper Palaeolithic	Bone and antler barbed points; points on stone blades	> 10,000	9260, 9230, 9160 1σ = 9785 (9260, 9230, 9160) 9053
early Mesolithic	Bone and antler barbed points; broad-blade microliths	10,000 to 8600	7570 1σ = 7691 (7570) 7534
later Mesolithic	Narrow-blade microliths, often geometric	8600 to 5000	3782 1σ = 3905 (3782) 3708

The lithics are highly simplified. Calibration is of a nominal date for each horizon, with an assumed standard error of ±100, 75 and 50 years on the three dates. See also P. A. Mellars (1990).

between an 'Early' phase (9700–9000 BP) with broad-bladed microliths and a 'Late' phase (8800–5200 BP) with narrow-bladed microliths. Table 1.2 sets out the major elements of these terminologies. Culture, lithics and chronology are all clearly set out in Christopher Smith's (1992a) textbook on the Mesolithic of the British Isles.

Environmental Context

The Late Devensian's last two phases form the precursors of Mesolithic time. Between 13,000 and 11,000 BP, the climate was warm, with temperatures reaching an average of 18°C in the English summer and allowing the development of pine-birch woodland. Towards the end of this warm interlude (termed the Windermere Interstadial), Britain and Ireland became separated. The final kick of the Pleistocene came with a return to colder conditions between 11,000 and 10,000 BP with the Loch Lomond stadial, which allowed the regrowth of an ice-field in the western Highlands of Scotland, with smaller glaciers in the eastern and northern Highlands, some of the Hebrides, the Southern Uplands, the Lake District, the uplands of both North and South Wales and some hills in Ireland. This period was however the last one in which glaciers appeared in the British Isles, and all traces of glacier ice seem to have vanished from these islands by 10,000 BP.

POST-GLACIAL CLIMATE

The succeeding period is often described as post-glacial and indeed may be *a* post glacial period, though it is not inevitable that it should be *the* Post-glacial. With it, Palaeolithic cultures were replaced by those called the Mesolithic, and these have occupied the first two sub-stages of the biostratigraphic divisions of the post-glacial or Holocene, which are called the Flandrian. The broad changes have been outlined in many books and monographs, such as Bell and Walker (1992), Roberts (1989) and Taylor (1975). Environmentally, there was a rapid warming rate over the first 1000 years from 10,000 BP of perhaps 1°C per century, and by 9500 BP temperatures similar to those of the present day were achieved. Evidence from the Greenland ice-cores suggests that some of the major warming took place within decades rather than centuries. By 8500 BP, the first elements of the deciduous forest biome had entered Britain and started the build-up that was complete by 7000 BP. From 8800–4500 BP, a Hypsithermal Interval or 'climatic optimum' can be recognised in which average annual temperatures were 1–2°C above the present; until ~7000 BP, rainfall was possibly 90 per cent of present but 110 per cent thereafter. Rising sea-levels in the present North Sea basin meant that the Dogger Bank was submerged about 7500 BP and the southern North Sea formed by 6500 BP. After then, the rate of rise of sea-level slowed up. After 5000 BP, some climatic deterioration towards cooler and wetter conditions set in. Short-term variations would no doubt have included very wet years with possibly 50 per cent additional precipitation above average, which would have produced flood hazards even in a forested landscape. As more detailed work on climatic history emerges, it seems likely that any picture of smooth changes between one climatic regime and another will be replaced by one in which there are many pauses and small-scale retreats. As yet, the effects which these had on human communities are not known.

For the uplands, Taylor (1975) provided a set of corrected curves based on an altitude of 500 m. The calibrations of radiocarbon dates adopted there have now been superseded, but the overall estimates are still useful. Average temperatures at 10,000 BP are of the order of –2.5°C but by 8000 BP rise to 4°C, with a slightly later maximum of 8°C. During the period of optimal climate, summer air temperatures for the lowlands were of the order of 17.5°C and in the uplands 15.5°C. Today's figure for the upland summer would be 13.5°C. Lapse rates would ensure that even in periods of better climate, an altitude of 500 m would have a growing season some 65 days shorter than at sea-level in the same latitude.

Careful interpretation of pollen diagrams, the dating of large collections of sub-fossil tree stumps and the measurement of stable isotopes are beginning to reveal some finer detail. For example, Tallis and Switsur (1990) may be able to detect in the South Pennines a climatic reversion at 5300–4000 BP which has a continental equivalent in the so-called Pioria Oscillation, with a recovery of forest and scrub after 4700 BP, though they acknowledge the difficulty of sorting out the climatic and the human-induced by that time. In the Scottish Highlands, with implications further south, workers have recognised that tree-lines may prove to be sensitive indicators of minor climatic variations and have looked in detail at the remains of pine (Lowe 1991). Together with work on the stable isotopes of hydrogen (Dubois and Ferguson 1985; Bridge et al. 1990), a picture can be constructed of 'pluvial' periods of higher than normal rainfall, followed by low frequencies of pine macrofossils (using stumps in peat as sources of evidence) in a lagged fashion. The radiocarbon years 7500, 6250–5800, 4250–3870 and 3300 have so far been suggested as wetter periods. Extension of such work to other uplands is highly desirable.

In passing, the effect of forest cover upon regional climate should be noted. The interception of rainfall and of insolation would have reduced heat and moisture at ground level; exposure to wind would have been ameliorated, especially in summer. Replacement by peat means the emplacement of a habitat with a very low heat conductivity, so that even a thin peat cover to a soil means, its growth season is reduced beyond the 'normal' local level and starts later: any early farmers seeking to use peaty-topped soils would likely experience a higher crop failure rate than those using the remains of forest humus, imported leaf litter or manure from stalled or corralled animals.

VEGETATION CHANGE

Thus the early Mesolithic was set against a period of rapid change of climate and vegetation, and saw especially the change from tundra through open woodland to the establishment of the deciduous forest, at any rate in the lowlands. The later Mesolithic took place in an overall environment of greater stability of major vegetation type, the best climate so far achieved in the last 20,000 years, and witnessed the final insulation of Britain from the European mainland. The continental matrix of forest types within which the British upland woods developed is described by Jahn (1991).

Forests

A universal finding of palaeoecology is that the climatic amelioration of the Flandrian period allowed the expansion of deciduous forests into EW. These formed the major ecosystem type of the lowlands and extended far into the uplands as well. The assembly of the forests has two main phases in the years 10,000–5000 BP. The first of these is the immigration of forest trees tolerant of relatively cold conditions and their colonisation of formerly open-tundra-like habitats. The second is the arrival of more warmth-demanding (thermophilous) tree species and the ways in which they compete with the existing species and form a woodland with a different species composition. This forest was in many respects a stable ecosystem except at its margins; that is, natural disturbances led to further deciduous forest, though not necessarily of exactly the same composition. Further, small changes of climate continued to shift the balance in favour of some species at the expense of others. So, Flandrian I is seen in the British Isles as a period of rapid change of vegetation type, Flandrian II of a slow change of composition.

The forests in the uplands were not all simply thinner variants of their lowland neighbours. A compilation from some of the sources which comment especially on upland forests in Flandrian I and II is given in Table 1.3. Close reading of the table and its sources suggest a number of points to be made about this 5000-year period. The first is that it is an exception to find an upland which was not substantially covered with closed-canopy woodland at some point before 5000 BP: Bodmin Moor stands out in this respect, with two investigations at Dozmary Pool reaching similar conclusions. Second, the idea of a Flandrian 'wildwood' which represents some form of mid-post-glacial climatic equilibrium is almost certainly mistaken. Adjustment to changes in climate on both glacial/interglacial and secular scales, transformation of soils under differing water and vegetation regimes, and inter-specific competition all brought about a vegetation characterised by 'patch dynamics' (*sensu* Pickett and White 1985) rather than an urge to follow predictable successions to a single climax of mixed oak woodland. A third feature is the importance of the hazel (*Corylus avellana*), which features strongly in the transitional woodlands of Fl I and in the slower-changing forests of Fl II. Its role is such that the uplands can be characterised during Fl II as belonging to a kind of oak-hazel province on a European scale (Huntley 1988), rather than the oak-lime province of the lowlands. Its ability to grow on a variety of soils (save perhaps gleys and podsols, though it will grow on free-draining acid soils) and to adapt to being a shaded shrub in closed-canopy forest, as well as forming the dominant at the forest edge and beyond, ensured for it the occupance of a variety of terrain. Several studies show that it was the woodland species which formed the upper edge of woody growth, even if in the form of a scrub. There are some hints of limitations to its growth in the Northern Pennines, where Turner and Hodgson (1979, 1983) detect lower proportions of its pollen along a north-easterly gradient of sites.

Another general point that emerges is the importance of soil type in determining the mix of successful tree species. This is shown especially in the Northern Pennines and in Craven (Bartley et al. 1990). It comes out in an extreme form in Upper Teesdale (Turner et al. 1973), where the crumbly Sugar Limestone (baked by contact with hot basalt) formed a substrate for pine when that species had been competed out from most other habitats; in a roughly similar fashion, limestone scars in Craven probably bore yew trees (Piggott and Piggott 1963). Limestone cliffs are one case of a more general category of openings in forest brought about by geomorphic processes. Steep and shifting slopes such as screes and landslides, and undercut river cliffs, are for instance unlikely to be stable enough to bear woodland. Mires and lakes are obviously unsuited for tree roots, though at the edge of both there may be trees, and both may dry out at the margins and become colonised by woody species. River channels themselves need to run in the same course without catastrophic floods for long periods if they are not to retain sub-woodland vegetation in which perhaps willows are the largest element.

Biotic factors are also at work creating gaps in forests. Senescence leads to trees falling over entire or to snapping off above the base of the trunk; windthrow may produce the same effect. In deciduous forests of North America, the magnitudes involved in studies of the Appalachians suggested that such gaps ranged from 8 to 1320 m^2 in area; that they may open 41–82 m^2ha^{-2} of the canopy per year (i.e. 0.4–0.8 per cent), with a resulting canopy turnover time of 100 to 278 years (Barden 1981; Collins and Pickett 1988). The role of these openings will need to be examined again in the context of human activity of the Mesolithic period.

TABLE 1.3 Woodlands during the Flandrian in the uplands.

Upland	Flandrian I	Flandrian II composition	Flandrian II physiognomy	Sources
Bodmin Moor	Early presence of oak (9050 BP). Birch and oak first, then elm-oak-birch (8229 BP) to which alder is added (6451 BP)	< 30% AP at DMP; oak dominant but hazel abundant: hazel scrub at DMP, oak only on hillsides	Scattered woodland at most	Brown 1977
Dartmoor	oak wood predates hazel rise (8250 BP); pine declines	Forest still climbing – oak with some elm. Hazel dominant at 490 m	Closed forest to 457 m	Caseldine and Maguire 1986
South Wales	Late alder rise mid-Glamorgan	WFF: hazel dominant but all trees present by 8000 BP except alder (7000 BP)	Well wooded at 530 m	A. G. Smith and Cloutman 1988; Chambers 1982a
Mid-Wales	Prolonged birch phase with low pine at 395 m. Birch taken over by pine and oak	Pine dominant locally, as is oak. Hazel very frequent in early Fl II, but oak and alder then more successful; low lime		Taylor 1980

TABLE 1.3 *Continued*

Southern Pennines	Birch-hazel-willow maximum by 7000. Mosaic of pine, birch, hazel in valleys	Pine disappears often, oak a replacement along with alder, ash and lime. Birch, oak and hazel in Nidderdale at 350 m	Forest not continuous above 400 m	Tinsley 1975; Tallis and Switsur 1990
Craven Pennines (Central Pennines)	Pine-hazel then elm. Tree spread dependent on soils. Alder rises at expense of pine	Alder-oak-elm dominant; some ash, lime. Yew on scars? Pine on limestone	Open: cliffs, screes, springs and flushes	Bartley et al. 1990; Piggott and Piggott 1963
Northern Pennines	Pine-birch-hazel; then oak with wide range; hazel has less penetration towards NE	Elm and hazel more at higher elevations in west; soils and elevation affect forest composition – alder lower down; pine on e.g. sugar limestone in Teesdale	Openings or low treeline permit Teesdale flora to survive	J. Turner et al. 1973; J. Turner and Hodgson 1979, 1983
North York Moors	Pine-hazel then oak-alder	Pine hazel wood above oak-hazel-alder forest	Pine-hazel probably open	Simmons, Cundill and Jones 1979; Simmons and Innes 1988a

Animal populations, too, can affect forest dynamics: a succession of poor mast years may mean that every acorn is eaten by herbivores and so regeneration to forest containing oaks is delayed; in hard winters, ungulates will eat tree bark and so effectively ring-bark individual trees. Any opening where herbivores concentrate is likely to be slow in regenerating woodland because the animals will feed selectively on young shoots. A last biological influence in mid-Flandrian forests is that of the beaver, *Castor fiber*. It is a doughty feller of small trees (especially aspen, *Populus* spp) and a dammer of streams, resulting in open areas of water within the forest with a fringe of dead trees where the water-table has been raised. Coles and Orme (1983) make a strong case for beaver being the cause of some of the forest recessions detected in pollen diagrams from Flandrian II, and this possibility will also need evaluation later.

Thus any image remaining from the earlier days of ecological theory of a more or less inert blanket of forest stretching unbroken from coast to coast must be dissolved. The 'wildwood' was in a constant state of change, though to any two or three human generations in Fl II these would have seemed relatively small scale and in overall terms predictable; in the earlier phase, however, the rate of change would have been rather faster and the directions of change, even if obvious, full of uncertainly. But one continuity is worth mentioning: that the current distinction in the landscape between upland and lowland which is so often defined by the limit of enclosure would have had no equivalent in the forests. Altitudinal zonations were undoubtedly present, culminating in some places in an upper forest limit; but the main forest type at say 400 m would have extended downwards to sea-level, so that the ecology of the uplands (though not exempt from physical processes such as the temperature lapse rate and orographic rainfall totals) is less distinct an entity than it now appears to be. The sea was the more obvious and important ecotone.

The Height of the Tree-Line

Just as visitors find it difficult to understand why our uplands are not tree-clad, native Britons find it hard to think of their uplands as being covered with deciduous forest, and the more aware of them ask: were they totally covered or were there areas bare of trees? This question has special pertinence here, since during the Mesolithic period the tree-line would be at its highest because that period also encompasses the Hypsithermal interval or Climatic Optimum of the Holocene. Maximum summer warmth in the uplands was probably in the years 9000–8000 BP. Given that plant growth tends to lag behind climatic changes, the period 8000–7000 BP was likely to have seen the maximum extent of tree cover in the uplands. This 2000-year period has been reviewed by H. J. B. Birks (1988), whose map of the percentage cover at the forest maximum is reproduced as Figure 1.2. Here, Bodmin Moor, the North York Moors and a part of the Pennines are rated by him at 100 per cent, but the other uplands of England and Wales fall below that maximum, with the mountains of North Wales achieving only an indeterminate '>59' per cent. Scotland, not surprisingly, nowhere exceeds 65 per cent, though the 54 per cent for Galloway seems exceptionally low. These data are in places estimates from macrofossils but in others are from pollen percentages, which are difficult to interpret in the context of open vegetation in exposed areas. The presence of tree remains in peat is the most definitive indicator of previous presence, but their absence is not a definite demonstration that the trees were never there, since deposits to preserve them from the mid-Holocene may well be absent. The complex relations between tree growth and death, peat growth and the preservation of Flandrian tree remains on the uplands are discussed by Tallis and Switsur (1983) and in a pan-European context by Holtmeier (1993).

For England and Wales, Birks' data are amplified by later work which is summarised as Table 1.4. For Bodmin Moor, Brown (1977) in fact thinks that there was only birch-hazel scrub at 265 m, a conclusion confirmed by the later work at the same site (Dozmary Pool) by Simmons, Rand and Crabtree (1987). Oak woods were confined to sheltered hillsides, according to Brown, though Keeley (1984) hinted that soil variability might have been a factor in Bodmin Moor vegetation. In the 9200–8500 BP period, birch and hazel scrub appear to have been dominant, with scattered stands of oak; limited elm and pine were confined to sheltered localities (Johnson and Rose 1994). On northern Dartmoor, there appeared to have been hazel-dominated woodland as high as 551 m. The investigators (Caseldine and Maguire 1986) point out that there is in fact very little evidence from the summits themselves but that they may have been open species-rich healths which later underwent acidification and species loss. On southern Dartmoor, oak-hazel woodland was present at 457 m, but above that level open ground can be inferred. In South Wales, at WFF, mixed woodland with a rising proportion of hazel is deduced for 530 m; elsewhere, open hazel woodland is suggested for 660 m, with no trees somewhere above 715 m. In the Lake

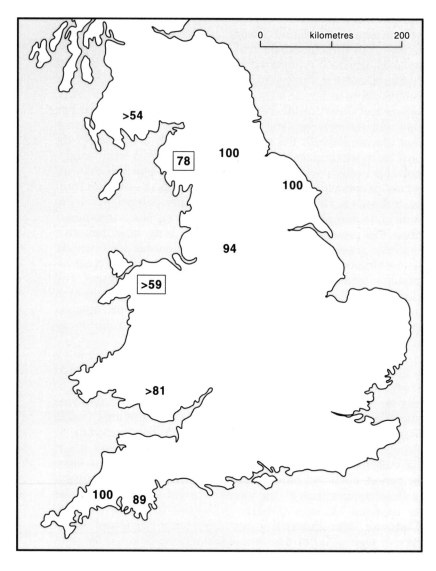

Figure 1.2   Estimates from pollen analysis and macrostratigraphy of
the percentage of uplands covered by trees during the
mid-Holocene (9000–7000 BP).

Source: H. J. B. Birks (1988), 'Long-term ecological change
in the British uplands', in M. B. Usher and D. B. A. Thompson
(eds), *Ecological Change in the Uplands*, Oxford: Blackwell
Scientific Publications; British Ecological Society Special
Publication no. 7, 37–56.

TABLE 1.4 Empirical evidence of tree-lines in Flandrian II.

Region	Date (BP)	Lowland	Upland	Scrub	Undiff	Ref
Bodmin Moor	6400	Oak woods on sheltered hillsides only		birch/hazel scrub at DMP (265 m)		Brown 1977 Simmons et al. 1987
North Dartmoor	up to 5000		in forest at 500 m	551 m has hazel scrub		Caseldine and Maguire 1986
South Dartmoor	7600		Oak-hazel wood at 457 m	Open not far from 460 m		Simmons et al. 1983
South Wales	7500		530 m at WFF: mixed wood with hazel, percentage rising			A. G. Smith and Cloutman 1988
	6000		oak-hazel woods	open hazel at 660 m		Chambers 1982b
South Pennines	6000	425 m limit of mixed woods with alder	500 m limit of pine and oak in continuous forest	over 500 m: scrub with hazel and birch		Tallis and Switsur 1990
North Pennines	8000				750 m is upper limit of evidence: not yet at tree-line	J. Turner and Hodgson 1979
North York Moors	5500	370 m limit of mixed forest with lime	woodland with birch and pine	Over 400 m hazel scrub		Simmons and Innes 1988a, 1988b

District, birch wood has been found in peat at 518 m and at Shelf Moss (Pennines) at 594 m. In Snowdonia, deposits in a tarn at 632 m suggested that closed forest was below that altitude but that some woodland was not far away (R. Walker 1978). Some of the only work specifically aimed at elucidating this problem comes from the South Pennines; the 1990 paper of Tallis and Switsur in particular repays close attention. Summarised in outline, the upper limit of mixed woodlands containing alder is postulated for 425 m, for continuous forest with pine and oak 500 m, and thereafter scrub with hazel and birch. In the North Pennines, Turner and Hodgson (1979, 1983) suggested that there was a substantial upland forest cover between 200 and 760 m ASL. Within this forest, there was more *Corylus* as altitude increased, and much less *Tilia* south of latitude 55°47′ N. Pine does not appear to have been confined to any particular soil type; elm (probably *U. glabra*) increased with altitude and may have decreased on the Millstone Grit's highly siliceous soils. They do not identify an equivalent to the hazel-dominated zone at the upper level like that of the South Pennines. In fact, the tree-line may have been higher than 760 m, for J. Turner's (1984) analyses from Cross Fell in the North Pennines (893 m) suggest that there was open herb-rich *Betula* woodland on the summit slopes during the optimal period for tree growth.

The substantially less high region of the North York Moors (highest point 454 m) might therefore be expected to be totally tree-clad at the Optimum, and Birks quotes Simmons (1969) to the effect that this was indeed so. Further work from that upland, however, often raises the possibility on pollen-analytical grounds that there was some open land during Flandrian II. At 402 m, for example during Fl II, ΣAP was generally less than 30 per cent of total pollen, whereas 1.5 km away at 346 m ASL, there was closed-canopy forest (evidenced by the trunks of birch, oak and pine) just after the elm decline. Calculations of tree pollen ratios exclude *Corylus*, and so an upper fringe of this may result from the 50 per cent of ΣP which is contributed by hazel at the upper site (Simmons and Innes 1988c). At 370 m, another set of profiles suggested a transition between mixed deciduous forest (oak-lime-alder) and more open pine-birch woodland (Simmons and Innes 1988b), but there is no indication in Fl II or early Fl III that the upper limit of woodland has been reached. Even at 200 m, Atherden (1979) found proportions of ΣAP in F1 II which allowed her to infer some open ground not far away.

Intra-regional variation may produce diversity. In the Craven

Pennines, R. T. Smith (1986) notes a difference in mid-Holocene vegetation patterns between the plain limestone areas and those covered with acid drifts. The former, for instance, had higher levels of pine and elm but were also subject to greater intensities of disturbance (and the subsequent increase in *Sphagnum* peat, sedges and bracken) during the Mesolithic. In some places, hazel formed more or less pure stands.

In summary, the most careful work shows that there were variations in the forest composition but that as upper limits were approached the proportion of hazel increased to the point where it may have formed a scrub altitudinally superior to the closed-canopy woodland with oak and pine below. Since *Corylus* is unlikely to grow on gleys and podsols, then increasing wetness and acidity of soils would likely produce a shift to birch and willow in this upper zone. For F1 II and the later Mesolithic, however, many authors (e.g. Chambers 1988) make the point that evidence of fire is often present in the deposits which also contain the micro- and macro-fossil evidence for the tree-lines. They thus raise the question (discussed more fully in Chapter 3) of whether the tree-lines might have been affected by the occurrence of natural, lightning-set, fire or whether human activity was involved. The evidence for Cross Fell suggests that on climatic grounds there is no reason why most uplands should not have carried open woodland (even if only a birch or birch-hazel scrub) in F1 II; if they did not, then the above two causes must be considered, or special local factors such as extreme exposure, or general processes such as soil acidification, for reasons why a particular locality did not fulfil its climatic potential. The *Calluna–Eriophorum–Sphagnum* communities of various kinds which now dominate upland vegetation, with subsidiary components like *Deschampsia flexuosa, Vaccinium vitis-idaea* and *Empetrum nigrum*, are individually described in Rodwell (1991b). He stresses that the present-day vegetation of these communities is much affected by frequent burning and heavy grazing together with draining and atmospheric pollution. They are not likely, therefore, to have been the same during prehistory.

COASTLINES

In one sense, the whole of the British Isles are a set of coastal environments, for the influence of the sea upon climate is pervasive. In a more detailed fashion, however, a number of the upland areas which are the special topic of this study abut onto coastal areas. Even where the uplands do not as it were fall directly into the sea (which they do, spectacularly, from some of the cliffs of Exmoor and the North York Moors), they often come within the kind of distance which is envisaged as being a possible part of a procurement territory of a hunter-gatherer group. Since the resource territories of mesolithic groups in the British Isles are imperfectly known (compared with Scandinavia for instance), it must suffice at present to include coasts within the possible living space of some upland groups and to mention briefly the possibilities and constraints which they represented.

Physiognomy

Today's picture is the obvious starting point; within 50 km of most upland areas in England and Wales, one or more of the following types of coastline ecosystem can be found:

- Very high cliffs, as at Boulby (NYM), which fall more or less directly onto a shoreline which is exposed at low tide but which may reach onto the foot of the cliff at high tide.
- Low and medium-height cliffs with a normal width of rocky, shingly or sandy beach, not all of which is covered at normal high tides.
- Low coastline with one or more parallel lines of dunes. These may pond back lagoons. They may be fronted by any of the normal kinds of foreshore.
- Sheltered bays, estuaries and other inlets with accretive inter-tidal areas such as mud-flats, saltmarshes and sandbanks.
- Near-shore islands, accessible by small boats.

Given the variety of geomorphological processes within small areas in Britain, more than one of these types is likely to be found within this wholly arbitrary 50 km distance or indeed within the postulated resource territory of any mesolithic group.

A key factor to be emphasised is the number of ecological transformations undergone by the coastline in F1 I and II. The period 9200–6800 BP was, according to Tooley (1978), the time of the most rapid post-glacial rise of sea-level, with the years 9000–8500 and 7800–7600 being especially fast. In the middle of F1 II (~8500 BP) in Lancs, for instance, sea-level (as indexed by reconstruction of mean tide level) was at –15.2 m OD, but by ~7700 BP its level was at –6.5 m OD. The rate of rise then slackened, and after 6980 BP the level fell to ~–4.3 m OD, with a band around 2 km in width at Downholland Moss being removed from marine influence. But between 6800 and 6300, sea-level rose again by over 1 m to −3.2 m OD, fell at 6000 BP and then rose again rapidly (at perhaps 0.6 cm/yr⁻¹) between 6000 and 5800 to −2.2 m, then falling again to −3.4 m by 5500 BP. Between 5500 and 5000 BP, the level rose again at a rate of 0.5 cm/yr⁻¹. Comparable patterns are recorded for many other parts of England and Wales, with the details varying according to topography and the degree of warping of the coastline following isostatic recovery.

Resources

The significance of such changes for Mesolithic populations cannot be dismissed. At the very least, some groups would find their familiar resource-yielding territories being rapidly attenuated by fast-rising sea-levels. Reconstructions of the coastline of Cornwall during the Mesolithic suggest that the rises of Flandrian I and II would have diminished the land area by 25 per cent. Marine incursions no doubt would have brought unpredictable hazards when for instance storms coincided with very high tides. Examples of habitat change would include the perimarine zone of peat mosses where such existed: these would have been flooded and peaty substrates replaced by clays and silts under the influence of rising water-tables on a regional scale. Tidal flats and lagoonal zones are invariably affected quite quickly, and their extent oscillated with the advance and withdrawal of the sea, provided that there was space for them to develop. Sand dunes, sandbanks and shingle spits develop little during eras of overall sea-level rise, for if they build up during times of falling sea-level, they are soon overtaken by later rises and their materials are dispersed. All these types of change are most developed in quiet-water environments where deposition can take place, and there is no reason to expect comparable complexity along for example coasts with high cliffs easily reached by high tides. In such places, however, it is reasonable to expect that any inlets would have an additionally important place in Mesolithic resource scheduling and that rapid changes would bring adaptational challenges. The overall story, though, is one of mean tide levels which have risen throughout the Mesolithic period, from ca −20 m in 9000 BP to ca −2 m in 5000 BP. This must mean that much evidence for mesolithic occupation of coastal zones is buried under later deposits, was washed away during periods of sea-level rise, or is beneath several metres of water as well as any other cover. Coastal sites such as those at Eskmeals, Cumberland (Bonsall 1989) which relate settlement to sediments (such as shingle ridges, peat-filled basins, and sand dunes) take on an added importance. Perhaps even more significant are regions like the coasts of south-west Wales where there appear to be no later Mesolithic lithic remains at all except at the present-day coastline (David 1989).

Excavations of Mesolithic sites in Scandinavia and other Baltic countries have led to attempts to formulate overviews of the likely resources available to mesolithic groups procuring subsistence from shorelines. In EW, few in the later Mesolithic (whether or not adjoining an upland) have yielded any density of either archaeozoological or archaeobotanical data, and so recourse has to be had either to analogous information from Scotland such as Mellars' (1987) work on Oronsay or Scandinavian discussions such as that of Paludan-Müller (1978).

The first point to be made is that the forests of Flandrian II would have reached to within tens of metres of the high-tide mark where the substrate was suitable and where exposure did not prevent the full growth of trees. This would exclude lagoons, but sand dunes would, after an appropriate succession, have been available for colonisation. No doubt there was attrition of the forest ecosystem on exposed cliffs, but in sheltered bays and estuaries the forest and its resources would have adjoined those of the coast and sea. So those who argue for the key role of plant resources in mesolithic economies (D. L. Clarke 1976; Zvelebil 1994) do not have their case diminished. Clarke suggested that the deciduous forests of Fl II would have provided as many as 300 species of edible plants in the form of roots, nut, berries, fungi and leafy material. He further argued that gathering would have been more productive than hunting. Evidence for the relative balance of plant and animal foods is however generally lacking, and most authors fall back on the general view from near-recent hunter-gatherer studies that such people ate as much plant food as was necessary and as much meat as they could get. Their subsistence base in the cool temperate zone of latitudes 45°–59°(using both coastal and inland groups) was typically 20–30–50 per cent of wild plants/small animals-land mammals/wildfowl-fish, shell-fish and small mammals. So the contribution of animal food from marine resources is nowhere negligible whenever the sea is within reach (and where it is not, then freshwater animals are used). The broad trends are: fishing is dominant in coastal locations; hunting is least important among groups which rely on fish; plant foods are usually the minor element in coastal calorie intake; at shorelines, seaweed enters the edible plant spectrum.

TABLE 1.5 Food value per 100 g raw edible portion.

Food	Water (percentage)	kcals	Waste (percentage)
Deer	68	271	53
Wild duck	61	233	42
Salmon	64	217	35
Eels	78	168	33
Mackerel	67	168	46
Cod	81	79	67
Mussels	79	95	80
Acorns	14	353	20
Hazel nuts	41	398	64
Sea kale	96	8	26

Source: Bonsall 1981, with figures rounded to nearest whole number.

These considerations flow to some extent from calculations of the food value of the plants and animals available to coastal groups (Bonsall 1981) and comparisons with other foods; a selection is given in Table 1.5. The evidence is clear: animals are a concentrated source of calories (and of protein as well) compared to all except a few nuts and seeds. Given that meat (and possibly fish) are more desirable to eat, then any Mesolithic group that had access to shoreline would almost certainly have used its resources.

In some places, it is conceivable that the coast was differentially attractive to animals at particular seasons. Modern red deer, for example, form larger groups in the winter, and in areas of high relief these congregate in sheltered and hence low-lying areas. If such conditions pertained in the largely forested environments of Flandrian II, then the coasts may well have been a favoured red deer habitat, though it has been argued that the differential between upland and lowland ecosystems was less apparent at that time. Inshore sea mammals are non-migratory and so available for capture at any season; whales and dolphins have been hunted with relatively simple technology and might at times have become stranded. Saltwater fish have varying distribution habits: some are offshore and in deep water seasonally, others are migratory. Considered in aggregate, one or other species is likely to have been available throughout the year. At estuaries, human groups were well placed to intercept migratory salmon and sea trout, which are especially abundant from April through November in the British Isles; but these can be taken anywhere along the river length as far as the spawning grounds. Many seabirds winter along British coasts; residents are vulnerable to capture if they nest or roost on cliffs. Eggs and young birds are scarcely ever totally inaccessible. Shellfish have the advantage of animal protein and calorie levels without the disadvantage of being able to run or fly away: mussels, limpets, cockles, winkles, oysters and whelks would all have been found in significant concentrations. They are however high in waste. Yesner (1980) quotes calculations to the effect that shellfish can withstand a cropping rate of 14 per cent compared with savanna ungulates at -2.5 per cent. Thus the exploitable biomass for shellfish might be 7.52×10^5 kg m^{-2}, well above the savanna ungulates at 0.6×10^3 kg m^{-2}. Even sea mammals can be cropped at higher rates than their terrestrial equivalents since recruitment rates are higher. Similarly, it can be postulated that biomass fluctuations are lower in oceanic than terrestrial environments, though these increase northwards even in the sea. The plants of the coastal zone offer no special attractions or advantages over woodland flora, but many are edible, and remains of *Atriplex patula, Polygonum aviculare, Scleranthus annuus, Spergula arvensis, Chenopodium album* and *Stellaria media* have been suggested as coastal plant resources in Scotland.

The lesson drawn by many workers is that coastal zones were plentiful sources of food and that they could therefore support sedentary populations and/or populations of a higher density than inland areas. If seasonal movement occurred, then it might have been within the coastal zone rather than a coastal–interior translocation. Thus there is a plentiful literature, especially from Scandinavia (but see also Mellars 1987), discussing the details of both presumed resources and the actual finds from excavations (Broadbent 1979; J. G. D. Clark 1983; Yesner 1980). Evidence is quoted (Yesner 1980) to the effect that people exploiting primarily inland resources in the circumpolar zone have lower population densities, shorter life expectancies and narrower population pyramids than their coastal neighbours. A better comparison with the European Mesolithic might be the Aleuts since these islands are ice-free: these people had the highest density of all the circumpolar groups. Part of the eco-social complex in such circumstances seems to be a high degree of sedentism in which many resources are harvested over a dispersed area but returned to a central settlement, though freshwater migratory fish (for example) might require the despatch of small parties of men to a particularly good catch site. Anthropologists seem agreed however that maritime hunter-gatherers are more territorial than other such folk. Endemic conflict between groups seemed to have been one consequence, though never at the level of a Malthusian factor. A coast which is undergoing rapid changes in habitat distribution due to rises and falls in relative sea-level is clearly one whose human populations are likely to be under stress if the whole of the resource base is taken up into territories; periods of greater stability of sea-level may well have been echoed in the human communities. Nevertheless, if Yesner (1980) is correct in arguing that 'marine foods do offer some distinct nutritional advantages in comparison with other subsistence regimes' then possibly no Mesolithic group would live anywhere else if it had the chance. Certainly, any group within travelling distance would make use of it if it had the opportunity. An extreme scenario would be to conjecture a coastline that was all occupied by sedentary groups, where the interior populations were unable to access the coastal resources except perhaps by trading. Could such a hypothesis be tested from the archaeological material?

3. ARCHAEOLOGY

In this section, the main distinguishing features of the Mesolithic period in England and Wales, as delineated by archaeologists such as Christopher Smith (1992a), will be set out. For the moment, it is necessary to see where it fits in the wider post-glacial context.

In England and Wales, the main characteristic is a paucity of evidence, compared with later prehistory and even with some Palaeolithic sites. This has meant that the presence of Mesolithic inhabitants and their lifeways has been primarily inferred from lithic industries. Ancillary materials such as bone and wood implements, and traces of settlement sites, have been added where possible. Once the presence of humans has been established, then a context for interpreting local and regional palaeoecological evidence as part of the eco-cultural framework is available. Nevertheless, even though the ecological context of Mesolithic people in Northern Europe has been discussed in a depth applied to few other prehistoric cultures in the region, the 'primary sort' (to use a database analogy) is on stone implements. This is so even where it is recognised that some limitations may be imposed by such an approach, since it inevitably foregrounds the kind of settlement at which stone tools are left behind (Mellars 1976a; Smith 1992a).

The next few paragraphs briefly put the material evidence into a regional chronological pattern and foreshadow some of the

aspects of our central theme which will be further developed later
in this book.

The Upper Palaeolithic

The transition to the Mesolithic is usually placed at 10,000 BP, with
some overlap of stone tool types into the later cultural period.
The lithics of this (Creswellian) culture are dominated by a range
of points made on large (40–90 mm long) blades, and these have
strong affinities with some cultures of mainland Europe, such
as the Brommian and Ahrensburgian. Close resemblance is not
surprising since mainland Britain was not then separated from
continental Europe.

The Early Mesolithic

The whole of the Mesolithic is characterised by the presence of
microlithic industries, which are rarely larger than 40 mm in
length and often smaller. None of the evidence for the entire
Mesolithic suggests anything other than the dominance of a food-
collecting (i.e. pre-agricultural) economy until possibly the very
end. The early phase also has larger implements reminiscent of
the preceding culture. The early phase is usually separated from
the later by the presence of broad-bladed microliths. Examples
of the early Mesolithic in England and Wales are dated between 9700 and 9000 BP. The culture is distributed throughout
England and Wales with the possible exception of the uplands
of Wales.

The Later Mesolithic

Physical separation from the rest of Europe was complete by
~8500 BP, though this does not totally require that all cultural
developments in this phase be indigenous (Jacobi 1976). Smaller
microliths with narrow blades and the appearance of more geometric shapes (including a small scalene triangle) are diagnostic
of the later Mesolithic, ~8800–9000 BP. However, separation from
the early phase is not always complete: narrow-blade industries
show up before the insulation from the continent. Equally, some
geometric industries are accompanied by larger, non-geometric
forms. This is especially so in south and east England and in
Wales. Pure geometric assemblages are especially common on
the uplands of northern England. In total, however, the later
Mesolithic presence is to be detected from upland, lowland and
coastal sites; it may be noted that there is every appearance

of some continuity between early and later Mesolithic periods, as indeed there is often some between the Mesolithic and the succeeding Neolithic.

Lithics

The hardest evidence of all comes from lithic material, and indeed this is, as suggested before, the foundation for the recognition and delineation of the Mesolithic in the whole of Britain, notwithstanding that palaeoenvironmental evidence and radiocarbon dating have now added further and integral structures which form a more complex whole. However, the lithic material is a constant, whereas the other sources of evidence may or may not be present for a given region.

In the early Mesolithic, in the period to ~8800 BP, the non-geometric industries include a restricted range of large microliths and a range of distinctive non-microlithic tools. Some uniserial barbed points of antler and bone are found. The later Mesolithic lacks any antler and bone technology but has a range of smaller geometric types such as scalene triangles and rod-forms. In both periods, the finds are mostly attributed to projectile technology, although wear studies at Thatcham in Berkshire, for example, have rejected the use of microliths as projectile points in favour of composite knives for vegetable processing. In the early Mesolithic, two or three large armatures on a projectile are postulated; in the later Mesolithic there appear to be a larger number of smaller armatures with a variety of numbers and layout. The raw material also differs: the later Mesolithic uses stones with a broader range of mechanical qualities including an increased use of low-quality chert and even flints from river and beach gravels. Closer analysis of the metric qualities of lithic assemblages of the later Mesolithic has been undertaken by Switsur and Jacobi (1979) and by Mellars (1978). The former study uses cluster analysis to define groups of stone material, which, although distinctively later Mesolithic, show some differences which may have interpretive significance. The clusters are:

Cluster E: Thirty sites from the Pennines and North York Moors of the early to mid-sixth millennium BP. All above 300 m ASL, variable size of spread; microliths limited to narrow rod-like points.

Cluster D: Thirty sites, all except two of which are in Northern England; dated 8750–5610 BP. Found in lowlands and on east coast, on flanks of uplands as well as on actual upland sites like White Gill, North York Moors. The microliths are dominated by scalene triangles.

Cluster C: Three sites: two on the South Pennines, one in the Kennet Valley. Dominated by micro-rhomboid microliths.

Cluster B: Twenty-four sites from the period 8540 BP until the beginning of the Neolithic, variously distributed in southern England, the Midlands and Wales. A high proportion of microlith shapes associated with early Mesolithic cultures is found. In general, a residual class of sites.

The authors make the point that many sites of flints and charcoal are the conflation of a number of apparent residential units, but it is impossible to extrapolate from these scatters to the social structures of resource procurement to which, presumably, they were directed. Microwear research for the early Mesolithic shows that no single tool type can be confidently correlated to a single usage or worked material at a scale greater than the individual site (Dumont 1987). Given the greater known diversity of tool-making materials at that time, this might apply *a fortiori* to the later period.

Mellars (1978) takes roughly the same body of source material and then produces a three-fold classification based on microlith proportions and on location. For Type A assemblages, some 88–97 per cent of the total tool inventory is composed of microliths. There are thus very low proportions of other tools, especially scrapers. A marked industrial specialisation is thus inferred. Most of the sites are from present-day moorlands in the Pennines and North York Moors above 305 m, but are not confined to such places. Three of them are found on the Lower Greensand of Hants-Surrey-Sussex.

For Type B assemblages, a wide variety of microlith shapes is found but only 30–60 per cent of the tools are microliths; 14–25 per cent are flakes and blade scrapers, and the total tool variety is high, with axes and saws in the repertory. Their locations are chiefly lowlands in south and east England; coasts of north and west Britain; and the uplands of the Central and South Pennines.

Type C assemblages occur at only three sites, all with an exceptionally high percentage of flake and blade scrapers: Blubberhouses Moor (Yorks) at 320 m; Kettlebury on the Lower

Greensand of Surrey at 91 m; and Freshwater West, Dyfed (with no microliths), at sea level.

Mellars also notes the absence of antler and bone projectile points from the later Mesolithic and suggests that the microliths form a substitute. An overwhelming proportion of later Mesolithic sites, however, are unfavourable environments for the preservation of organic materials.

Closer analysis of form, function and distribution of Mesolithic stone technology has been undertaken by Myers (1987, 1989). He notes that the frequency of sites from the later Mesolithic suggests a filling-up of the landscape, though with smaller sites. The shift to microlith-dominated tools indicates the need for reliable projectiles, capable of functioning without the need for time-consuming repair. From this analysis, conclusions about resource scheduling can be drawn, but for the moment one fundamental distinction must be remembered. This is between 'encounter' hunting, when animals are found in small numbers and with a largely scattered distribution, and the other types, where for example a large migratory population is hunted in a predictable set of times and places. An example of a more complex settlement pattern and its translation into resource scheduling is given by T. D. Price (1978).

Settlement Pattern (see Plates 2 and 3)

At the scale of the individual site, Mellars' type A spreads are mostly below 20 m² in area, but an area on Snilesworth Moor (NYM) totally exposed after a fire showed 5000 flints within an 8 m radius of a spring-head. At Cock Heads (NYM), an area 30 × 17 m yielded only 33 tools. Over 50 m² is common for type B assemblages: at Upleatham (NYM), the main area of flints was 100 × 60 m, thinning towards the edges (Spratt et al. 1976). Most of the upland spreads of stone tools and charcoal are near water, in the form of streams, spring-heads or standing water. Examples of proximity to contemporary lakes include WFF in South Wales (A. G. Smith and Cloutman 1988), the Malham Tarn area of the Craven Pennines (D. J. Williams et al. 1987), Cefn Gwernffrwd and Rhosgoch Common in mid-Wales (Chambers 1982a; Bartley 1960); on the NYM, most of the sites are near the spring-lines (Spratt and Simmons 1976; Innes and Simmons 1988; Wilson 1988). In Swaledale (NP), scatters of flint artefacts are found above the spring-line and on south-facing slopes (Laurie 1985). A sheltered aspect not far from the tops of hills and ridges seems also to have been sought: in south-west Yorkshire, most of the sites are found in the 415–500 m zone, on sites facing east through south

Plate 2   On the Black Mountains north of Abergavenny, looking
north. The moorland plateau is dissected by streams at
the heads of which mesolithic flint scatters of Mellars'
type A are typically found.

Plate 3   The Eston Hills overlook the valley of the Tees, and the North
          Sea is just off this northward-looking photograph. The more
          complex material scatters are often found in such localities:
          Upleatham (Mellars' type B) is a few kilometres to the east.

and off the crests (Radley and Marshall 1963). This is also evident in the hills east of Manchester (Stonehouse 1987/88) where the areas above 450 m are mostly devoid of the worked stone that is plentiful between 350 and 450 m, in a terrain which has been extensively worked over. There is a concentration of sites along the edges of some of the steeper valleys (see Figure 1.3) which might reflect peat erosion, though in a wider context it seems to be a valid distribution. This narrow strip of gritstone between Skipton and The Peak has a very high concentration of sites which are regularly revisited by local archaeologists, and so patterns are probably reliable. Stonehouse (1990) comments on the microlith spreads that where rods are dominant, the microliths are usually concentrated in a small part of the site; that triangle sites are more often in groups than rod sites; and that some parts of the moors attract triangle sites while others that are not obviously different attract rod sites. In the North Pennine valley of Upper Teesdale, flint is most often found on alluvial flats or on limestone shelves overlooking streams (Coggins 1986); to what extent blanket peats obscure other sites is uncertain. On the limestone uplands between Shap and Kirkby Stephen, most sites are in the range 275–350 m but show no obvious relation to the topography; like several other places, they do show some degree of continuity between implements associated with both Early and later Mesolithic periods (Cherry and Cherry 1987).

At a regional scale, Mellars (1986) points out that in northern England, a transect from east to west reveals a clustering of sites between 350 and 480 m. In the Central Pennines, Stonehouse (1990) calculates the average altitude of narrow-blade lithics sites at 385 m (n = 49). There is discussion about whether this is an artefact of land-use type, peat erosion and the concentrations of amateur archaeologists and of flint-collectors. It seems likely that these distributions are reliable where many sites have been found, but absence of finds should not be taken axiomatically to mean absence of mesolithic presence. That is, the high densities of charcoal and stone tool sites on the Pennines and NYM are real (though both individually and collectively they may represent a considerable chronological depth), but absence of comparable sites in the lowlands may be due primarily to lack of discovery. In Wales, Jacobi (1980) suggests that one Mesolithic site in six is above the 300 m contour in the uplands which comprise about 40 per cent of the Principality. In the uplands of south-east Wales, these have been classified by Tilley (1994) into locations around former small lakes, those on river terraces, those commanding

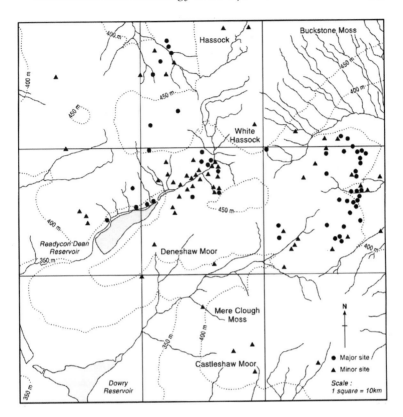

Figure 1.3   An area 30 × 30 km east of Manchester in the South
              Pennines (SP) showing the Mesolithic sites discovered
              by intensive survey and hill-walking. Some of the
              area is still peat-covered and may not therefore have
              yielded all its information. The 'edge' distribution
              to the east is especially notable.

              Source: P. B. Stonehouse (1987/88), 'Mesolithic
              sites on the Pennine watershed', *Greater Manchester
              Archaeol. J.* 3, 5–17.

views across valleys and the localities at the heads of valleys near
passes in the mountains. This last situation has been put forward
for Pennine passes and routes (Faull and Moorhouse 1981) and for
Galloway (Edwards et al. 1983).

Most sites which have been seriously investigated have evidence of charcoal concentrations which are taken to be the remains
of hearths. These are typically at the junction of the mineral soil,
and overlying peat, and so radiocarbon dates lack conviction as

to the real age of the organic material. Some places have a concentration of several of these spreads within a small area and are
presumably the result of either a number of groups camped near
together or repeated visits by smaller groups. At March Hill South
(CP), there is a group of eight sites of which Stonehouse (1987/88)
says that they are 'so close to each other that it would have
been confusing to plot them individually'. The radiocarbon dates
(mostly on charcoal) from this 3 × 3 km area are between 5610±120
BP and 7545±140 BP. Stonehouse (1992) notes that a number of
Early Mesolithic sites on the central Pennines occur in pairs, as
close as 20 m apart, and further that one site at least (Pule Hill
Base, 361 m ASL) was probably reoccupied in the later Mesolithic.
On Mynydd Hiraethrog in North Wales, there is a complex of later
Mesolithic bowl-shaped pits with scorched sides in which layers
of charcoal are each covered with layers of fresh soil. When the
pit was full, a new one was dug (Lynch 1993). The lithics show a
Mellars type B assemblage (see above), and the radiocarbon dates
suggest the Mesolithic/Neolithic boundary: 5700, 5350 and 5250
BP are quoted.

A few places have been deemed to show evidence of structures.
At Broomhead 5 (~8570 BP, SP), there are five stake-holes as if to
form a windbreak, and the charcoal areas are all within or adjacent
to the flint distribution. At Deepcar (mid-tenth millennium, 12 km
north-west of Sheffield), stones are arranged in an oval to circular
pattern, and Dunford Bridge A exhibits an oval area of stone
paving (Radley and Mellars 1964).

Outside the immediate region of investigation, the evidence is
not much more plentiful. Areas of stone paving are said to be
common in mainland Europe where they are integral parts of
dwellings. A similar feature at Bonsall et al.'s (1989) sites on the
Cumbrian coast is interpreted merely as paved areas overlying
clays. His area E1 shows evidence of a raft-type foundation of
branches overlying a foundation of brushwood and also a level
area of earth and stones behind a timber revetment. This possessed a floor of birch bark. The timbers were of a good size and
were dead some time before their incorporation into the structure,
suggesting the use of driftwood. Radiocarbon assays centred
upon ca 5500 BP. At Morton in Fife (~6380 BP), small stake-holes
delineated a possible structure 2–3 m in diameter, interpreted as
a windbreak or a hut of an insubstantial kind.

Taken overall, the evidence is difficult to split into easily-
delineated sub-groups to which functions can be clearly attached,
but it looks very likely that there is some difference in function

along the spectrum of size and diversity of tool types. This much can be fed into more complex models which also incorporate other types of evidence.

Organic Materials

There is a dearth of these at upland sites. Wood is very scarce, and bone totally absent. Peat is generally thin, burnt and abraded. Organic muds are scarce, with Stump Cross (CP) one of the few exceptions. Charcoal spreads at the interface of mineral soil and peaty top are difficult to date and unrewarding to identify to species. Commonest are the shells, often burnt, of hazel nuts. These were found even at 350 m ASL, for example on Blubberhouses Moor, CP (J. Davies 1963). Hints of worked lengths of wood are given by the layout of microliths: these are generally interpreted as arrowheads, though D. L. Clarke (1976) argued for their consideration as aids to gathering plant material. A very interesting organic upland structure is found on Bodmin Moor, though its dates of 9250±85 BP and 8655±85 BP argue for Early rather than later Mesolithic. Birch bark strips were laid horizontally over a layer of *Betula* stems and twigs and then the bark layer was covered with roots and branches of willow. M. J. C. Walker and Austin (1985) suggest that the structure was a platform overlooking a marsh and used for wildfowling.

The Neolithic

In EW, a first cluster of Neolithic sites is plotted at 5300–5100 BP (E. Williams 1989) showing little overlap with radiocarbon dates for Mesolithic sites. Some constancy of stone tool types is, however, mentioned by other investigators.

The most striking feature of the advent of the Neolithic is without doubt the explosion of indices of human presence: structures, pottery, different types of stone tools (e.g. axe-, adze- and chisel-heads) and more human remains themselves. The overwhelming finding of a move to food production based especially on cereals first domesticated in south-west Asia has provoked a lively debate over the relative probabilities of the development of agriculture by indigenous cultures or the large-scale immigration of a new culture-economy complex from continental Europe. Most commentators place the earliest Neolithic sites in England and Wales in the lowlands rather than in the regions of most concern in this book. Sites bearing the characteristics of Neolithic culture in terms of stone tools and diagnostic structures replace the lithic assemblages labelled as Mesolithic during the fifth millennium

BP. Using E. Williams' plot, the last Mesolithic date in Britain was ~5375 BP.

British Isles' Context

For many years, it was thought that the occupation of Scotland and Ireland during the Mesolithic was both exclusively coastal and very late in the period compared with EW. More recent discoveries, however, are filling out that picture. In Scotland, for example, later Mesolithic sites have been discovered in inland locations in Galloway and the Southern Uplands (Edwards et al. 1983; H. Mulholland 1970). In Ireland, the site of Lough Boora in Co. Offaly has yielded dates between 8980±360 and 8475±75 BP, right at the beginning of the mainland later Mesolithic period. So the previous perception of these regions as having depauperate Mesolithic sequences is almost certainly wrong; and, where evidence from Scotland and Ireland appears germane to the present collations, it can be used with greater confidence of its relevance than ever before.

The Continental Context

The disparities in the intensity of archaeological work of the appropriate age and of terminology make it difficult to construct a unified account of the Mesolithic in Scandinavia, the North European Plain and France. Four-and five-fold divisions are found as well as simple bifid classifications. A major similarity with the British scene is the existence of a major shift in technology in the millennium 8450–7450 BP. This is accompanied by the appearance of more and larger settlements, and altogether it is envisaged that some kind of adaptation to changing environmental social conditions had occurred, with population growth as the favoured explanation of the latter (T. D. Price 1981; Gendel 1984; Bogucki 1987). A major difference from Britain is that the density of sites and diversity of recovered material allow inferences about the regions or territories within which Mesolithic bands operated. In the case of Denmark, for instance, stylistic groups of flake axes (with differences in size and shape) have a regional patterning which is said to reflect the social divisions of territory in the later Mesolithic (Petersen 1984). Hence, findings from continental Europe may be of outstanding value in formulating hypotheses about the Mesolithic in EW. But assumptions about the direct transfer of findings, making the presumption that the only difference is that the evidence is missing from England and Wales, are difficult to sustain. This is particularly so in the case of the uplands since there is nothing similar to them, in most of Europe, given their proximity to the sea.

There is no gainsaying the unpalatable fact that currently the quantity and quality of evidence for the period is low compared with, for example, parts of Scandinavia or the North European Plain. This makes inferences at once easier since there are fewer 'hard' points of reference that have to be built into models, and more difficult in the sense that a very little extra information has the potential to require a great deal of revision. Nevertheless, an occasional appraisal of what there is may at the very least suggest target areas and topics for further research, rather than just waiting for additional evidence to turn up.

4. INFERENCES ABOUT LIFEWAYS

Because the upland evidence is rather scanty, attempts to suggest how the culture and economy (and in particular the resource procurement) of the later Mesolithic was arranged have made use of inference from richer sources and from analogy. The major sources have been:

- The archaeology of Scandinavia and the North European Plain;
- Palaeoecology: 1. Pollen analysis from excavated sites and nearby;
  2. Extrapolation from the richer sites such as those of the Vale of Pickering, even though they are lowland and early Mesolithic;
- Ethnographic parallels from near-recent hunter-gatherers, with an emphasis on North American groups, closely followed by the Ainu of Hokkaido and Sakhalin.

Ideas from the above sources now suffuse writing on this period so much that they form a virtual theory in the light of which evidence is *ab initio* assessed: many papers and chapters mix the recording of lithics and speculation about hunting patterns in the same paragraphs. Difficult though it is, some attempt to keep the evidence and the overt theory apart until later will be made here.

5. POPULATION

Using a 10×10 km^2 grid and radiocarbon dates, C. Smith (1992b) has noted a rapid increase in sites for the whole of Britain after 9000 BP which slowed up by 8000 BP and showed little increase during the seventh millennium. Assuming a population density of 0.01–0.02 persons/km², he suggests that by 9000 BP, lowland Britain was densely occupied. The population of the uplands cannot be inferred separately from these data, even supposing that they were in fact a separate population of some kind.

6. CHAPTER SUMMARY

1. The moderation of climate after the end of the Late Devensian was rapid, and temperatures like those of today might have been established as early as 9500 BP. Optimal temperatures were reached in the period 8000–4500 BP, known as the 'Climatic Optimum' or 'Hypsithermal Interval'.
2. Lapse rates ensured that temperatures in the uplands were lower at all times than at sea-level; altitude ensured that precipitation was always higher, which may have meant very high totals when the general rate (as in the Atlantic period) was possibly 110 per cent of today's values.
3. Within the general trends, minor variations such as the ~400-year-long 'pluvial' periods may have existed. These probably affected tree-lines (at any rate in the Scottish Highlands) and may have had significance for a number of plant and animal species.
4. Fl I was a time of rapid vegetational change, Fl II less so.
5. The main forest type in the uplands in Fl II was oak-hazel, but there were many variations depending upon altitude and soil type, for example.
6. The forests were dynamic in their ecology, not least in containing gaps from dead trees and from beaver lodges.
7. The lower levels of the forests on the uplands merged undetectably into those of the lowlands.
8. The evidence for Fl II tree-lines is difficult to interpret: tree remains depend upon the presence of peat for their preservation, and pollen ratios for the presence of this phenomenon do not command universal acceptance.
9. Tree-lines may lag behind climate but should have fulfilled their climatic potential during Fl II.
10. Some places have documented forest right to the top at nearly 900 m, but others have no evidence beyond 460 m for an upland forest with a scrub zone above it.
11. The causes of sub-potential tree-lines are to be sought among factors such as climatic change and paludification, acidification of soils, natural fire and human-directed vegetation management.

12. Lithics are of primary importance in classifying the Mesolithic cultures, with other data used in ancillary ways.
13. In most of northern Europe, a shift in tool types (often accompanied by other evidence) is found in the 9000–7500 BP period.
14. On the continent, but not in Britain, the density of lithic and settlement evidence more readily allows the recognition of social and territorial units, though attempts to define 'provinces' have been made.

CHAPTER TWO

Palaeoecological Evidence for the Uplands

This chapter will deal with the palaeoecological evidence for the period of the later Mesolithic between ~7500 BP and 5000 BP, equivalent to the Atlantic period (zone VIIa) of Godwin's pollen-analytical scheme or the Flandrian II stage of later biostratigraphic divisions. It generally starts with the expansion of alder in large quantities (though that is not a synchronous horizon in Britain) and ends with the marked decline of elm characteristic in much of Europe; that too is not a totally synchronous horizon. It will be recalled that mixed deciduous forests form the dominant vegetation type on well-drained soils, and that the climate was perhaps 1–2°C warmer than at present, though this may not have been so marked in the uplands, especially those facing west, as in Wales. Though the rate of marine rise had slowed up, the period saw the final separation of Britain from the continent.

1. TYPES OF EVIDENCE

The evidence for human activities in the later Mesolithic uplands comes overwhelmingly from pollen analysis, supported by macrofossil remains in peats and lake deposits, charcoal, and peat stratigraphy itself, especially where tree remains are preserved. A large number of sites have been published, while some remain in thesis form and others in reports of varying degrees of completeness and accessibility. No attempt in this account will be made to compile a gazetteer nor to make quantitative deductions; rather, examples of possible scenarios will be suggested. However, at the end, some remarks will be made about the apparent proportions of different scenarios. In this chapter, only the ecological interpretation of the evidence will be given; no inferences about mesolithic activities or lifestyle other than those directly inferable from the biological evidence will be made.

Interpreting Pollen Analysis

There is no shortage of material on the techniques and interpretive methods of pollen analysis. A few points are made here to draw attention to particular features of the techniques which need to be borne in mind when considering human-initiated activity and the special context of the uplands. Special mention should be made of multiple-profile analysis, when several profiles no more than tens of metres apart which cover the same period of time are subject to pollen counting (Edwards 1983). The work at Waun Fignen Felen (WFF) described later in this chapter is of this type. Some of this work has helped with the establishment of the reliability of replicability in closely-spaced pollen profiles (J. Turner, Simmons and Innes 1989). The other technique of value has been Fine Resolution Pollen Analysis (FRPA), which entails the counting of samples with a very low vertical interval, often of 1 mm (D. G. Green 1983). A temporal resolution as low as 2–3 years has been obtained with this method, and it can be combined with multiple profile analysis as at North Gill (NYM), discussed in this chapter and in J. Turner, Innes and Simmons (1993).

There are still difficulties of interpretation, especially those relating the spatial distribution of pollen fall-out to the spatial distribution of human activity. The review of problems of detection of prehistoric agriculture made by Edwards (1979) applies *ceteris paribus* to pre-agricultural disturbance of woodland as well: the key relationship is clearly the relative positioning of the pollen analysis site to that where the human activity occurred (Jacobsen and Bradshaw 1981). These relationships for bogs, soils and peats were amplified by Edwards (1982) in his study of the detection of woodland edge from pollen analysis. The models of Tauber (1977), as expanded and formalised by Prentice (1985), are based on distance decay and also take into account complications such as the filtration effect of woodland or lakeside carr that might for example take out the larger pollen grains, which would be a factor in the representation of early cereals. So a fen-girdled lake in an open landscape could give a rather inaccurate picture of the regional vegetation. Lakes are complicated by the effects of stream inflows with their pollen load; one consequence seems to be the smoothing-out of differences between profiles. The important finding, as emphasised by Bradshaw (1981), is the need to try to relate the deposit and the deposition conditions spatially to the scale of pollen catchment area. A pollen-analysis site may, for instance, change its catchment area from regional in the Late-glacial, through very local in the forests of the mid-Holocene, and back to regional after human-caused deforestation.

These complications are particularly noticeable in the uplands where the wind patterns are different from the lowlands. M. D. R. Price and Moore (1984) suggest that for Wales, the winds blowing up either side of an interfluve result in an uneven deposition of pollen on the plateau top because of an eddy effect over the plateau. A model of predicted pollen influx from forest and non-forest communities in different altitudinal zones of the SP assisted Tallis and Switsur (1990) with their differentiation of climatic and fire-driven movements of the vegetation zones.

Generalisations that might be placed like a template over all that follows are hard to find. A basic maxim might be that as forest cover diminishes in area, the catchment zone increases in size. More extra-local pollen is then recorded, though it might have been present anyway. Some events are likely to be under-recorded in the sense that their visibility post-dates their presence.

Relations of Palaeoecology and Archaeology

Two main types of relationship between palaeoecological evidence and mesolithic remains can be delineated. The first (section 2 following) is the less common and consists of those sites where appropriate palaeoecological investigations have been undertaken at sites where lithic material is stratified into peat. The second type (section 3), much more frequent, is where an investigation is in the vicinity of Mesolithic finds but not directly related to them stratigraphically or spatially. Within this type, some authors note changes in peat stratigraphy, charcoal presence and type and pollen frequencies which they attribute to Mesolithic activity, and others either ascribe natural causes to the same analytical phenomena or note their absence. Given the large number of investigations, the differences in sampling interval, the differences in pollen sums used for frequency calculations, the presence or absence of absolute pollen frequency calculations and many other variables in the actual quality of the evidence, the compilation of a single quasi-comparable database seemed unlikely to yield answers to the questions which will be posed, and it was not attempted. It would form a good M.Sc. project.

2. PALAEOECOLOGY OF SITES DIRECTLY INVOLVING LATER MESOLITHIC FINDS

As remarked above, these are not frequent in the uplands. They are also often difficult to interpret: are soil/peat sequences prone to chronological hiatuses, for example? Do flints which fall onto accumulating peat sink to levels which would yield a different age in terms of pollen content and radiocarbon dates?

The main examples, which must then be construed with care, are given below.

Microliths in Shallow Peat

These are sites where a microlith has been found stratified into a shallow peat section (<100 cm) with no suspicion of the artefact having come from the soil/peat interface. The best examples are White Gill 3 (Simmons and Cundill 1974) and Botany Bay (Simmons and Innes 1988b), both from the NYM.

WHITE GILL AND BOTANY BAY (NYM)

White Gill is at 416 m, facing north-east, lying on the plateau surface above the source of the White Gill itself. It is an area of known Mesolithic industries (Radley et al. 1974), and Dimbleby (1961) carried out soil pollen analysis from this vicinity. The microlith reported at White Gill 3 was deemed to have come from a minero-organic layer above the actual soil rather than being at the actual soil/peat interface, though only 5 cm separates the artefact from the mineral soil. Although there is a clear indication of woodland decline at higher levels in the 50 cm profile, the only indication of disturbance at the level of the flint itself is a small peak of 'shrubs' (= *Corylus/Myrica* type). Heather pollen remains steady.

Botany Bay is at 335 m in the shallow basin which forms the head of the valley of the Bonfield Gill. The microlith comes from a piece of detached peat 8 cm in length which had enough rootlets in it to be placed right way up; the authors delineated three pollen zones, in the middle one of which (BB-D1) elm and hazel pollen appear to diminish, with alder gaining, as does birch. Oak is more or less constant but gains a little above the level of the flint. Plants of open ground or unshaded forest floor appear (including *Plantago lanceolata, Melampyrum, Succisa, Artemisia, Pteridium*) along with shrubs of opened woodland such as ivy and honeysuckle. Total tree pollen, however, falls little, and what remains is the hint of an opening of a forest canopy: the lack of response of the *Calluna* curve suggests that no acidification or paludification of soils took place.

Artefacts in Soil/Peat Sequences

These are sites where the artefact is stratified into a soil/peat sequence but where there is the suggestion that there has been a continuous sequence of deposition, and comparison with non-microlith sites of similar stratigraphy can be made. Recent examples include Dunford Bridge A and Broomhead 5 (Radley et al. 1974); Rocher Moss South 2, Dean Clough 1 and Warcock Hill South (Barnes 1982), all from the sp and cp. Remarks on the difficulty of interpreting many such sequences are made by Cundill (1988).

The pollen analyses from Broomhead Moor (433 m) and Dunford Bridge (500 m) are from soil/peat profiles and have to be interpreted with care, as the authors note. Broomhead Moor was on a broad, convex hill cut by a clough which cuts across the interfluve, and five stake-holes were excavated as well as three hearths and a paved area. The second site is on the brink of a slope, in 'a slight hollow cut by a small streamlet'. A hearth was found upon excavation, with a stone surround; the charcoal yielded a date of 8573±100 BP. Pollen analyses were taken through the soil/peat transition at places where the stratification level of the microliths could be determined, and then the profiles were compared with analogous sites from the region which lacked the stone tools. The main finding is that at the stone tool sites, the ΣNAP began to rise at the level of the microliths. This is attributed to 'the degradation of mineral soils on the steeper slopes following upon destruction of the forest cover' rather than the growth of peat. At Dunford Bridge A, pollen of *Plantago lanceolata* is found, which is unique for this stratigraphic level in the South Pennines, and this permits the inference of 'fairly intensive woodland clearance'. Changes in vegetation initiated at the microlith level seem to be carried through into later time, and Neolithic material is found in association with Mesolithic tools at 380 m at Warcock Hill, Marsden, which is 15 km to the north. At a further profile, Dunford Bridge B (20 m away from A), birch twigs and charcoal (5380±80 BP) occur in association with the microlith layer, and at site A there is a temporary decline in *Betula* pollen at the microlith layer, so local clearance of birchwood seems to have taken place. The *Calluna* pollen sharply rises at the same horizon, and this feature can also be seen at WFF in SW in the mor humus horizon of the profile closest to the Mesolithic remains.

The presence of charcoal in the excavations allows the suggestion that human presence and controlled fire were involved. This appears to have taken place in an open forest and scrub environment dominated by *Corylus* and *Betula* with shallow peat communities on the flatter ground. Woodland clearance may have promoted soil erosion and favoured the spread of heather and moorland ecosystems, which took over from wooded areas.

The sites of Warcock Hill South, Dean Clough I and Rocher Moss South have been investigated by R. Louise Brown, with results incorporated in Barnes (1982). These sites lie within 2 km of each other at ~400 m but off the plateau summit; Warcock Hill, at 9210±340 BP and with a broad-blade industry, is probably early Mesolithic. At Dean Clough there is a large increase in ΣNAP at the mineral/organic boundary, and this is, like Broomhead Moor, mostly *Calluna* pollen; here it is attributed to peat growth rather than human influence; there is a radiocarbon date on charcoal of 7595±140 BP. Rocher Moss pollen assemblages are quite clearly of Atlantic zone date, and a radiocarbon date of 5830±100 BP is very near the Dunford Bridge B date of 5380±80 BP. The author does not in the end draw any definite conclusions about the possibility of human impact on the vegetation during Mesolithic times, but the similarity with the sites further south might allow the same interpretation.

Artefacts in Long Organic Sequences

These are profiles where the artefact is stratified into a long (> 100 cm) sequence of organic materials. For obvious reasons, this is very rare. The best example is still that of Stump Cross in the Craven Pennines (D. Walker 1956), but Hard Hill at the head of the Tees (G. A. L. Johnson and Dunham 1963) is also germane. The Waun Fignen Felen site of A. G. Smith and Cloutman (1988) is also relevant but is dealt with as a whole later in this section.

STUMP CROSS, CRAVEN PENNINES

At 400 m, a Millstone Grit erratic is split in two, and the cleft once contained a pool of water which went down 1.2 m below the surface of the mineral soil surrounding the rock. This pool has filled up with organic muds as if it were a small pond. At 130 cm, a flint flake was found 10 cm to the side of the sampling profile. The flake clearly belongs to an early Atlantic part of the section, and three others are attributed to the same pollen zone. The horizon of the flint (which along with other local material was attributed by J. G. D. Clark to a tradition now generally labelled as later Mesolithic) has a radiocarbon date of 8450±310 BP and shows a number of fluctuations in relative pollen frequencies: elm kinks downwards, the rapid rise of alder is slowed down, and there is a peak of *Corylus*. Oak is apparently unaffected. Of the NAP, Ericaceae (probably nearly all *Calluna*) responds the most positively, though smaller increases are seen in bracken spores and there is an isolated occurrence of *Artemisia*. The AP/NAP ratio is declining by this time and continues downwards above this level. In terms of conventional interpretations, a horizon 10 cm below the flint has stronger indications of interference with the vegetation, with sharp peaks in heather, followed by grasses. Oak has a sharp reduction, paralleled by a peak in *Corylus* and the introduction of alder to the profile. So the horizon of the flint flake may not be the first indication of Mesolithic presence in the vicinity. The rise in *Calluna* proposed for the other Pennine sites appears in a limited form in this profile, but pollen rain into a cleft 2–3 m high between solid rocks may not be of a typical pattern.

HARD HILL, NORTH PENNINES

In the course of investigating the peat deposits of the Moor House NNR, Johnson and Dunham (1963) undertook biostratigraphic analyses not only from the large Valley Bog (see p. 74) but also from a section of blanket bog at Hard Hill (NZ 727331; 750 m). This hill is a north-east-running spur of the crest ridge of the North Pennines above the Tees, and the sampled profile is in 224 cm of peat. At 136 cm in this profile, an unspecified number of Mesolithic flints of later Mesolithic type were found along with some horn-cores from *Bos* sp. No ^{14}C dates are available, though the dates from Valley Bog (Chambers 1978) are helpful. From the diagram, it is difficult to place the flints: depending on where the elm decline is placed, the industry might be ca 5000 BP or 5840 BP. The level is marked by some diminution in oak and birch pollen and an increase in *Corylus* and *Artemisia* pollen as well as other herb types. There is a sharp upward kink in the AP/NAP ratio which hitherto had been at ca 50 per cent, followed by increased NAP levels. A limited effect on the vegetation is all that can be inferred.

COMPARISONS

At all three categories of site, the evidence is difficult to interpret but a common theme of a minor recession of woodland can be discerned. In the NYM, there is no response from the *Calluna* curve, whereas in the Pennines it seems to be a clear beneficiary. In two uplands, the ruderal plant *Artemisia vulgaris* and the bracken fern *Pteridium* increase their frequency whenever microliths are found. Overall, there is very little drop in the representation of trees. The difference in *Calluna* frequencies between the two areas can only be the subject of speculation: the degree to which soils were already acidified (though a key role for paludification is ruled out for the SP sites by the author); the role of rock type; and the vegetation type (open woodland/scrub or high forest) could all have been influences on the response of heather to what can at most have been small openings in woodlands or scrub.

3. SITES NOT DIRECTLY INVOLVING LATER MESOLITHIC TOOLS OR STRUCTURES

By far the bulk of the palaeoecological work comes from places where the pleasure of finding an artefact stratified into organic materials is absent. In some places, however, Mesolithic sites are nearby (an arbitrary distance of 200 m is adopted here); in others they are found locally, within 2 km; in yet others there are none. This section will examine the palaeoecological evidence for sites with Mesolithic sites nearby, then for those with no Mesolithic sites nearby, with no effects on vegetation or where there are postulated effects on vegetation before the *Ulmus* decline, first without cereal pollen and then with cereal pollen.

Palaeoecological Investigations Near to Mesolithic Sites

Whereas the majority of pollen-analytical investigations from the uplands have looked at a phenomenon (such as the inception of peat growth or the regional forest history) and noted if there appeared to be disturbances to the forest during Flandrian II, a few sites have been granted special attention because they were close to Mesolithic artefact concentrations. This may not have been the primary reason, but it stands along with the others as a main theme of the investigation.

A good example is Dozmary Pool on BM. The industry there has been assigned to the early Mesolithic and so is outside the main period of concern in this book; nevertheless, pollen analysis there by Brown (1977) and later by Simmons et al. (1987) covers the later Mesolithic. Two other lakeside sites fall more closely into the current category: WFF in the Black Mountain regions of SW (Smith and Cloutman 1988), and Malham Tarn in the Craven Pennines (Piggott and Piggott 1963; Simmons and GreatRex unpublished material on palaeoecology; D. J. Williams et al. 1987 on Mesolithic remains).

DOZMARY POOL, BODMIN MOOR

Carbonised material is present through Fl I in a vegetation which lacked any serious development of woodland. Brown (1977: 295) preferred to attribute this to a less than obvious cause: 'Although

Plate 4   The Black Mountain in South Wales, showing that
moorland will develop over craggy limestone country.
The site of Waun Fignen Felen lies just over the horizon
of this westward-facing photograph.

carbonized material is found in younger, even Late-Devensian
sediments, in small quantity, there is no certainty that it is
produced as a result of fire'. Later fluctuations in pollen curves,
around 6800–6500 BP, were interpreted as an indication that
upland fires had altered the woodland composition. Coincident
with these fires is an abundance of *Hedera* and *Lonicera* pollen.
Brown explained these as the result of climatic dryness, but it is
also possible that they were responses to a more open canopy:
this is a time of lower oak and higher birch frequencies than the
zone before ~7500 BP. Though the spectra are complicated by the
peat-forming taxa, it looks as if a set of fire-related disturbances
has been detected. Attempts to amplify these findings (Simmons
et al. 1987) foundered on the use of profiles which appeared from
their radiocarbon date sequence to have been inverted, possibly
by peat-cutting. Yet even the lowest horizons of this profile, with
an accepted date of 7590±110 BP, have charcoal present in the samples, with size classes of > 180μ and < 180μ being represented. So
the earlier (rather than 'younger' *pace* Brown) carbonised material
looks as if it was from fire, and so the whole of the Dozmary Pool
catchment area appears to have been subject to fires throughout

Fl I and much of Fl II. The wider context of the palaeoecology of Bodmin Moor is discussed by Caseldine (1980).

WAUN FIGNEN FELEN

WFF is a site (see Plate 4) where flints of both early and later Mesolithic have been found. They lie close to a small upland bog which was in Late Devensian times a small lake basin and which is now in an area of dissected blanket bog. The investigated area lies at ~450 m ASL and has been subjected to very detailed pollen and stratigraphic analysis so that a reconstruction of the vegetation history for the period 8000–3700 BP can be mapped, that is, laid out in three dimensions. The chief concentration of artefacts is near profile B125N; at profile GG0, stone tools are found at the base of the peat along with charcoal. Pollen-analytical evidence suggests that at ~7500 BP there was a clearing some 120 m from the shore of a shallow, reedy pool (see Figure 2.1). The surrounding woodland is characterised by high hazel values, but heath vegetation is already established, and most of it persisted until 6200–6000 BP when it was overtaken by blanket bog. Given (a) that around the Mesolithic find sites, the heath succeeded an open birch woodland; (b) that the heath was not colonised by birch or oak; and (c) the presence of charcoal in many of the profiles sampled, then the role of fire in keeping open the vegetation within the local pollen catchment area seems indisputable. Smith and Cloutman indeed argue that the presence of open birch woodland at 8000 BP when the record starts is evidence for earlier human activity. Similar sequences are observed in Scotland, for example, and where fire is involved then it is argued that human agency is most likely.

The maps produced for WFF are among the most detailed evidence that exists for the Mesolithic period, and their story can be summarised as:

- The presence of open woodland and grassland in a mixed woodland matrix at the site of Mesolithic artefactual material.
- The presence of charcoal at the base of most organic profiles and the strong linkage between fire and the inception of blanket peat.
- The presence of mixed woodland in close proximity to the focal basin until between ~4700 and 3700 BP (though the pool was by then covered in acid peat), some of it adjacent to the main area of Mesolithic finds. At 3700 BP, only a small hill seemed to have remaining woodland, however.

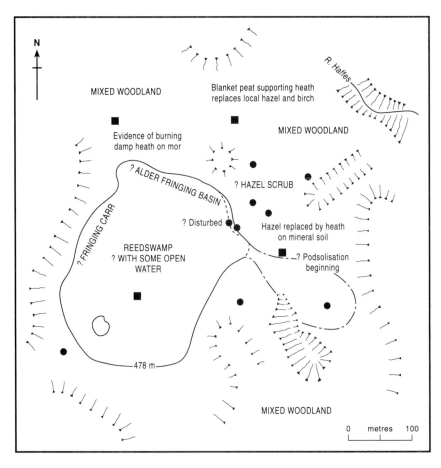

Figure 2.1   The immediate vicinity of the site at Waun Fignen
Felen in South Wales, reconstructed for ~7500 BP.
The pond has subsequently been covered by blanket
bog, which may have happened to a number of
small lakes in the uplands. Both circles and squares
indicate the pollen-analytical profiles taken at the
locality.

Source: A. G. Smith and E. W. Cloutman (1988),
'Reconstruction of Holocene vegetation history in
three dimensions at Waun-Fignen-Felen, an upland
site in South Wales', *Phil. Trans. Roy. Soc. Lond.* B
322, 159–219.

This suggests that Mesolithic impacts may always have been sporadic in their effects: even if fire was used as a tool to prevent tree regeneration, there were areas at WFF which escaped and where tree regeneration was possible for 3000 years.

It is clear that WFF evidence is also very helpful in elucidating the processes surrounding the onset of the growth of blanket peat, and it will be considered again in that context.

MALHAM TARN (CP)

Malham Tarn is in the Craven Pennines at 375 m. It is in a basin of Silurian rocks but surrounded by Carboniferous Limestone. Both rock types are plastered with glacial drift. The tarn is adjoined by a mire (Tarn Moss) almost as big as the Tarn, and the tarn also receives drainage from two other mires (Ha Mire and Great Close Mire), both smaller than the Tarn Moss. Great Close Mire has few open-water deposits, but Ha Mire was open water in Late-glacial times, and Tarn Moss was open water until the end of chronozone Fl I. The systematic collection of surface material has led to the identification of six (designated A–F) sites at ~380 m on areas of flat or gently sloping land near the wetlands of the locality.

Site A, on the north bank of the Tarn, is ca 70 m square and is situated around the largest of the springs which feed Malham Tarn. The flint is probably derived from tills some distance away (Holderness coast, East Yorks and Lincs Chalk outcrops are the likely sources), but cherts come from the local limestones. The proportions are 8210 items of flint out of a total 11240, that is ~73 per cent of the total. Williams et al. (1987) think that some tools belong to an Early Mesolithic type (and that other early sites may have been covered by peat growth) but the majority of the microliths are of the narrow-blade type associated with the later Mesolithic. Truncated blades are also found (only) on site A. Site A also has a balance of chert and flint materials, with chert (reckoned the poorer material by most interpreters) the more common on other sites. These typological considerations add up to an archaeological case for the presence of Mesolithic people at the edge of the Tarn/Moss basin (with the Moss having open water until being colonised by fen shrubs in Godwin zone VIa (i.e. ca 8000 BP).

Pollen analyses from Tarn Moss consist of the published material by Piggott and Piggott (1963) and profiles analysed by Dr P. A. GreatRex and published here for the first time. The Piggott profile is from the Moss some 300 m south of the Mesolithic site A; Tarn Moss A (see Fig 2.2) was taken as near as possible to the Piggott site but only a proportion of the material was subjected to analysis, in order to concentrate on mesolithic time. The 1963 paper notes that in Flandrian I there were moraine hillocks protruding from the fen and these were covered with hazel scrub which led to drift lines of nuts in the peat. As *Sphagnum* and heather became established, thin seams of charcoal are found (with carbonised twigs of *Calluna*) and there is a rise of herb pollen, including *Urtica* (nettle), Chenopodiaceae and *Plantago lanceolata*, 'probably associated with the Mesolithic site on the mound by the north shore of the fen'. There is also a small peak of grasses at a time when this taxon is declining, and some response in AP can be seen, though it must be remembered that the spectrum at this point predates the mesocratic trees. Hence, since birch appears to be affected, pine frequencies must rise as these are the only two trees in the pollen sum. Hazel is in the middle of a rapid expansion phase, which seems to be pulled back one sample above the main interference level. In the Atlantic period, mixed deciduous forest is established in the normal sequence. In the peats at this level, thin charcoal seams are reported by the Piggotts, but few coherent sequences of a 'clearance' nature can be discerned except perhaps at 500 cm (early in Fl II) when a peak in *Plantago* coincides with the sudden and virtually final demise of pine. So it can be deduced from this work that mesolithic activity in Godwin zone V (ca 9000 BP) has left more convincing traces than later occupation.

The Tarn Moss A diagram was part of a project focused on the impact of the later Mesolithic and so covers Flandrian II. It was counted at a standard interval of 4 cm, with 2 cm samples at one point, and charcoal frequency and size were routinely noted. All the deposits are acid peats, and the analysis starts in late Fl I time before the rise of alder. The local zone TM (i) of Fl I exhibits a substantial fall in Coryloid pollen, followed by a secondary peak, and at 628 cm there is an increase in birch and bracken, followed at 620 cm by high charcoal. Some of this latter is macroscopic and so has not travelled far. There is also an *Artemisia* record and relatively high herb frequencies associated with falling *Corylus*.

Local zone TM (ii) ends at an elm decline at 472 cm and can be equated with Fl II. Evidence for vegetation disturbance in this zone can be seen at 604 cm with a charcoal peak associated with *Artemisia* and Compositae-Tubuliflorae, but increases from 520 cm with a notable charcoal peak at 520–522 cm. There is no plantain in this diagram before the elm decline, but the charcoal at 520–522 cm

TABLE 2.1 Clearance at Malham Tarn Moss.

Years BP	Piggott and Piggott 1963	Tarn Moss A	Tarn Moss B
5000			
		Sporadic but increasing	
6000			
		Minor clearance	
7000			
	Minor clearance	Minor clearance	Minor clearance
8000			
9000			
	Major clearance		
10,000			

is accompanied by taxa associated with open ground (including *Rumex* and *Euphorbia*); the trees are relatively unaffected though there is a general increase in ash. Overall, the later Mesolithic period appears to have seen small-scale recession of forest only, probably of a highly localised sort. The probable relations of the two investigations are set out in Table 2.1.

Pollen analysis from closer to site A might, if the deposits cover the right period, yield a more sharply-focused picture. In fact, Tarn Moss profile B (Figure 2.2) was undertaken in that spirit except that it was then thought that Spiggot Hill on the south side of the Moss was a major mesolithic site, which has subsequently turned out to be a wrong assumption. Tarn Moss B seems however to record the earlier disturbance phase with some clarity and at the same pollen-analytical horizon, namely the transition from Fl I to Fl II. Local zone (ii), the equivalent of Fl II, shows more herb taxa diversity and higher values than at Tarn Moss A, but no 'phases' as such can be distinguished.

A good degree of concordance between archaeological and palaeoecological evidence can be agreed for the Mesolithic. The probability of early Mesolithic occupance is confirmed. Its impact seems to have been greater than that of the later occupants of the site unless there is a pollen rain effect which allowed more pollen from the mire edge settlement site and its immediate environs to reach the middle, when the dry land forest was more open than when it was a mixed deciduous forest. For the later Mesolithic, human presence is attested, though its impact seems to be small-

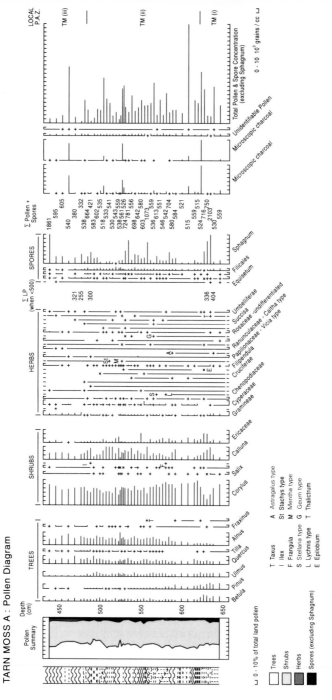

Figure 2.2 Pollen diagrams from Tarn Moss, Craven Pennines. Hitherto unpublished work, with analyses by Dr P. A. GreatRex in 1982. Profile A is from the north bank of the Tarn, profile B from Spiggot Hill on the south side. Note that only parts of each profile are examined; for the total picture from the Tarn, see Piggott and Piggott (1963).

TARN MOSS B : Pollen Diagram

scale and local: no immense attempts at landscape management can be inferred from the investigations summarised here.

COMPARISONS

There are similarities between WFF and Malham Tarn. Although the majority of the industry at the latter site is later Mesolithic rather than early Mesolithic, both show distinct phases of disturbance in early Mesolithic time; and, at both, mixed woodland persisted through the later Mesolithic until ~4700 BP or later. At both, however, there were phases of disturbance during later Mesolithic time, almost as if the focus had changed away from the lake itself at MT; at WFF the shallow pool had by this time been covered with ombrogenous peat. For the early Mesolithic period, more or less the same can be said for Dozmary Pool, but its history during the later Mesolithic is open to severe problems of interpretation of the deposits.

Palaeoecological Investigations 200 m to 2 km from
Mesolithic Sites

A fuller heading would read 'from *known* Mesolithic sites', since many occur in environments where the evidence is so patchy, especially where it depends upon peat erosion and accidental fires. However, for present purposes, these two limits will be set, though since they are arbitrary some flexibility will be granted if it seems helpful.

The first sub-category is the easier to describe: it consists of those pollen diagrams which, while in upland areas known to have Mesolithic occupation and while covering the appropriate part of Fl II, do not (according to their original investigators) exhibit traces of the recession of forest or scrub, or demonstrable burning of open vegetation. Examples include the eastern-central area and St Helena B on the NYM (Atherden 1979; Simmons and Cundill 1974), sites in South and Mid-Wales (Chambers 1982a, 1982b, 1983; M. J. C. Walker 1982), southern Dartmoor (Beckett 1981; K. Smith et al. 1981), the East Moor of Derbyshire (Hicks 1972), Upper Teesdale (J. Turner et al. 1973) and Northumberland (G. Davies and J. Turner 1979). These profiles appear to have no linking features, and indeed it is often possible to find within the same region pollen analyses which show forest disturbance during Flandrian II. If it is accepted that quantitative analysis of positive and negative sites is unlikely to be fruitful, then there is more evidence for the notion that here is a small-scale phenomenon. These negative profiles will then be considered again after those which yield positive indications during the later Mesolithic period.

This second category, then, is of sites in regions of known Mesolithic presence (usually from spreads of lithic material and charcoal) but where no detectable spatial association occurs between the occupation debris and the palaeoecological profile. The phrase 'in an area where flints of Mesolithic type have been found' occurs quite often in the literature, and the general context is set by P. A. Mellars (1986) in Darvill's review:

> Evidence for relatively extensive, systematic exploitation of upland areas first comes into focus . . . around the middle of the 8th millennium BC. Throughout the Mesolithic period there is comparatively abundant evidence for occupation in most if not all the upland areas of England and Wales.

There are a number of relevant pollen analyses, and extra consideration will have to be given to those profiles where, in clearances not long before the elm decline, cereal pollen is detected (cf. Edwards and Hirons 1984). The database is in fact very variable since it could consist of pollen diagrams from the 1930s onwards (if only tree pollen curves are inspected, which is not now acceptable) to thesis and report material not yet published. One major source is a conspectus of profiles with pre-elm decline disturbances catalogued and described from thesis and published material up until the mid-1970s. This was compiled by Dr J. B. Innes but never published. To this can be added the work published in major journals and some of the theses until the early 1990s. This gives a database of nearly 60 examples of episodes in pollen diagrams which by the interpretation of Dr Innes, the present author or the original author(s) represent disturbances to the vegetation during the latter part of Fl I or in Fl II. It is a very variable set of data: pollen sums differ, as does the sampling interval and the use of absolute counting; the recognition level of taxa develops through time, with attempts to quantify charcoal presence coming only recently; the quantity of radiocarbon dates ranges from the totally absent (the major category) to the relatively close; the presence of Mesolithic remains may be quantified to the nearest 10 m or dismissed as 'elsewhere on the moor'. On the other hand, the very variety of interpreters and materials is a safeguard against too easy acceptance of a ruling hypothesis.

From such a set of non-comparable judgements, often verbal rather than numeric, it seems otiose to draw anything other than

TABLE 2.2 Frequencies of occurrence within episodes.

Numbers: Σn = 58; [Percentage: to nearest whole number]

Charcoal layer: macro	Y	22 [37]	*Salix*	Up	4 [7]
	N	21 [36]		Down	1 [2]
Charcoal presence: micro[1]	Y	8 [14]	*Calluna*	Up	18 [31]
	N	21 [36]		Down	4 [7]
Silt	Present	4 [7]	*Pteridium*	Up	18 [31]
ΣAP	Up	2 [3]		Down	1 [2]
	Down	18 [31]	Gramineae	Up	13 [22]
Quercus	Up	0	Herbs	No. of occurrences	
	Down	27 [46]	*P. lanceolata*	32 [55]	
Ulmus	Up	1 [2]	*P.major/media*	3 [5]	
	Down	8 [14]	*Rumex acetosa/sella*	19 [33]	
Betula	Up	8 [14]	*Melampyrum*[2]	13 [22]	
	Down	7 [12]	*Artemisia*	9 [15]	
Pinus	Up	3 [5]	*Urtica*	5 [9]	
	Down	2 [3]	*Succisa*	13 [22]	
Alnus[3]	Up	2 [3]			
	Down	8 [14]			
Fraxinus	Up or enters	18 [31]			
Corylus	Up	36 [62]			
	Down	9 [15]			

Notes
1. Many earlier studies did not recognise this material.
2. Not recognised in earlier diagrams.
3. The 'down' figures are skewed by the Bodmin Moor sites.

Source: unpublished literature scans by Dr J. B. Innes for
the period 1965–80, with later additions by I. G. Simmons.

the grossest generalisations. Yet a few inferences can be made
by inspection of the variability within the whole data-set, using
the numbers extracted into Table 2.2. It is surely significant, for
example, that 74 per cent of episodes were associated with detectable layers of charcoal of macroscopic size, where that most likely
means fragments identified with the naked eye, either in the field
or upon examination of samples in the laboratory. Microscopic
charcoal at 50 per cent is very likely to be an underestimate, since
in many of the pre-1975 publications this was not recognised on

the microscope slides nor during sample preparation. So, finding 1 might be:

> Forest disturbance during late Fl I and during Fl II took place in an environment in which fire was a common feature. (The presence of either macro- or microscopic charcoal does not of itself, however, point inexorably to the causative agency of the fire.)

If the ΣAP data are inspected, the overall proportion affected (33 per cent) is unimpressive, but there is a big majority of cases in which the NAP expand at the expense of the trees, and this can be assumed to be a real phenomenon, even given the exigencies of upland pollen catchments. Within the AP, oak never seems to benefit but in fact suffers more than any other tree in these episodes; elm is affected only in a small number of places (it may never have figured very greatly in the upland woodlands anyway) but is never a winner. Birch and pine are different in the sense that there is more of an even balance between benefit and loss; birch however responds in only about one quarter of all episodes, and pine moves in only 8 per cent. Alder is affected in 17 per cent of all episodes and by a factor of four is adversely influenced. Ash, by contrast with all the others, is always a gainer: at several sites it actually enters the pollen spectrum at a disturbance episode, but otherwise it establishes a higher frequency. Finding 2 might be:

> The forest tree most likely to have suffered in these episodes was oak, with birch and alder also possible losers. Birch and ash are the most probable trees to gain or improve their representation.

The woody genera *Corylus* and *Salix* are found differentially, with the latter only changing its level in 9 per cent of episodes, with gains outnumbering losses by 4:1. Hazel changes its frequencies in 77 per cent of all episodes (the highest representation in this analysis), and again by 4:1 this is in a positive direction. Yet the 9 per cent of all episodes at which it diminishes cannot be ignored. So, finding 3 could read:

> In the course of a disturbance episode, hazel is likely to contribute more copiously to the pollen rain, but there are also cases where it appears to have lost ground.

This leaves the ground flora to be considered, including woody species such as heather, *Calluna vulgaris*. The 4:1 ratio is approximated here (18:4), with heather gaining in that proportion. This is outpaced by the bracken fern, where all but one of its 19 movements are positive. In the case of the grasses (Poaceae), all movements are positive. A number of herbs which are normally considered to reflect the presence of open or disturbed ground also turn up. The most frequent is *Plantago lanceolata*, followed by *Rumex* of the *acetosa/acetosella* type. Third equal are *Melampyrum* and *Succisa*; the genus *Urtica* (nettle), not a widespread find in pollen analysis, turns up in 22 per cent of episodes. The plantain is sometimes a sporadic grain or at 1 per cent frequency and tends to appear in higher frequencies along with an expanded suite of open-ground plants; this may mean that its frequency is a guide to the 'intensity' of the episode in terms of the degree of disturbance of the ground or possibly in terms of the proximity of the profile to the epicentre of the disturbance. *Plantago major* is a plant of trodden areas such as tracks. For finding 4, these grains might be interpreted as meaning:

> If trees or shrubs diminish during the disturbance episodes, then grasses are a likely replacement. But heather and bracken are also colonists, indicating a lack of shade and, in the case of heather, acid soils. The 'weedy' herbs are well known from Neolithic and later contexts to be present when clearings are made, but there is no direct evidence to prevent them from implying openings of a different kind.

No doubt more sophisticated probes into the significance of these numbers might be made. But bearing in mind their provenance, it might be more profitable to examine a few episodes more closely, especially where the work has provided a good level of detail of pollen and stratigraphic analysis. Events over long periods from the following investigations will therefore be examined more closely. Equivalent phases from the North York Moors will be examined below.

Site	Region	Reference
Blacklane Brook	Dartmoor	Simmons, Rand and Crabtree 1983
Waun Fignen Felen	South Wales	A. G. Smith and Cloutman 1988
Robinson's Moss	Central Pennines	Tallis and Switsur 1990
Soyland Moor	Central Pennines	C. T. Williams 1985

BLACKLANE BROOK, DARTMOOR

This profile records a shallow pool which was colonised by birch and willow; this was then (~8000 BP) submerged beneath acid peats which became cotton-grass blanket bog shortly before the elm decline. By extrapolation from the three radiocarbon dates, the later Mesolithic (8500–5000 BP) is contained in 185–121 cm of the 220 cm profile, making some broad assumptions about the stability of accumulation rates. ΣAP is highest at the wood layer (190–175 cm), and mixed oak forest is established at the level of the base of the wood layer (~9000 BP).

Attention is drawn to the possibility of disturbance by the continuous presence of microscopic charcoal in the deposits from 7660±140 BP until and beyond the elm decline. Estimates of relative quantity of charcoal leap from 1 at 175 cm to 3 in the next sample, a level maintained until 123 cm (with a couple of 2 levels) when a sequence of 4–2–3 leads into the elm decline. There are no traces of silt. Using this period of charcoal presence as a primary indicator, inspection of the pollen analyses allows the following subdivisions (not in the original paper).

Phase A (levels 175–148 cm, ~8000–6010 BP): ΣAP is not as high as when the wood layer is present but seems to be at a regional maximum; it drops in the middle of this phase and rises again. There is birch but very little alder, and a little ash. Hazel is high, and oak rises through the subzone; *Calluna* is at a low level. Peaks of bracken, grasses and *Succisa* are seen, and there are grains of honeysuckle (*Lonicera*) and a grain of hawthorn (*Crataegus*). Σherbs (14 taxonomic groups) rises towards the top of this phase.

Phase B (levels 148–118 cm, 6010–~5200 BP): ΣAP is above that of phase A and steady; Σherbs contract slightly overall, though 14 groups are found, albeit more sporadically found than in phase A. *Quercus* drops at the beginning, then peaks and rises again: there appear to be 3 peaks in ca 800 years, at 270 years per cycle. Elm rises as oak drops after phase A. As oak drops, then alder rises then drops towards the next zone. *Fraxinus* is sporadic or absent. Birch is highest at the start of the phase, then drops irregularly and rises again at the end. The Poaceae climb steadily through the phase but fall at the end. Heather is climbing from very low values in phase A and is significant only at the end.

Phase C (level 118 cm upwards, ~5200–4500 BP): Most of

the disturbance indicators pick up again: there are higher frequencies of herb pollen though from fewer (9) taxonomic groups. *Plantago lanceolata* occurs for the first time. *Pteridium* is noticeably peaked but declines soon thereafter; heather frequencies rise.

Interpretation

These three phases can be regarded as a sequence in which phase A represents an initial set of disturbances with a rapid onset. Phase B is more of a maintenance stage, with ΣAP steady and regional acidification taking place. Phase C is an intensification (note the presence of *P. lanceolata*) just before the elm decline. Inspection of the curves for *Pteridium* and the *Prunus-Sorbus* type in an early diagram from Blacklane (Simmons 1964) shows the same sequence in a rather cruder form. The levels of alteration and of open-ground plants suggest that the pollen rain has a large extra-local component and that the effects of a number of disturbances are being integrated. It can be noted that one of the Scottish 'pluvials' (Bridge et al. 1990) is given as 6250–5800 BP and that its beginning is roughly coincident with the end of phase A at Blacklane Brook. Evidence of increased wetness is not present in either stratigraphy or pollen spectra.

WAUN FIGNEN FELEN, SOUTH WALES

At 480 m, this site occupies an area of blanket peat, part of which is underlain by a basin containing pool muds and blanket peats. There are no counts of microscopic charcoal, though larger material is recorded in the stratigraphic register. However, Figure 32 of Smith and Cloutman (1988) plots the pollen frequencies of elm and open-habitat plants (excluding *Calluna*) for all the 13 profiles from the site, and the deepest (Goo: 500 cm) allows the kind of divisions attempted above, with the help of seven radiocarbon dates.

> *Phase A*: As previously discussed, a flint flake was stratified into this profile near the base, and this comes from a period (~9500--~8400 BP) of high representation of non-tree pollen, with heath plants like *Calluna* and *Empetrum*, a big peak in *Potentilla*, *Rumex*, and groups like the Tubuliflorae. There is more or less no grass pollen, nor any *Succisa*.
> *Phase B*: This can be distinguished at ~8400--~6250 BP, with the transition to ombrogenous peat taking place at the upper contact. Alder enters the profile and hazel is slightly up,

and the open-habitat group is distinctly lower than phase
A. Within the group, there are indicators of the continued
presence of open ground in the pollen of, for example,
Melampyrum, Rosaceae, *Potentilla* and the *Prunus-Sorbus*
type. A grain of *Viscum* (mistletoe) is also found. There
appears to be a minor interruption ending at 7460±90 BP,
which contains herbs like the Chenopodiaceae, and higher
levels of *Pteridium* and *Calluna*.

Phase C: The pre-elm-decline phase of higher herb
frequencies dates from ~6250–~5250 BP, with the decline of
Ulmus at 5000 BP in this profile. Filicales and *Calluna* rise, and
there are small peaks of Labiatae, Caryophyllaceae, *Rumex*
and *Lotus*. At ~6000 BP there is a small peak of the bog-bean,
Menyanthes.

Interpretation

The initial phase of high open-ground frequencies lasts about
1100 years, ending at the conventional transition between early
and later Mesolithic cultural periods. The phase of less obvious
disturbance, though by no means one in which these indicators are
absent, is about twice as long, with a minor interruption ending
~7500 BP. The pre-elm-decline intense phase is long, at about 1000
years. The only connections with the Scottish 'pluvial' periods
are perhaps the peaks of *Menyanthes* at ~7500 and ~6250 and the
change to ombrogenous peat accumulation at 6240±90.

ROBINSON'S MOSS, CENTRAL PENNINES

Tallis and Switsur (1990) record the pollen and stratigraphic
analysis of peats from a shallow saucer-shaped basin at 500 m
on the Pennine moors of Derbyshire; the hollow is filled with
blanket peat 3.0–4.7 m deep. A feature of the analyses is the
systematic recording of two sizes of carbonised material as relative frequencies. All fragments with one axis >50μ were counted
on the microscope slides, and burnt twigs were counted in the
macrofossil washings. In a profile ca 410 cm deep, the levels
240–410 cm were subjected to analysis at 1–2 cm intervals, with
six radiocarbon dates. Flandrian II occupies the horizons between
360 and 265 cm. As with Blacklane, the carbonised material can act
as a primary indicator of disturbance; it seems also to be possible
to recognise three sub-zones or phases.

Phase A: Just before the opening of Fl II, beginning at an
extrapolated date of ~8200 BP, there is a phase of high

carbonised material of both sizes. This is accompanied by peaks of *Calluna*, *Poaceae*, *Potentilla*, *Rumex* and *Pteridium*. Hazel diminishes but birch and willow rise. This represents, according to Tallis and Switsur, repeated burning at the upper edge of *Corylus* scrub and expansion of a range of heather, grass and sedge communities, depending upon the local drainage. At ~7500 BP, the pollen and charcoal begin to fall off, and by 345 cm (perhaps ca 7000 BP) a different phase can be recognised.

Phase B: Here, from 345–295 cm (295 cm = 5470±50 BP), ΣAP remains steady, and oak builds up its frequencies (albeit with some peaks and troughs), as do alder and *Fraxinus*. Grasses remain at high levels, but heather falls markedly from the previous phase, and many of the herb groups are absent or at best sporadic. There is a continuous but low presence of bracken spores. The combined total of tree and shrub pollen is the highest for the whole of the Flandrian stage at this site. Tallis and Switsur suggest that 310–300 cm represents a short extra disturbance phase with a coincidence of high carbonised material (especially the larger size), some herbs, and Cyperaceae. By extrapolation, this would be in the range 5900–6100 BP.

Phase C: At 295 cm, with a radiocarbon date of 5470±50, and with an elm decline at 275 cm (4875±60 BP), NAP rises sharply, as does the frequency of the carbonised material, especially the smaller fraction. Hazel appears to be diminished, and *Calluna* rises. Herbs such as *Rumex* increase representation, but there is neither *Succisa* nor *Potentilla*, both prominent in phase A. However, at the 5470 level, *Plantago lanceolata* appears for the first time, though there is no continuous curve until 4875. One sample below the elm decline contains Chenopodiaceae and a grain of Cerealia.

Interpretation

With the exception of the peaking of non-woodland indicators at 300–310 cm, the three-fold interpretation of this diagram advanced here is very similar to that of the original authors. The sequence of initial disturbance (ending ~7400 BP), steady phase, and pre-elm-decline resurgence of interference (starting here at 5470) is not forced upon the evidence. It can be noted that the end of phase A is not too far off the Scottish 'pluvial' date of 7500 BP and that the episode in phase B with extrapolated dates of 5900–6100 is within the 'pluvial' dates of 5800–6250.

SOYLAND MOOR, CENTRAL PENNINES

This site is at 390 m and is almost all ombrogenous peat, surrounded by Mesolithic find-sites. In the pollen analysis, C. T. Williams (1985) herself distinguishes three phases, derived principally from the SM 'C' profile, which has 700 cm of deposit and eight radiocarbon dates. It is claimed that there is no direct evidence of fire, and the initial zoning criterion used in the original monograph is that of peaks in the pollen of the *Potentilla* type.

> *Phase A*: This is dated ~7900–~7150 BP, that is, 750 years and firmly in the later Mesolithic. The smooth pollen curves allow a claim of a single phase, with hazel being affected by the disturbance, and several taxa of open-ground plants seeming to benefit, including *Melampyrum* (early in the phase), *Succisa*, *Rumex*, *Pteridium*, *Lotus* and *Calluna*. A grain of *Ligustrum* (wild privet) suggests shrub growth.
>
> *Phase B*: From ~7150–6600 BP, only some 550 years, with ΣAP at its highest in the profile ~6975 BP. Birch, heather and hazel all appear to gain ground during this phase. Within it, there is a minor *Potentilla* peak at 6975±40 BP.
>
> *Phase C*: Williams identifies this as a second *Potentilla* peak, with dates ~6600–~4965 BP, but suggests that it represents a number of disturbances, with the pattern of pollen curves showing several fluctuations. At 5280±95 BP, cereal pollen appears, with a suite of herb types but very little *Plantago lanceolata*.

Interpretation

There appear to be no relationships to 'pluvial' phases except possibly the transition to cotton-grass peat around 7500 BP. Finds of tree remains in the peat above Soyland Moor itself suggest that the site was below the tree-line for much of its history and that the disturbances therefore record events in nearby woodlands. Phases of disturbance are often marked by the appearance of wetland taxa; the observations of Holstener-Jorgensen (1967) on the paludification of Danish woodland floors under conditions of only partial deforestation seem relevant here.

COMPARATIVE FINDINGS

Despite the apparent similarities of the three-phase division, it is not difficult to point to differences between this small sample of profiles: *Calluna* rises in three of the four A phases, and is low in

TABLE 2.3 Pollen in short disturbance phases at Dufton Moss, North Pennines.

	ΣAP	AP components	ΣNAP	NAP components (a)	NAP components (b)
Above 515 cm	30–40%, up to 85% at top	Huge Be peak, Co gains. All else down	30–40%, down to 5% at top	Group below have rapid increase, then fall	Present above but not below charcoal: Compositae, Chenop, Rx
Betula charcoal (0.5 cm thick)					
Below 517 cm	50% declines to 10% just below charcoal	Sx is dominant; Be and Pi; a little Co	50% rising to 65% just below charcoal	One group rising rapidly: Gram, Umbell, Filip, Rosac	Cyps rising fast, then cut back at charcoal

Source: Squires 1970.

one phase B and high in another (see Table 2.3). The length of the phases is variable: phase A has a range of 750–3250 years, phase B of 550–2150 years, and phase C of 605–1635 years; and a time-plot (see Figure 2.3) merely shows that in absolute terms, they start at different times (no doubt influenced by the peat accumulation chronology at that particular place) and that interruptions to phase B (present at all except Blacklane, DM) happen at different times. Each profile has some event that can be loosely connected to the Scottish 'pluvials', but the events are often different. For the pluvial event of 7500 BP, WFF shows a *Menyanthes* peak, Robinson's Moss possibly shows the end of phase A, and Soyland Moor shows the transition to ombrogenous *Eriophorum* peat. For the pluvial 6250–5800, WFF shows a *Menyanthes* peak and the inception of ombrogenous peat, while Robinson's Moss shows a minor disturbance of phase B. Later events are not considered in this account.

So, the event of 7500 BP has the most candidates for connections, but they are perhaps tenuous, and further discussion must await the refining and extension of the work on stable isotopes. There is nonetheless a challenge to present an ecological interpretation of

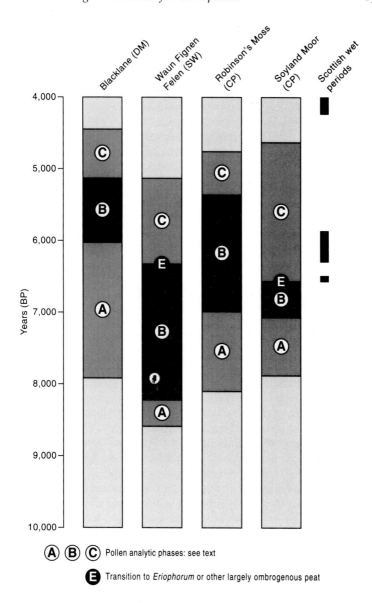

(A) (B) (C) Pollen analytic phases: see text

(E) Transition to *Eriophorum* or other largely ombrogenous peat

Figure 2.3   The pollen-analytic phases detected for Fl II at a number
of sites plotted in a comparative chronology. They seem
to have no general significance; if real phenomena,
then they seem to be related to local sequences of
events rather than larger-scale occurrences.

the A–B–C sequence, including the interrupted B. This might run as follows.

> *Phase A*: Intense disturbance of local woodland or scrub, with fire an attested feature of the processes except at Soyland Moor. It is not, however, an ephemeral event, since it seems to last for at least 750 years and for over 3000 at WFF, where it has the earliest start (~9500 BP). The range of starting dates, at 1600 years, is higher than the range of ending dates at 990 years.
>
> *Phase B*: A more stable phase, with a range of 550–2150 years. Tree pollens often improve their position (including alder), and the Σherbs total usually falls, though it is rare to have a phase totally dominated by the tree pollen. At three sites, there is a non-synchronous interruption; at the fourth (BLB), there are a series of fluctuations through the phase.
>
> *Phase C*: A resurgence of the open-ground indicators suggests a renewal of disturbance, though there are no consistent losers among the tree pollen, for instance. But almost everywhere, *Calluna* pollen is up and the intensity is confirmed by *Plantago lanceolata*. On the Central Pennines, cereals occur just before the elm decline, though in short-lived episodes about 1000 years apart.

It is necessary to avoid a naïve interpretation of these phenomena as simply being the reflections of human activity. The expansion of NAP in these environments may well be bound up with the extension of blanket bog and other mires, and so careful attention to the local site factors as interpreted by the original investigators is needed. For that reason, any further explanations of this apparent three-fold division will be held over until more palaeoenvironmental evidence has been brought into play.

Not every profile has a detectable three-fold sequence and enough radiocarbon dates to make the above kinds of statements. Sufficiently detailed pollen and stratigraphic work exists nevertheless on a number of profiles where it is worthwhile examining the disturbance in some detail to see what ecological information may be garnered. In each case, there is a definite layer or layers of macroscopic charcoal or silt in the profile sufficient that the epicentre of the disturbance is likely to be relatively close to the site. The examples considered are all in areas of known Mesolithic occupation, though of varying density.

Site	Region	Reference
Dufton Moss	North Pennines	Squires 1970
Bonfield Gill Head	North York Moors	Simmons and Innes 1988b
Black Ridge Brook	Dartmoor	Caseldine and Hatton 1993
Ewe Crag Slack	North York Moors	Jones 1976
Valley Bog	North Pennines	Chambers 1978

DUFTON MOSS, NORTH PENNINES

At 368 m in Upper Teesdale, this is one of a number of sites investigated by Squires (1970, 1971, 1978), and there is a specially detailed study of a charcoal layer towards but not at the base of the ~5 m of deposits under this former raised bog. The charcoal layer is some 5 cm thick and so dense that there was no pollen in it; pollen was analysed at 1.5–2.5 cm intervals below and above the layer, in a wood peat, mostly of *Betula* with some *Phragmites* remains. No radiocarbon dates exist from these samples; the main Dufton Moss profile has a number of them, but they do not reach low enough to compare directly with these layers. Using the earliest of them and comparing the pollen assemblage with other radiocarbon-dated sites in Upper Teesdale, the phase appears to pre-date ~8000 BP but post-date ~10,000 BP, with the highest probability (based on a *Betula-Corylus* PAZ delineated by Squires (1978) at Fox Earth Gill, 3 km due west) of a date shortly before 8000 BP; thus later Mesolithic culturally. The context is that of a wood peat throughout, and no assumptions about accumulation rate can be made: the duration of the burning episode cannot be estimated.

The pollen assemblages can be summarised in tabular form (see Table 2.3), bearing in mind that there is a gap where the charcoal is devoid of pollen. This format does not adequately describe the commonest pattern in most pollen groups: most are rising or falling steadily until the sample below the charcoal, when they abruptly rise (e.g. Rosaceae undiff. 5 to 15 per cent of AP in two samples). Above the charcoal layer, sharp peaks are recorded, for example of birch (30 per cent below the charcoal, 90 per cent above it) and of *Filipendula* (20 per cent to 35 per cent). Then in the next sample, even sharper drops occur, so that affected taxa have their lowest levels in the diagram: pine disappears, as almost does hazel. Rosaceae fall to <5 per cent; *Filipendula* to 5 per cent. A more or less 'normal' set of trends is resumed for the remaining three or four samples. The base does not represent closed woodland (ΣAP = 10–20 per cent), but the rising ΣAP suggests that it was closing slightly, with an accelerating rate; pollen of open ground species was increasing as well as the trees, including those of, for example, *Rumex*, undifferentiated Rosaceae and the Compositae, which together suggest some disturbance even if the birch was gaining as well. After the charcoal, the first sample implies open ground with willow and many herbs. In the second, birch wood shades out or otherwise replaces oak, hazel and willow, plus many of the herbs; the AP:NAP ratio is very high. Samples 3, 4 and 5 above the charcoal see the restoration of a more steady state: all the taxa are present; but, although values are not steady and ΣAP is dropping, *Corylus* rises in what appears to be a 'normal' expansion pattern. So there is:

1. a rapid (though no absolute time-scale can be given) interruption of an ongoing process of colonisation by birch wood;
2. either a very quick recovery of the birch or a second woodland-interruption, this time removing pine, willow and hazel from the locality (but many herbs also fall, so shading is the most likely explanation);
3. a position more like the base, though with more birch, pine and hazel, and less willow. (It is possible that the willow is one of the prostrate species and so ought to be treated more like a woody low shrub such as heather.)

In all, there seems to be a major disturbance event recorded at a site where others are also being recorded in a less intense form, probably because they were further away: microscopic charcoal was not routinely identified when this work was done in the 1960s.

BONFIELD GILL, NORTH YORK MOORS

At 364 m on East Bilsdale Moor, the head of a branch of the Bonfield Gill runs into a patch of blanket peat from under which eleven sub-fossil tree stumps and five trunks (of birch, pine and oak) are emerging as the peat erodes. Some are stratified into the peats and a section was analysed to determine their age and ecological relations (Simmons and Innes 1988b). The tree remains proved largely to be of elm-decline age (one *Betula* stump has a radiocarbon date of 4890±90 BP), but the pollen and charcoal analysis shows earlier phases of forest disturbance, with an emphatic stage at 5670±90 BP, which is marked by a distinct peak in microscopic charcoal and large fragments of charcoal in the peat. This local fire seems to have affected pine, oak and alder most among the trees, with birch gaining ground. *Corylus* is also favourably affected, as are *Pteridium*, *Calluna*,

Salix and *Prunus-Sorbus*. Those appearing for the first time or having enhanced frequencies are *Melampyrum*, *Rumex*, Cruciferae and Chenopodiaceae, Rubiaceae, Umbelliferae, *Scabiosa*, *Succisa* and *Urtica*. Afterwards, hazel and ash diminish almost to zero, although ΣAP rises to its highest level in the profile. Herbs in general diminish, though they are not totally absent.

The picture is then of an relatively open oak-alder wood in a state of succession which is affected by fire, after which birch-alder wood (with very little hazel) colonises the site. The canopy appears to be largely closed, with herbs restricted to types which are almost certainly from damp habitats, like *Filipendula*, and those that might be, like *Potentilla*. Apart from the detailed ecology of the disturbance, the profile as a whole shows at least three such phases between ~5670 and ~4890 BP, giving a return period of $^{780}/_3$ = 260 years.

BLACK RIDGE BROOK, DARTMOOR

Near 440 m on northern Dartmoor, Caseldine and Hatton (1993) report a pattern of charcoal in the peats which reflects that of Bonfield Gill in the sense that there is a continuous record of MI from ~7600 BP to 6300 BP. Pollen analysis enabled the authors to compile 'snapshots' of the vegetation from the brook up to the higher moor in 7700 and 6300 BP. This showed a gradual expansion of open summit areas and higher slopes, which mostly replaced woodland. The NAP during the burning phase contained large amounts of grass pollen, often coincident with high values for charcoal, and *Calluna*, which in general seemed to flourish best in the absence of fire. The pollen-analytical phenomena are interpreted as 'the continuous effects of fire within the upland vegetation communities' (Caseldine and Hatton 1993: 123). Some variations in intensity of charcoal production can be inferred from the diagram: their relation to other events must be speculative, but there is a low level of MI about 7510 BP and its absence after 6200 BP; the Scottish 'pluvials' are dated at 7500 BP and at 6250–5800 BP. The cross-sections also show the expansion of *Sphagnum* bogs on streamside flats and blanket peat on the upland plateaux. The sequence of events leading to the latter is incorporated into the discussion in Chapter 3 on paludification (section 4).

EWE CRAG SLACK, NORTH YORK MOORS

Though not dated by radiocarbon, this site is interesting since it affords evidence of forest recession which resulted in the inwash of silt into a deep channel. The NYM have many sub-glacial drainage channels trenched into the moorlands, and they usually have several metres of biogenic deposits from the Holocene: at Ewe Crag Slack on Danby Moor at ~235 m, there are a maximum of 4.74 m of peats intercalated with silt layers, which in fact occur throughout the prehistoric period (Simmons et al 1975). The lowest of the Ewe Crag Slack examples is in the middle of Godwin's pollen zone VI, which would be expected to be about 8500 BP.

In the middle of the channel, the silt layer is 15 cm deep, contains charcoal, and lies within wood peats. Alder has not yet begun to rise and is apparently unaffected by other tree-pollen diminutions, which are of pine and oak. Reciprocally, hazel and birch rise and there is a peak of willow. Whereas the wood peat below the silt is almost free of herb taxa, with the exception of *Succisa* and some Compositae, the silt zone has many herbs (*Artemisia, Filipendula, Melampyrum, Rumex* and the Ranunculaceae), most of which vanish or diminish in the wood-peat horizons above. Bracken, the Filicales and *Polypodium* all rise during the silt phase. Local burning of forest previously dominated by *Pinus* seems to have occurred; and, as Jones (1976) puts it,

> The small cleared areas which were created as a result [of disturbance and fire] yielded sediment deposited as colluvium within the nearby mire, leaving patches where a mosaic of plant communities including ruderals, grassy sward and *Corylus* thicket soon developed in regeneration complexes.

The history of this deposit suggests, therefore, that the kinds of disturbances examined so far need not be confined to mixed deciduous forest or to the upper edge of forest and scrub, but can occur within the last coniferous woodlands to be found in the uplands during the early to mid-Flandrian.

VALLEY BOG, NORTH PENNINES

On the Moor House NNR at 549 m, this mire (NY 763331) is one of the highest to have a detailed pollen diagram, with the investigation by Chambers (1978) amplifying the earlier work by G. A. L. Johnson and Dunham (1963). The present bog overlies a small lake which was formed in Fl I and which became peat-covered during the Boreal period (zone VI of the Godwin scheme.) The disturbance phase, unaccompanied by any recorded charcoal, is most obvious at 430–415 cm when *Ulmus* undergoes an unsteady set of falls as *Corylus* rises. Many herbs increase their frequency: Rosaceae, Umbelliferae and *Filipendula* notably; others achieve a continuous presence, like *Rumex* (cf. *acetosella*), *Succisa* and Ranunculaceae. Occasional grains of Labiatae, Scrophulariaceae, Chenopodiaceae, *Artemisia* and *Urtica* are found, and there is subsequently a single grain of *P. lanceolata*. Radiocarbon dates for 421–426 cm of 5950±60 BP and for 426–431 cm of 5945±50 BP are virtually identical. Not remarked upon by the author, there is another scatter of herb pollens in the profile during zone VB II, at 6779±75 BP. As at Hard Hill (see above), a limited disturbance only can be inferred, though it may be noted that mixed deciduous forest with elm was present at this altitude.

Comparative Findings

The two earlier examples show that disturbance associated with fire is not confined to mixed deciduous woodland and its upper edge: it also happened before the assembly of the mixed forest and in the last coniferous woodlands in upland England. The disturbances show a wide range (10–40 per cent) of drops in ΣAP, reflecting either the intensity of the episode or the proximity of the sampling site. The trees most affected are pine and oak, with hazel and birch the beneficiaries. Even in the early examples, there is a wide range of herbs which respond to more open conditions; *Plantago* spp are usually absent, however.

A last feature is that of disturbance of the vegetation during the mid-Holocene even in areas where Mesolithic finds are absent. A good example of this is upland Ardudwy (NW), where at Moel-y-Gerddi (280 m) a phase at 7510±95 BP shows charcoal along with big peaks in grasses, sedges and some wetland herbs. The trees are much diminished, and any recovery is from alder and willow but not *Corylus*. The pattern is sufficiently comparable to others in upland EW, however, for the authors to predict the eventual discovery of mesolithic material in the area (Chambers and Price 1988; Chambers et al. 1988). But all the above sites are subject to the interpretive constraint that, presumably, any openings which were favoured by large mammals would not also be the exact places where humans chose to make their fires, sleep and curate tools.

Sites with Disturbance and Cereal Pollen Before an Elm Decline

For many years, the onset of the major declines in *Ulmus* pollen which occur ~5000 BP in so much of north-western Europe was taken to mark the onset of Neolithic economies in which farming

TABLE 2.4 Selected Pennine Mesolithic radiocarbon dates.

Site	Uncalibrated Date BP	Cal. BC
March Hill II	5875±75	4832 (4770) 4685
Rocher Moss	5830±100	4801 (4720) 4545
Lominot IV	5610±120	4545 (4460) 4342
Dunford Bridge B	5380±80	4334 (4240) 4086
Soyland Moor D	5820±95	4790 (4710) 4461

Source: E. Williams (1989), where the laboratory numbers and reasons for selection are given. Calibration at 1σ from Stuiver and Reimer (1993).

was practised. The key indicator was the presence of grains of domesticated cereals (usually wheat, *Triticum* spp). Intensified interest followed the detection of forest disturbance before an elm decline (albeit in the last few hundred years before 5000 BP) when cereal pollen was also found.

Great care has to be exercised in the identification of disturbance-with-cereal before the elm decline. The size of the grains and their shape are especially important since confusion with wild grasses with similar pollen morphology is possible and other considerations, as detailed by Edwards (1989), should be evaluated before an episode is admitted. Indeed, when using as filter the following criteria,

- more than one grain of cereal pollen is present in the unit in question;
- the grains have been positively identified as cereals using more than one criterion;
- there is no evidence of contamination of the horizons being examined;
- there are clear indicators of vegetation disturbance including ruderals indicative of arable activity;

then E. Williams (1989) allows only three satisfactory sites. Of these, the North Gill site to which she refers has now been dated by radiocarbon and thought to be post-Mesolithic in Turner, Innes and Simmons (1993), so that Soyland Moor D (C. T. Williams 1985) is the only English upland site to fulfil all the requirements. It can be put in the context of dated wood or wood charcoal from other upland sites (see Table 2.4). Later work includes Robinson's Moss (Tallis and Switsur 1990), which shows cereal-type pollen immediately prior to a drastic fall in elm at 4875±60 BP. The dates in Table 2.4 show that the Soyland Moor cereal-type phase is within the range of dates for the regional Mesolithic though it must be recalled that the other dates are from wood or charcoal and not from peats yielding evidence of cereal-type pollen.

At Soyland Moor, the early cereal-type pollen is at 5820±95 BP in profile D. Three grains were found in one sample and a repeat core also yielded one grain at the same level. (Poor preservation did not allow identification to genus level, although one grain is tentatively referred to *Hordeum*, barley.) At this level, ΣAP declines from 40 to 34 per cent. There is a small peak in *Fraxinus*, with all other tree species except alder falling. Hazel suffers a rapid fluctuation: it is at 55 per cent of ΣAP at 499 cm, then 35 per cent at 500 cm (the level of the cereals) and then reverts to 40 per cent, which was the pre-499 cm level. The cereals are accompanied by peaks and/or continuous (rather than sporadic) presences of *Plantago lanceolata*, *P. major/media*, *Rumex*, *Artemisia*, *Pteridium* and some wetland groups. The phase appears to be very short, with values returning to their pre-disturbance levels quite soon; there is no long-term rise in *Calluna*. Williams interprets this as the result of the selection of patches of base-rich soils for agriculture, which afterwards became waterlogged (ca 5820 is near the end of one of the Scottish 'pluvials').

COMPARISONS

This episode is not dissimilar from many phases very much nearer to elm declines (here it is at ~4865 BP): it is short-lived and accompanied by peaks in a ruderal flora not different from other disturbances. Its main interest lies in the strongly-argued case for the presence of cultivated grasses ca 1000 years rather than 100 years before an elm decline and 520 years before the first group of attested Neolithic dates given by E. Williams (1989).

4. GENERAL FINDINGS

A brief attempt to draw out generalities from the whole this chapter will be made here, using two major divisions into features in common to many of the phases described and those which are different. In each of these, attention will be paid to time, space and ecology.

Features in common to the episodes of all types chronicled here include the fact that they may be found at any time during later Flandrian I and throughout Fl II. There is usually an episode shortly before the first (if there is more than one) elm decline, though there may often be a period of woodland stability before such a phase. In spatial terms, all the episodes seem to represent small-scale changes in the vegetation; the standard of comparison is the movement of ΣAP and Σherb pollen frequencies in dated clearances from the Neolithic and later prehistory. It is, though, necessary to remember that pollen catchment characteristics will have changed as the area of high forest diminishes, and the admission of more pollen of open communities will probably have exaggerated the record of the progress of non-forest vegetation. The small-scale changes mean, as would be expected, that recovery back to forest is common, though by no means ubiquitous since some sites become paludified.

The location of the episodes has much in common with actual Mesolithic sites, in the sense that 'edges' of all kinds are favoured: topographic edges overlooking valleys but usually off the crests, near springs, and at the edges of lakes. Work in the South Pennines especially suggests that the upper edge of closed woodland is a favoured site to find evidence of burning and of peat initiation. The ecology of disturbance phases yields a very similar suite of ruderal indicators whatever the place and time; the concomitant presence of wetland plants is not universal but happens sufficiently often that an explanation needs to be sought.

What differs among these palaeoecologically discovered episodes? Their spacing in time lacks regularity: the three-fold pattern which was discussed for a number of sites is limited in its occurrence. Nor is there in most regions any increase in the number or intensity of the disturbances as the first elm decline is approached. This could be a facet of the density of work undertaken: where many diagrams exist in a region like the NYM, it appears to be the case that there is an increase in frequency of disturbance towards the elm decline (Innes and Simmons 1988, Figure 5). Though work on the Scottish 'pluvials' needs to be expanded, evidence so far accumulated allows no ubiquitous inferences of connections between wet periods and the presence of stable forest phases, though there are some suggestive coincidences here and there. Finally, the regrowth of woodland over peats at the end of Fl II (apparently caused by a lower frequency of fires), as documented in the Southern Pennines and at Bonfield Gill Head in the NYM, is limited in its occurrence.

So there are a number of general points which call out for explanatory mechanisms. Before discussing these, however, the body of work on the North York Moors will be transmitted in some detail since it is particularly focused on the last 1000 years of Flandrian II and may therefore suffuse some of the patterns so far discovered with more detailed evidence.

5. THE NORTH YORK MOORS

Although work from the Bonfield Gill and Ewe Crag Slack areas of these moorlands has been examined above, there is a great deal of other work from this relatively low and dry upland. Pollen analysis started here with a visit from the Swedish pioneer Gunnar Erdtman in the 1920s (Erdtman 1927) and was given a great boost by the innovative work of G. W. Dimbleby (1961, 1962) on soil pollen analysis. Modern investigations of organic materials started with Simmons' (1969) paper on both channel and blanket mire deposits and was continued through the 1970s and early 1980s with a series of theses and subsequent papers on all types of organic deposits. The Bonfield Gill Head profile (Simmons and Innes 1988b) has been of considerable interest in the present context. In the mid to later 1980s and early 1990s the emphasis has been on the North Gill area (discussed in detail below) of blanket peat, with a database of considerable size having been accumulated for an area about 500 × 100 metres. (All this work except the very detailed FRPA from North Gill is discussed in Spratt (1993) and updated in Simmons (1995).) The overall result has been the accumulation of a regional picture for the whole of the Late Devensian and the Flandrian, though the detail for different times and places is variable: there are few pollen diagrams for the limestone hills of the southern third of the upland, for example, and few radiocarbon dates for Bronze and Iron Age times. Happily, Flandrian II is very well covered on the northern moors and in peripheral deposits such as Seamer Carrs, Cleveland (not to be confused with Seamer Carr in the Vale of Pickering), and the North Gill work has brought a good density of radiocarbon dates.

The Mesolithic Archaeology of the North York Moors

This was brought together in Spratt and Simmons (1976) and has not changed in essence since then, though recent and current excavations in the Vale of Pickering by P. A. Mellars and by T. Schadla-Hall are adding greatly to the picture of both early and later Mesolithic in that adjacent region. A summary account of both the archaeology and the palaeoecology appears in Innes and Simmons (1988); the latest account of the archaeology of this and other periods is found in Spratt (1993). There appears to be no great difference between this upland and most of the others, and the occupation may be summarised as follows.

For early Mesolithic a high density of remains has been found in the peripheral lowland zone to the south (Vale of Pickering); this includes the much re-examined site of Star Carr (ca 9500 BP). R. M. Jacobi (1978) has confirmed that the same period is represented in the stone tool industries of the uplands as well.

For later Mesolithic the uplands have yielded two types of site: (a) the classic spreads of flint and charcoal at the mineral soil-peat interface, with a small range of tools; and (b) the larger sites such as Upleatham, with a wider range of tool types. Upleatham is on the edge of the upland, whereas the others are usually found at or near the spring-line, below the crest of the watershed, though 'crest' is not a term easily applied to the wide, flat interfluves of this upland. A small number of implements have been found in the lowlands peripheral to the North York Moors, and it is assumed that sea-level rises will have submerged most of the evidence of coastal settlement.

For Neolithic occupation, the periphery of the uplands has a few long barrows, but the concentration of many Neolithic finds is on lower ground, as near Whitby and in the dales and major river valleys like the Tees, Esk and Leven. The Corallian rocks of the southern part of the upland may well have been the most attractive soils for farmers in terms of their nutrient status, though it is reasonable to assume that even the siliceous rocks of the northern moors developed a brown earth soil when under deciduous forest. Arrowheads and tranchets have been found on the moors in some numbers and sometimes occur in conjunction with mesolithic material albeit in unstratified contexts. On Snilesworth Moor, fire exposed Mesolithic, Neolithic and Bronze Age stone tools within a radius of 25 m (D. Clark 1973). A certain continuity of occupance is usually inferred.

Evidence from North Gill (see Plate 5)

In his first paper from the region, Simmons (1969) recognised the complexity of the deposits towards the base of the peat in the sections of blanket mires exposed in the upper stretches of the North Gill on Glaisdale Moor at 350–370 m ASL (NZ 726007). A second phase of investigation by J. B. Innes (1981) and Simmons and Innes (1988a, 1988c) investigated that complexity and tried to set out a conspectus of alternating phases of disturbance and stability of the vegetation. A third phase, undertaken by J. Turner, Simmons and Innes, has resulted so far in a thesis (Innes 1989), a basic data-reporting paper (J. Turner, Innes and Simmons 1993) and detailed papers on the disturbances, the charcoal, and small

Plate 5   The Grain Beck area of the North York Moors. Land whose
         woodland was first opened in the later Mesolithic period has here been
         carved into field systems during the Bronze Age. The heather in the
         foreground is a characteristic feature of the local landscape but is a
         product of 19th-century moor management rather than of prehistory.

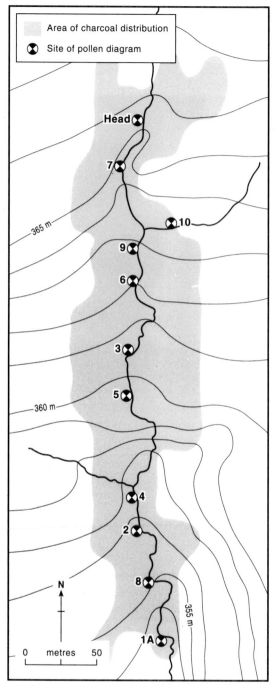

Figure 2.4   The pollen profile sites from the North Gill on Glaisdale
Moor (North York Moors). The contours are for the
current land surface, not the pre-peat surface. There is
no implication that the 'area of charcoal distribution'
is necessarily a single, synchronous, spread.

fluctuations of tree-canopy pollen (Simmons and Innes 1996a, b, c). This latter project described was undertaken with the aim of investigating in more detail the spatial diversity at North Gill during the mid-Flandrian and in particular the spatial and temporal dimensions of the disturbance phenomena. Ten pollen diagrams from eight new profiles have been added to the earlier data-sets. Profiles 2, 3 and Head are from the original set, and Profile 1A is close to the original NG1. Profiles 4, 5, 6, 7, 8, 9 and 10 are new profiles (see Figure 2.4). One diagram has been prepared from each, except for profile 5 which has two from parallel monoliths, 5A and 5B (J. Turner, Simmons and Innes 1989) and profile 9 which also has two, 9 and 9A. In total, the profiles are spaced at more or less regular intervals along 350 m of North Gill; but, in order to facilitate comparison with the earlier publications, he profiles have not been renumbered in order along the transect. The order from south to north is therefore 1A, 8, 4, 2, 5, 3, 6, 9, 10, 7, Head. Because the diagrams have been prepared at different times and with slightly different objectives, the sample interval varies. The more recent mostly have an interval of 1 cm. However, in addition to these 1 cm interval diagrams, selected portions (such as the disturbance phase described in earlier publications as D2 at sites 1A, 4, 5B, 6 and 7) have been analysed at 1 mm intervals. The pollen-analytical techniques used are described by Simmons, Turner and Innes (1989). Peat from selected levels at profiles 1A, 8, 4, 2, 5B, 6, 9 and 7 has been radiocarbon dated. Hence, all the diagrams have been rezoned, and this new zonation supersedes that in earlier publications.

The geology of the area shows that the peat is mostly underlain by solifluction deposits which are related in texture to the underlying solid. In the upper part of the Gill, around profiles Head, 7, 9, 10 and 6, the solifluction deposit is a clayey silty ferruginous sand containing rotten sandstone. At site 9 it is leached, and at profile 6 it is less deeply stained and more sandy. It overlies a calcareous sandstone with numerous mollusc shells, part of the Grey Limestone series of the Middle Jurassic, from which it was largely derived. Between-profile variations in the *Ulmus* and *Tilia* pollen frequencies indicate that the pre-peat soils around this upper section of the stream were more calcareous than those around profiles 6, 3, 5 and 2. In August 1989, during an exceptionally dry summer, the water-table came to the surface just south of profile 9 and this may well indicate the precise position of the boundary between the calcareous sandstone and the Middle Deltaic shales shown on the Geological Survey 1-inch map No. 43. In the middle portion of the Gill, around profiles 3, 5 and 2, the solifluction deposit is light-grey or buff-grey and clayey with only small and variable amounts of silt and sand. It overlies shattered shales of the Middle Deltaic Series. Near site 3, there are numerous large sandstone boulders on the surface of the clays. In the lower section of the Gill, around profiles 4, 8 and 1A, there is a sandy layer between the light-grey solifluction deposit and the peat. South of profile 1, it contains large stones.

One reason for the choice of the North Gill for detailed investigation was that previous work had shown that the majority of the peat represented Fl II, with some earlier and some later deposits. Most profiles have therefore a period of time in common, and so it becomes possible to compare spatial differences in the intensity of forest recession, for instance, or in the incidence of paludification. Because of this overlap in time, the diagrams from many of the profiles have three features in common: a section with high *Alnus* frequencies; an *Ulmus* decline; disturbance phases characterised by higher values for the *Betula, Pinus, Salix* and *Melampyrum* frequencies and lower values for that of *Quercus*.

The zonation used here (and in J. Turner, Innes and Simmons 1993) is based on the *Alnus* and *Ulmus* frequencies and not, as in previous publications, upon the taxa associated with the disturbance phases. Because no two diagrams are totally alike and neither the high *Alnus* zone nor the *Ulmus* decline is synchronous, the pollen assemblage zones are not chronozones. They simply highlight vegetational processes that were occurring at different times in different parts of the stream's course. The zonation is as follows.

> NG1: characterised by high frequencies of *Corylus* and low frequencies of *Alnus* pollen and considered equivalent to Godwin's zone VI or Flandrian Id. It is represented at only three profiles: by three samples at profile 2, two at profile 5B and one at profile 9. Interestingly, at each of these the peat began forming later than at a neighbouring profile. This early pollen assemblage is best explained by assuming that the samples represent forest mor humus which accumulated while the ground was becoming damper.
>
> NG2: characterised by a mixture of *Betula, Pinus, Ulmus, Quercus, Alnus, Corylus* and *Salix* pollen and considered equivalent to Godwin's VIIa or Flandrian II. It occurs at the base of the profile at sites 4, 2, 5B, 3 and 6, a time when there was some alder in the regional forests but no local alder carr in the channel of the gill.

TABLE 2.5 Radiocarbon dates for the end of zone NG4 at North Gill.

Site	depth	Lab. code	date BP
1	79	SRR-3635	5105 ± 45
8	85	SRR-3637	5755 ± 45
4	74	SRR-3643	5405 ± 45
6	74	SRR-3651	5515 ± 45
5A	76	estimated	5740

NG3: characterised by high *Alnus* frequencies, it occurs at all sites except 7, 9, 10 and Head. The high *Alnus* frequencies represent an alder carr lateral to the peat in that part of the gill. Asynchrony is demonstrated by the range of radiocarbon dates for its end (see Table 2.5): actual dates assayed are 5405, 5515 and 5785 (all±45) BP; estimated dates, ~5740 and ~5881 BP.

NG4: similar to NG2. It occurs at all sites and represents the period when peat had spread to the edge of the channel of the gill and was abutting dry ground, with no room for a bordering carr. (Because there is no zone NG3 at sites 7, 9, 10 and Head, NG2 and NG4 cannot be separated and in these diagrams the relevant section is referred to as NG2/4.) Dates for the *Ulmus* decline (of which there are ten: see Table 2.6) range from 3490±45 to 5995±45, a difference of at least 2505 radiocarbon years.

NG5: characterised by low values for the *Ulmus* frequency and considered equivalent to Godwin's VIIb or Flandrian III. It occurs in all the profiles except NG2.

RECESSIONS OF THE FOREST

Unlike for example, the sites investigated by Tallis and Switsur (1990), it seems from the pollen frequencies that the North Gill in Fl II was a dominantly forested environment into zone NG3, after which there are some longer-term diminutions in the ΣAP/NAP ratio. This has certain implications for the pollen catchment areas of the sampled profiles. At some sites, for example site 5, disturbances are very clearly expressed, indicating that they affected much of that site's pollen catchment. At others, for example site 8, they are more weakly depicted because they were affecting less of that site's catchment. In attempting to define the area of any one episode of disturbance, it is helpful to envisage two distinct possibilities. If the area disturbed had been approximately the same as that of a site's pollen catchmen that is, a few tens of metres

TABLE 2.6 Elm decline calibrations.

Sample	Radiocarbon years BP	cal. age years BC	cal. age ranges BC at 1σ
NG1A 59 cm	3600 ± 45 (SRR-3632)	1936	2016 (1936) 1885
NG1A 60 cm	4640 ± 50 (SRR-3868)	3370	3501 (3370) 3353
NG8 72 cm	3645 ± 45 (SRR-3870)	2015, 2006, 1979	2113 (2015, 2006, 1979) 1934
NG4 55 cm	5290 ± 45 (SRR-3638)	4214, 4204, 4136, 4125, 4082, 4053, 4048	4223 (4214, 4204, 4125, 4082, 4053, 4048) 4003
NG5B 30 cm	4595 ± 45 (SRR-3646)	3355	3370 (3355) 3339
NG5B 30 cm	4730 ± 80 (HAR-6620)	3610, 3510, 3390,	3634 (3610, 3510, 3390) 3372
NG6 58 cm	3490 ± 45 (SRR-3649)	1859, 1847, 1772	1880 (1859, 1847, 1772) 1741
NG9 67 cm	5690 ± 45 (SRR-3871)	4518	4549 (4518) 4465
NG9 68 cm	5595 ± 45 (SRR-3872)	4454, 4414, 4405	4464 (4454, 4414, 4405) 4360)
NG7 69 cm	4625 ± 45 (SRR-3653)	3365	3496 (3365) 3349

Calibration according to Stuiver and Reimer 1993. In national terms, dates of > uncal. 5375 BP/cal. BC 4237 are likely to be Mesolithic; younger dates, Neolithic.

in diameter (or equivalent dimension), each episode would have been recorded at only one site. Alternatively, if the area had been many hundreds of metres or more in diameter, each disruption would have been recorded at several adjacent or all sites, and the data, as summarised in Figure 2.5, would have shown a more regular pattern. The absence of such a pattern (as illustrated by the contrasts between sites 7 and 9, 9 and 6, 6 and 5, and 8 and 1) argues that any area of disturbed vegetation was of the order of tens rather than many hundreds of metres in diameter.

Inspection of the longer profiles for an equivalent of the three-fold sequence detected at Blacklane Brook (DM), Robinson's Moss (CP) and Bonfield Gill Head (NYM) reveals no consistency of pattern. Profile NG5B (which has something of the status of the 'standard' diagram of the set) has a pattern of charcoal content in which there is a basal phase of high values for both macro- and

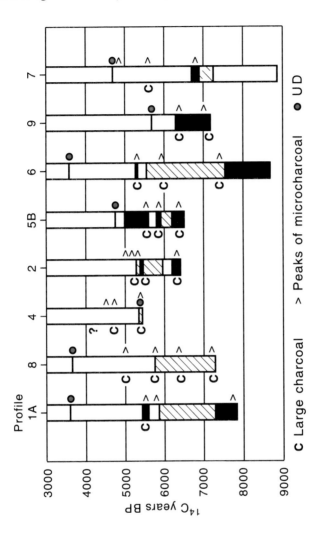

Figure 2.5   A synthesis of the radiocarbon dates of certain
             phenomena in the North Gill profiles. UD = *Ulmus*
             decline. Note that peaks in large charcoal are always
             accompanied by peaks in the microcharcoal (< 180
             μm) but the reverse is not always the case. The dense
             shading indicates periods of forest disturbance;
             diagonal lines show the presence of alder woodland.

             Source: I. G. Simmons and J. B. Innes (1996b),
             'Prehistoric charcoal in peat profiles at North Gill,
             North Yorkshire, England', *J. Archaeol. Sci.* 23, 193–7.

microscopic fragments, after which there is a continuous presence of microscopic charcoal in which there are two small peaks that coincide with the presence (after an absence) of larger material. There is then a pre-elm-decline peak (5480±50 BP) of microscopic carbonised matter but unaccompanied by the larger solids. On the other hand, at profile NG7 (150 m upstream), which records the same time-span, there appears to be only one disturbance phase, at 5645±45 BP. If it is accepted that each of these profiles is likely to have had discrete pollen catchment areas (at any rate at a time when forest predominated the landscape), then any three-fold division is clearly a restricted phenomenon rather than some nationwide epic event driven by climate or culture: the picture given above is confirmed. In passing though, it can be noted that the NG5B phase just mentioned is more or less the same as a pre-elm-decline phase at Robinson's Moss (CP: 5470±50 BP) and the NG7 is very close to an emphatic phase at Bonfield Gill Head (NYM: 5645±45 BP). If the first phase in any three-fold sequence is at the base of the profile, then it suggests that fire and forest opening are implicated in the inception of peat growth and that thereafter disturbance processes at varying distances from the collecting site and/or in catchments with differing degrees of openness are recorded. The presence of intensified evidence of disturbance just before the elm decline is, however, very widely recorded in the NYM.

The Pattern in Time

Inspection of Figure 2.5 shows that the forest disturbances (as detected by changes in pollen frequency and the presence of charcoal described above) are not synchronous down the gill, nor do they each last the same length of time. The main types are:

1. Basal disturbances: those which occur at the base of the accumulation profile and thus which appear to be either coincident in time and space with the inception of peat growth or causally implicated in it. The phenomenon occurs in profiles 1A, 2, 5B, 6 and 9.
2. Relatively long periods of disturbance in mid-profile. The best examples are at 5B, 1A and 7, with a length of hundreds of years.
3. Short periods of disturbance in mid-profile, lasting decades at most, as at site 4.

The intervals between disturbances can usually only be estimated since the radiocarbon control over whole profiles is not close enough to give more precise appraisals; but the orders of magnitude are: as follows Profile 1A, 1700 yr; Profile 2, 980 yr; Profile 5B, 300 yr, 100 yr; Profile 6, 2300 yr; Profile 7, 1100 yr. But any discussion of the significance of these numbers is best postponed until after the later discussion of the spatial pattern of disturbance, since it is conceivable that some of these are the same disturbance expressed in different profiles.

Ecological Sequences at Disturbances

Here, an attempt will be made to describe the ecological progression during a disturbance phase of the above types 1 and 2, using extrapolations from the available radiocarbon dates to give chronological estimates of the durations involved.

(1a) A basal phase at profile 2, ca 6250–5900 BP (detail in Innes 1981: 107–15) in zones NG1 and NG2 of the present book. It comprises three samples at 72–78 cm (NG1) and four samples in NG2, 64–70 cm. The latter is an amorphous peat, but the lowest levels are composed of a charcoal-and silt-rich material with very small fragments of charred wood and bark in the lowest levels. These particles extend into the uppermost few centimetres of the yellow sand below the organic profile. The pollen content of NG1 and NG2 shows that ΣAP is only 25 per cent of total pollen (mostly pine and birch, with a significant rise in alder during the zone); shrubs are dominated by *Corylus* and declining values for *Salix* with representation of four other genera of shrubs. *Calluna* frequencies are low. Most of the herb pollen is of sedges and grasses, with some other damp-habitat plants like *Filipendula* and *Ranunculus*. Dry ground is indicated by *Pteridium*. In NG1, there is a sparse presence of *Artemisia* and Chenopodiaceae. There is very little *Sphagnum* in this profile until zone NG4, after ~5210 BP. The zones are terminated by a layer of birch wood about 5 cm thick, mostly rootlet material and apparently slightly charred. After this horizon, ΣAP (if alder is included) rises to 70 per cent of ΣP by the end of NG3 at 5220±75 BP. The picture, then is of open birch and pine woodland with hazel and several other small trees of the *Prunus* and *Sorbus* genera, ivy and honeysuckle. Some areas of the ground are damp but other parts dry, and fire has been a common local occurrence though it might not have been at that very place since no larger fragments occur. The whole habitat mosaic was however wet enough to accumulate peat rather slowly, as shown by the amorphous peat of NG2; the layer of wood suggests that the peat was susceptible to drying out and recolonisation by birch. Some resemblance to the Dufton Moss phase in Upper Teesdale can be seen.

(1b) The basal phase at profile 9 is higher up the gill at a point where microtopography contains no water-accumulating sites and has relatively steep gradients. Dating is difficult since in a 98 cm profile the lowest radiocarbon date is at 80 cm (6260±45 BP). Extrapolation here is especially risky since there is a sandy layer at 86–88 cm and much charcoal in the amorphous matrix below 85 cm. If it is assumed that the largely amorphous matrix has grown at a constant rate, then the base of the organic material is ca, 7000 BP. The pollen and charcoal content would then show a disturbance lasting from 7000 to 6260, that is 740 years. The evidence for this (Innes 1989: 246–54) consists especially of the continuous presence of high values of small and microscopic charcoal from the base of the profile as high as 80 cm, with large charcoal at the base which is coincident with sand in the peat at 86–88 cm. Oak and alder are low, while hazel, pine and birch are high. Ruderals are present (including *Plantago lanceolata*), and there is a high *Melampyrum* curve. As ΣAP is about 20 per cent, the catchment is unlikely to have been closed forest. The sandy layer is attended by rises in oak, hazel, heather and Cyperaceae; there is a single grain of *P. lanceolata* and a two-sample peak in *Sphagnum* followed by a sharp drop. All types of charcoal are present. There are also falls in pine, birch and *Melampyrum*, Rosaceae and Filicales, and *Rumex*. Thus, in spite of the stratigraphic evidence of burning and erosion, the pollen evidence is of recovery of woodland: there is no obvious explanation for this dichotomy except to guess that the sand and charcoal are allochthonous, though the presence of large charcoal in a non-collecting area does not sit easily in such a frame.

The very base of profile 9 (90-100 cm) has been additionally examined at 5 mm intervals[1], as profile 9A. This shows the disturbance indicators to be strongest in the 897.5–1000 cm zone, with much lower frequencies of them between 897.5 and 890 cm. Once again, the actual inception of the accumulation of organic material is associated with disturbance phenomena.

(2a) A good example of a non-basal but far from evanescent disturbance is found near the opening of zone NG4 at profile 5B. The horizons from 68–75 cm have been counted at 1 mm intervals, and a 1 cm slice at 73 cm has a ^{14}C date of 5760±90 BP. The main disturbance phenomena last from 687–734 mm, which at a profile-long accumulation rate of 0.039 cm/yr is a period of 120 years. There are thirty-seven samples within this period, so that each sample contains pollen rain from ~3 years. At 734 mm per cent the ΣAP is 60 per cent of ΣP; if hazel is added, then canopy-formers are at ~90 per cent of ΣP. This tree pollen is mainly *Alnus*, with other woody genera at low levels. With wood peats present at 820–860 cm, it seems likely that an alder carr formed a significant fraction of the local vegetation, though by the time of the start of zone NG4, it had given way to amorphous peat *in situ*. A major change occurs at 730 mm, where there is silt (2 mm thick) in the profile, and for the next five samples (= 15 years) there are high microscopic charcoal frequencies. These five samples neatly define a peak in *Pinus* and *Corylus* and falls in *Alnus*, *Quercus* and in *Betula* a 3-year peak followed by a sharp drop and a 12-year recovery. The NAP in this 5-horizon (= 15-yr) time-slice also change sharply. Rapid rises in *Calluna*, *Hedera* and *Pteridium*, Poaceae, Rosaceae, Filicales and *Sphagnum* are seen, and the ruderal-open-ground taxa such as *Melampyrum*, *Plantago lanceolata*, *Rumex acetosa/acetosella* type and *Succisa* become present.

The rest of the disturbance phase is capable of two interpreta-tions. The *first* (as laid out in J. Turner, Innes and Simmons 1993) stresses the high level of resolution of the data and the likelihood of yearly variations in the accumulation rate. This sees a period of $20 \times 3 = 60$ years' stability of an opening in the woodland; at 708 mm the *Melampyrum* decreases and heather increases, and then after 9–12 years the tree-pollen concentration rises at the expense of shrubs and open-ground plants. So, by 697 mm the oak-pollen frequency is restored to its 730 mm level. The ΣAP is then at about 40 per cent (ΣAP + shrubs = 70 per cent), so recovery of cover is not complete. A *second* representation squeezes the content of the data into sub-phases which can be shown as in Table 2.7. This presents a virtually classic position of a double sequence of disturbance-recovery phases, with the charcoal coinciding with the high levels of disturbance indicators, of which *Melampyrum* is perhaps the best integrator in the pollen curves. In both cases, the charcoal peaks last ~15 years, but a reasonably high level of charcoal is present in the intermediate recovery phase and in the highest one as well, though almost absent above 690 mm. Choice between these interpretations must await the examination of other examples.

(2b) Profile 1A is from the lower end of the gill. A largely steady-state zone NG3 is followed by a disturbance phase which can be tied to two radiocarbon dates in successive 1 cm slices of 5680±50 BP and 5515±45 BP. As at profile 5B, enhanced levels of charcoal are a first clue to the presence of a disturbance phase, and

TABLE 2.7 Profile 5B 1 mm count zone: 700–730 mm.

	Up	Down	Up	Down	
700–708 mm = 27 years	Qu, Al	Be, Pi, Co, Sx	Poly	Mel (but present); Gram, Call, Cyps, P. lance, Rosac, Sph, Pterid	Recovery of woodland
709–717 mm = 27 years	Charcoal 710–714 Be, Pi, Co, Sx	Qu a little, Al	Rx, Call, Pterid, Rosac'e, Mel (big), Succisa at end; Epilobium with charcoal		Disturbance phase
718–726 mm = 27 years	Be gains, Qu recov,	Co	Potentilla, Ranun'e, Rosac'e	Melam down but present, Filic, Pterid, Succisa	Recovery of woodland
727–730 mm = 15 years	Charcoal peak Be at end, Pi, Co, Sx, Cal, Ul (slight)	Al	Pterid	Potentilla	Disturbance phase

Note: at 718–720 mm there is a sharp downward kink in ΣAP without any obvious sharp rises in NAP; *Calluna* and Filicales are the main beneficiaries. The pollen concentration figures for trees rise sharply.
Source: Innes 1989, Figures 31–6.

in this case the horizons 69–76.3 cm encompass the phenomena. These levels have been counted at 1 mm intervals. Calculation of the times involved are difficult because of the necessity of rejecting two of the radiocarbon determinations from further up the profile. Use of a date of 4640±50 BP at 60 cm allows the inference of an accumulation rate of 0.015 cm/yr; in that case, 76.3 cm is equivalent to ~5766 BP and 69 cm to 5240 BP. So 73 mm of deposit contain 526 years and 1 mm = 7 years of pollen rain. The FRPA at 1 mm evidence (Innes 1989: Figure 67–72) allows a division on pollen content into three, set out in Table 2.8. This presents the appearance of a classic three-fold sequence of a forest environment (ΣAP is 45 per cent below 765 mm, with ΣAP × shrubs at 80 per cent) being subject to disturbance with the loss especially of oak and the accession of a large suite of open-ground plants, followed by a recovery of the woodland though with a greater component of hazel in the resulting cover. A special feature of this phase, however, is the appearance of large grains of Gramineae subject to very careful examination for their possible determination as Cerealia. As Table 2.9 records, some of them satisfy the conditions for referral to the genus *Triticum*, the wheats.

(2c) Profile 7 is near the head of the gill. The time-span covered by the peat is one of the longest in the stream section: in a 94 cm profile, the lowest date is at 82 cm and is 6735±45BP. An overall accumulation rate of 0.006 cm/yr would then place inception at ~8735 BP, though since alder is already established, this looks rather late and some slowing-up of growth rate at the base is likely. Inspection of the pollen curves shows a number of possible disturbance phases, and the one between 77.5 and 83 cm was subjected to FRPA. Radiocarbon dates of 6710±50 BP at 80 cm and 6735± at 82 cm were obtained. The local environment at ~6710 was different from other profiles discussed, since ΣAP was only 30 per cent; ΣAP + *Corylus* was 80 per cent, suggesting that hazel was no mere understorey shrub but an important component of the woody vegetation. The same is true at North Gill Head, the highest-altitude profile examined: here there was charcoal at the base of the profile, suggesting that the lack of high forest was due to pre-deposition disturbance (Simmons and Innes 1996a). A similar history is found at a profile at Bluewath Beck Head (NZ 739006; 375 m; Innes 1981: 161–79) some 750 m east of North Gill Head.

As with some other profiles, the 1 mm counting allows for degrees of fineness of interpretation. Inspection of the curve for

TABLE 2.8 Profile 1A 1 mm count zone: 690–763 mm.

	Up	Down	Up	Down	Cereals
690–721 mm = 189 years; 690 mm = ~5240 bp	Qu, Al, Tilia	Co, Be, Pi, Sx, some effect on Cal		Ruderals, Rumex, Melam after 719	717 and 718: Cereal-type only. Early disturbance followed by recovery
722–746 mm = 175 years	Minor charcoal 720–725; Major at 730–740 (70 years) Be, Pi, Co, Sx, Cal = shrubs; charcoal, high at 746	Qu	Mel, Rx, Pterid; large suite ruderal herbs 722–727 inc P. lance		723–730: 1 + *Triticum* or *Elymus*; 3 *Triticum* type, 1 Cereal type Disturbance phase
747–763 mm = 119 years; 763 mm = ~5766 bp	Qu, Al, Ul all high; Gram				Stable woodland

Source: Innes 1989, Figures 49–54.

TABLE 2.9 Cereal-type pollen grains from North Gill profile 1A.

Depth	Size (microns)	Ratio	Annulus (microns)	Morphology
725 mm	51.5 × 35	1.47	8.7	cf. *Secale*
725 mm	42 × 32	1.25	9.0	
725 mm	43.6 × 36	1.20	8.2	
725 mm	43.7 × 41.6	1.05	12.0	*Triticum*
725 mm	51.5 × 41.1	1.25	12.8	*Triticum*
730 mm	52.5 × 41.2	1.27	10.3	? *Triticum*
730 mm	36 × 35	1.05	10.0	*Triticum*
730 mm	51 × 41	1.24	11.0	? *Triticum*
730 mm	39.1 × 36	1.08	8.0	
723 mm	36 × 36	1.00	7.2	
723 mm	fragment only		10.3	
719 mm	41 × 38	1.07	8.7	
718 mm	41 × 38	1.07	10.2	

Melampyrum, for example, might suggest a single disturbance phase from 786–820 mm (at the profile-long accumulation rate of 0.006 cm/yr, this would be 56 yr, each sample containing 1.6 yr pollen rain. In this can be seen a relatively simple sequence in which oak and alder decline at the expense of birch, pine and hazel; there is a corresponding presence of plants of open ground. The height of the disturbance is in the middle, when peaks of charcoal are found at 790, 803 and 807 mm: in the same portion can be found grains of *Artemisia* and the only Chenopodiaceae of the profile. Small quantities of all except the microscopic charcoal size and the absence of *Neurospora* at all except the three horizons designated above suggest that the fire was not at this actual profile location.

However, the detail of the diagram will allow a more refined set of sub-phases, based on the *Melampyrum* curve. In this, three disturbances can be separated, with recovery in between. The mirroring of the tree and open-ground pollen is virtually complete, with oak and alder declining most. The detectable phases are set out in Table 2.10. The disturbance phases are ca 10 yr, 27 yr and 10 yr long respectively, and each is associated with peaks in microscopic charcoal, but only the 27-yr phase has any larger material. This phase has higher values of bracken fern, for example, and more herb taxa than the other disturbances.

In fact, this 27-yr phase can itself be subdivided using the *Melampyrum* curve: a set of sub-phases is laid out in Table 2.11. If

TABLE 2.10 Profile 7.1 mm count zone: 775–828 mm.

Depth	Years	State	Notes (1)	Notes (2)
775–786	19.2	Recovery	Arbitrary top	
787–792	9.6	Disturbance		
793–795	4.8	Recovery		
796–812	27.2	Disturbance	Most intensive D phase: Small charcoal at 799/803/807; peaks in Micros 800–801/804–805/807	Capable of further threefold division
813–817	8.0	Recovery		
818–820	4.8	Disturbance		
821–828	12.8	Stable	Arbitrary base	

Source: Innes 1989, Figures 103–14.

it is accepted that this is not a distortion of the evidence, then there is a classic three-fold history:

1. A disturbance phase of 7 yr in which *Melampyrum* and bracken rise rapidly but fall after about 4 years; indicators of acidity like heather and *Sphagnum* fall.
2. Some recovery (nearly 5 yr) with a fall in *Melampyrum*, but bracken is at its highest; heather rises and is accompanied by rising *Sphagnum*. Some micro-charcoal for 2–3 yr and a suite of ruderals including *Epilobium*, *Cirsium* and Chenopodiaceae; *Artemisia* near the top.
3. More disturbance (6 yr) with small and micro-charcoal in early 2–3 yr phase. Bracken steady. *Melampyrum* imitates its sub-zone (i) behaviour, *Calluna* is a mirror image; *Sphagnum* falls. Fewer ruderals but single occurrences of *Artemisia*, *Epilobium*, *Urtica*.

Clearly, any recovery was short-lived in (ii), and any processes of forest recession leading to acidification seem at this stage to be reversible, though after 786 mm *Calluna* rises to very high levels; *Sphagnum* does not however follow it.

Acceptance of the various levels of interpretation of profile 7 gives some insight into the scale of processes producing disturbance and raises the possibility that accumulation rates are critical in the amount of detail which they yield to 1 mm sampling and

TABLE 2.11 Profile 7 1 mm count zone: 797–812 mm.

mm	Number of samples	Yr	State	Small charcoal	Micro charcoal	*Melamp* curve	Graminaea curve	*Pter* curve	*Call*	*Sphagnum*	Ruderals
797–801	5	6	**Disturbance**	X	XX	Rises→falls: > shape	Rising steadily	± steady	Falls→rises: < shape	Falling	Urt Art Epi
802–805	4	4.8	Intensification	X	XX	Lower but high	low high high low	Highest	Rising	Rising	2 × Art; 2 × Epi; Ci; Ch
806–812	7	8.4	**Disturbance**	X		Rises→falls: > shape	Low	Rises→falls	Falling	Falling	Epi Art

Note: ΣAP/NAP ratio is ± constant except for a sharp dip at 809–804 mm; *Corylus* is ± constant except for a minor peak at 803–805 mm

Abbreviations: Art = *Artemisia*; Urt = *Urtica*; Epi = *Epilobium*; Ci = *Cirsium*; Ch = *Chenopodiaceae*.

Source: Innes 1989, Figures 109–14.

thus that other disturbance phases may in fact be composite. The four 1 cm horizons at profile 2 (41–44 cm; 5220±75 BP) could be such a phase: at 0.036 cm/yr accumulation, they last 111 years, of the same order of magnitude as the 700–730 mm double phase at 5B, for instance, or the disturbance phase itself at 1A, or the 775–828 mm horizons at profile 7.

The Pattern of Charcoal Layers

Figure 2.5 summarises the incidence of major finds of charcoal in the North Gill profiles (Simmons and Innes 1996b). The 'large' material is deemed to be the result of *in situ* burning or very local inwash and is usually in discrete layers. The microscopic material is in fact present throughout most profiles, but its concentration is notably peaky and these high values are plotted on the diagram. This plot reveals a number of features:

1. Both 'large' (LA) and microscopic (MI) charcoal are found at the base of most profiles. The plot only shows the peaks of MI, and there is normally a constant background rainout of lower frequencies.
2. LA and MI are often found together, which is not surprising since a fire will create charcoal fragments of many different sizes according to its intensity and fuel load.
3. MI occurs without LA but not the reverse: this is as might be expected.
4. The time intervals between LA layers and MI peaks are not regular but their variation is not extreme: the average for local fires leaving evidence in the profile is 786 yr and for peaks of MI it is 742 yr. The range is from a 10-yr interval to 2000 yr, so the average is not a very meaningful figure.
5. If it is recalled that only 350 m separates North Gill Head profile from profile 1A, then an area of 350 m × the catchments (MI might well behave like a very large pollen grain) has been subject to fires and their aftermath for the total period of peat accumulation until 5000 BP. If this strip is regarded as one landscape element, then combining the LA and MI peaks gives a virtually constant presence with main events at intervals of never more than 400 years: interval of 100 years, 2 examples; 200 years, 6 examples; 300 years, 7 examples; 400 years, 2 examples.
   Dates of one episode (rounded) are 7600, 7500, 7200,

TABLE 2.12 Estimated dates for onset
of peat accumulation at North Gill.

Profile	Date (years BP)
1A	7824
8	7276
4	5412
2	6389
5B	6469
6	8631
9	7130
7	8800

7000, 6800, 6500, 5000 and 4800; dates of two episodes are
6300 and 5800; and dates of three episodes are 5500 and
5200. (There is a 400-yr gap between 6300 (2 examples)
and 5900 (1 example), then 100 years to 5800 (2 examples). Without the 5900 example (MI in profile 6), then
there would be a 500-yr gap corresponding largely to the
Scottish 'pluvial' of 6250–5800 BP.)

Note also that the period 6300–5200 encompasses all
the dates with more than one phase, suggesting a higher
fire frequency during those years. This concurs well with
evidence in the earlier part of Chapter 5 suggesting the
common occurrence of disturbance in the 1000 years
before the elm decline.

Peat Growth

A date for peat inception at each profile was calculated from its
age/depth plot and estimated increment. The results (see Table
2.12) indicate that peat began forming at profiles 7 and 6 in
the upper section of the gill during the first half of the ninth
millennium BP and spread to the other parts of the upper, and to
profiles 1 and 8 in the lower, section of the gill during the eighth
millennium. Eventually, the gentler slopes around profiles 2, 5
and 4 in the middle section were colonised some time during the
sixth and fifth millennia, a variation of some 3000 years.

The lack of a neat correlation with the underlying deposits
indicates that peat inception was influenced by several factors.
Peat began forming in the upper course of the gill on the solifluction deposits derived from the calcareous sandstones (profiles 6
and 7) shortly after 9000 BP. Charcoal at the soil/peat interface
and the *Melampyrum* pollen in the first few centimetres of peat

indicate that the woodland was already subject to disturbance at that time. This may well have contributed to the initiation of the peat at both sites, which for different reasons were damper than elsewhere in the gill: profile 6 because it is just south of where water surfaces today during dry periods, and profile 7 because it is near a spring. Meanwhile, peat began forming at the most southerly profile (site 1A) just after 8000 BP, again with associated evidence for forest disturbance. By 7000 BP, it had spread upstream to the neighbouring profile 8. This profile is unusual in having very little *Melampyrum* in the first few centimetres formed, indicating perhaps that its peat inception was influenced more by waterlogging than by disturbance of the vegetation. Waterlogging would have begun as soon as the developing peat at profile 1A had started to block the channel. When peat began to form in the middle section of the gill during the sixth and fifth millennia, there is again evidence for disturbance.

It seems therefore that, irrespective of the millennium in which peat inception occurred, disturbance of the forest was the most direct contributing factor. Only near existing patches of peat, for example at profile 8, was autogenic paludification the immediate, though indirect, cause. The climate must have been suitable for peat accumulation, but it is clear from the long period involved that neither climatic deterioration nor local variations in soil contributed in any significant way.

COMPARATIVE FINDINGS FROM NORTH GILL

Comparing the length of time occupied by disturbances is not easy since not all of them are susceptible to accurate estimation: the distribution of radiocarbon dates and obvious changes in accumulation rates prevent this. It can be said, however, that they are mostly of the order of hundreds of years rather than simply of decades (and none reach the thousand mark) if the full stretch is measured and relatively minor internal variations as chronicled for profile 5B are ignored.

The most detailed diagram is in fact that from profile 5B. The first samples represent apparently undisturbed woodland, with some light-demanding species. There are high concentrations of the pollen of *Corylus*, *Quercus*, *Ulmus* and *Calluna*. There are then further increases in the *Corylus* and *Calluna* together with increases in *Pinus*, Poaceae, *Melampyrum*, *Succisa*, various other herbs and Filicales. Also found is a single high concentration of *Betula*. This perhaps represents an initial opening of the canopy, allowing either *Calluna* and several of the tree species to flower more abundantly, or easier access of their pollen to the accumulating peat surface, followed a few years later by further opening of the woody canopy together with burning of the ground vegetation, thus encouraging *Melampyrum* and grasses rather than *Calluna* in the newly-created glades.

During the main part of the disturbance, there are only minor (but repetitively patterned) changes in the increased concentrations. There is charcoal in many of the samples and also some mineral material. The period of stability appears to have lasted for 40–60 years at this site, and the continued high pollen concentrations for light-demanding herbs and shrubs allows the inference that these woodland glades with their more grassy ground flora were being maintained. The minor variations discussed above (pp. 94–8) suggest the renewal of the maintenance process or processes. Continued opening of the canopy and burning of the ground vegetation would produce such a pattern in the pollen rain.

At the end of the disturbance, there is a decrease in the *Melampyrum* pollen concentration and an increase in that of *Calluna*, indicating that the nature of the ground flora was changing. The cessation of the disturbance processes may well have encouraged the growth of *Calluna* rather than *Melampyrum* for a few years until the canopy began to close. An estimated 8 to 12 years later, there is a sharp decrease in the Poaceae, *Melampyrum*, *Calluna*, Rosaceae, *Corylus* and Filicales concentrations and a more gradual one in those of *Betula*, *Pinus*, *Ulmus*, and *Quercus*, as the amount of pollen reaching the peat deposit returned to the original values. Finally, after another 8 to 12 years there are increases in the concentrations of *Sphagnum* spores and Cyperaceae and Poaceae pollen, probably representing a lateral encroachment of peat at the edge of the disturbed area.

Comparison of pollen analysis at different levels of resolution at North Gill, where it is possible to compare the patterns shown by counts at 1 cm and 1 mm, suggests that many of the phases identified on earlier diagrams from this and other uplands are of episodes comparable to the North Gill sequence. Multi-profile analysis (to establish spatial patterns) and FRPA to establish detailed pollen-taxonomic orders would very likely show patterns which differed only in the detail which would be expected in, for example, the differences in the proportion of a herb taxon in a series of comparable grassy glades, or the growth rates of woody shrubs not subject to any disturbance.

6. CHAPTER SUMMARY

This chapter has covered the palaeoecological evidence from a number of upland sites. These have been of two main types.

1. The first group contains work done over a long period until the recent past from a variety of locations. It reminds us of the small scale of the changes in the forest, the apparent paludification of some of the disturbed areas. Also characteristic are lakeside and streamside and -head locations. But distribution in time is more often random than not, with the exception of a greater intensity just before the transition to Fl III.

2. Much of this is confirmed by the more concentrated FRPA from the North York Moors, especially North Gill. Detail from North Gill contains additional minutiae like the evidence for the lightening of the canopy early in one disturbance phase. Finer resolution suggests a more important role for grasses in the ground flora of the disturbance patch than earlier investigations. Neither type of work has the sort of spatial coverage which would enable an estimate to be made of the area disturbed at any one time.

NOTE

1. Where FRPA is used, horizons are numbered as millimetres (mm) rather than as decimalised centimetres: 89 cm becomes 890 mm, for example.

CHAPTER THREE

Detectable Ecological Processes

In examining a large number of palaeoecological investigations from the uplands during the later Mesolithic, a number of eco- logical processes have been identified at many sites. This chapter will attempt to discuss the nature of these common patterns of change, using all the sources so far introduced and where helpful amplifying these with new examples. Attribution of cause between natural and human-induced processes is mostly avoided until section 7, when the relative probabilities of natural and human-directed origins are introduced.

1. RECESSION OF WOODLAND

The kind of information that can be drawn out of the previously discussed work includes the kind of woodland which has been disturbed, how much of it was thus affected and where it was in terms of the local topography.

Types of Woodland Disturbed

The main conclusion to be reached is that no type of woodland was necessarily immune from disturbance at that time. For example, because of the nature of upland climates, pine-birch- hazel woodland is sometimes found in the later Mesolithic when at lower altitudes a mixed deciduous forest had developed. Thus at Dufton Moss in Upper Teesdale (NP), at 368 m and ca 8000 BP, there is evidence for the sudden burning of a woodland (ΣAP = 50 per cent) of willow, birch and pine, which results in the better establishment of the *Corylus* component and a gain for *Betula* of 30→90 per cent of AP. At West House Moss (NYM; NZ 635095, 178 m), in the centuries before 6650±290 BP (Jones 1977), peaks of *Melampyrum*, *Succisa* and other herbs, together with *Pteridium*, in PAZ WH-5 suggest that the birch-pine-hazel woodlands were being disturbed: in that PAZ (120 cm of sediment), there is clearly more than one episode of that character. Pine seems to decline at the ex- pense of birch, and *Corylus* begins its familiar rapid expansion to the accompaniment of the pollen of *Artemisia, Rumex acetosa* type, Umbelliferae, Caryophyllaceae and several types of Compositae.

The main type to exhibit the process is the mixed deciduous woodland on mesic sites dominated in the pollen spectra by that of *Quercus,* which combines the pollen of *Q. robur* and *Q. petraea.* The mixture of woody species usually reflects the local soil and drainage conditions, with a high proportion of alder (*Alnus glutinosa*) reflecting damp conditions; it is possible to infer that there was a streamside plant community dominated by alder with other deciduous species present: elm, aspen and possibly hazel would have been tolerant of the damp soils and occasional inundation, though *Tilia* and the oaks would have been restricted to the drier ground beyond. More moderate pollen levels probably imply that alder was present throughout the woodland. The mixture of tree species does not directly reflect the pollen frequencies, and correction factors are sometimes applied. In the North York Moors at North Gill, later Flandrian II corrected spectra have very high proportions of elm and alder at North Gill Head, of oak, elm and alder at North Gill II, and of oak, elm, lime and alder at North Gill I (Innes 1981: Figure 39). Oak is very often affected in any disturbance, but elm much less so, especially when compared with post-Mesolithic times. Disturbance and recovery often afford a foothold for species like ash (*Fraxinus*) as well as letting hazel flower more abundantly. In heavily wooded catchments, opening of the forest canopy also allows the greater representation in the pollen rain of 'minority' species. There is a sub-type of this woodland, consisting of wet places such as streamsides where alder-dominated woodland became established during Flandrian II. At North Gill, this inception seems to vary over 2000 years, which probably reflects some degree of topographic control; and this is reflected in its demise as well, which occurs over a period of 500 years during the sixth millennium BP in conditions of both disturbance and its absence. The actual influence of topography is transmitted through the growth of the blanket peat which swamped the alder woodland.

Lastly, the upper edge of the woodland was the scene of disturbance. Such an ecotone is of course always the most susceptible to climatic change and the growth of blanket bog, but some investigations have asserted that this zone is also prone to the kinds of disturbance in which fire is implicated. The clearest indications of the processes at work come from the central Pennine sites investigated by Tallis and Switsur (1990) and Tallis (1991). At 6000 BP, a pollen-influx diagram for Robinson's Moss (500 m; SK 104943) proposes that the upper level of the 'lowland forest' was at 425 m and that of the 'upland forest' at 460 m. This date, however, coincides with a [second] temporary retraction of the limit of the upland forest which is associated with evidence of burning. This is seen by Tallis and Switsur (1990) as just one of a series of fires in which burning 'probably prevented the upward spread of the component tree taxa . . . right from the time when upward forest expansion was just commencing in the early Flandrian'.

The principal woody species at the tree-line at 6000 BP was probably *Corylus*. In spite of the fires, the tree-line moved up slowly between 6800 BP and 5500 BP, which probably signifies a continuing response to climatic change. Ecotones would also have been sites of soil deterioration along the lines proposed by R. T. Smith and Taylor (1989), moving towards a situation where gleys and podsols were more likely to bear birch and willow (and possibly pine) than hazel or oak, and certainly not lime or elm. Given that exposure, rock type and slope are all additional variables, it is to be expected that the impacts of burning at the upper edge of woodland are highly variable from place to place. Between 8000 and 6000 BP on Dartmoor, interestingly, hazel is dominant in the woodland community, but its values appear to have been negatively influenced by fire after ~7500 BP (Caseldine and Maguire 1986). These authors talk indeed of the removal of woodland and its replacement by blanket peat, with burning as a key factor in the process.

Quantities of Woodland Disturbed

In many papers, estimates of areas involved in disturbance rely simply upon the degree to which certain pollen frequencies alter. Given that pollen rain will vary according to the distance between the sampled profile and the disturbed area, and also according to the degree of openness of the sampled catchment, this is not very precise. More accurate estimates depend on spatially coherent sampling strategies or at the very least upon the detection of syn-chronous macro-charcoal layers which can be traced from profile to profile. The number of investigations in upland EW during Flandrian II which supply such data are, understandably, limited. The outstanding example of a reliable data-set comes from Waun Fignen Felen in South Wales (A. G. Smith and Cloutman 1988), where analysis of multiple profiles within a small basin has allowed the construction of a series of diagrams (Figures 26–31 in the original paper) reconstructing the vegetation at 8000, 7500, 6500, 5700, 4700 and 3700 BP. The actual edges of the vegetation mosaic are not mapped, but at 8000 BP, for example, the mixed woodland shows a burned-over opening which is beginning to accumulate mor humus; a part of this area is a grassy clearing being recolonised by birch and hazel. The opening abuts a small shallow lake, contains an 'early mesolithic' flint knapping site and is ca 200 × 200 m. This site forms a nucleus for the spread of blanket bog to the north-west but on other sides continues to be set in mixed woodland until 4700 BP, when mixed woodland appears to form islands in a sea of blanket bog (the lake being now covered with acid peats), a reverse of the position at 6500 BP. Local topography is clearly important in determining the actual sites of vegetation change, but it is clear that fire is implicated in the basal layers of the blanket peat and played a role in its inception.

The multiple profiles at North Gill have too few radiocarbon dates for the type of accurate time-slice mapping displayed for Waun Fignen Felen; but if we accept that in a wooded environment the catchment area for the pollen rain was probably no more than 25 m in radius, it can be inferred that the disturbance episodes discussed in Chapter 2 were themselves confined to such a space. The fact that the 1 cm interval diagrams from the North Gill differ from each other also suggests that each catchment had its own history. It is possible to plot the outer limits of what appears to be a coherent charcoal layer (although the dating and stratigraphic controls are not good enough to make a strong statement about this, the best guess is that it dates from the 5700–5400 BP period) focused on the length of the gill (400 m) and extending at most 60 m normal to it on one side. The position of this macro-charcoal spread in accumulating deposits then may be interpreted as a result of inwash into accumulating peat rather than as the remains of an individual burn. Even if it were the trace of a single burn, 400 m long and 100 m at its widest, the size is not incommensurate with the Welsh example.

Topographic Locations

The complications which surround the relation of a pollen-receiving site, its surrounding vegetation and the total pollen catchment have been discussed early in Chapter 2. They make it difficult to be certain that some topographic locations are more likely to experience Flandrian II disturbance than others. Nevertheless, the following upland situations occur frequently in the literature as the locations of such events:

- Near lakes. There were a number of small lakes in the

uplands during Fl II which are now overgrown with blanket peat and near the margins of which fire seems to have been frequent. In the few riverside sites which have been subject to analysis, forest recession is usually seen, as investigated by Wiltshire and Edwards (1993) at Buxton (SP) at some 300 m.

- In the zone between hill-tops and the spring-line, where the latter is altitudinal and under geological control. The actual exposed interfluve 'ridge' (something of a misnomer over many of the swale-backed hills of upland Britain) is a less common site.
- Near to the spring-line, and especially just above it altitudinally and then along stream-sides.

For all of these, however, the role of preserving environments has to be remembered. They are in general the places where peat has accumulated in sufficient depth to be a source of evidence. But following the due cautions expressed by Tallis and Switsur (1983) in their analogous study of tree remains, it seems that there is now a sufficient quantity of evidence to allow general conclusions of the type expressed above.

2. REGENERATION OF WOODLAND

The western European literature has embedded in it something of a classical model of what happens after a disturbance. Derived from studies of prehistoric (especially early Neolithic) agriculture and suffused with near-recent descriptions of swidden agriculture in tropical forests, it divides neatly into phases:

1. High values of open-ground indicators (e.g. herbs, bracken and heather) are joined by woody shrubs like *Rubus*, *Prunus*, *Sorbus* and Rosaceae.
2. The open-ground indicators decline, and dominance of the spectra is taken over by shade-intolerant tree species such as *Betula*, *Corylus* and ash.
3. The high forest dominants reassert themselves: oak and lime especially. The renewed woodland may provide a habitat for more ash and alder than had previously existed in that place.

Within any phase, there is likely to be inter-site and inter-regional variability. The amount of pine in Flandrian II, for example, varies considerably regionally; there are chance variations in the

relative frequencies of open ground taxa; the acidity and drainage characteristics of the local soils will affect the rate of any
progress towards mire formation and the degree of resistance to
colonisation by any tree species unable to grow on acid peat,
which is most of them. Table 3.1 gives a number of examples
of regeneration sequences from 1 cm or closer counts. There are
few departures from the classic model except perhaps to note
the importance of willow as a pioneer at two locations and the
almost universal involvement of *Corylus*, though there are exceptions. Elm too appears at a relatively early stage rather than in
high forest.

General findings also include the following. The species available depend partly upon the stage reached in the Holocene: for
example, the quantity of pine or alder present may be variable
through time. In many places (see pp. 110–11), disturbance leads
to heath and/or mire rather than the recovery of woodland. Even
when progress towards woodland takes place, it is not always
complete since there may be renewed disturbance. Thus there
are some types of woodland which appear to be 'held' at a
particular stage.

3. THE VEGETATION OF DISTURBED AREAS

Most of the pollen diagrams examined have a phase in which the
authors remark upon the diminution of ΣAP and its replacement
by the pollen of shrubs and herbs and by spores such as those
of ferns and mosses. The interpretation of these spectra has its
complications, not the least of which is the need to try to separate
autochthonous pollen contributed by the peat-forming vegetation
from that of dry areas nearby or adjacent. Pollen identified as
Gramineae, for example, might come from a peat-forming species
such as *Molinia caerulea* (Purple moor grass) or from any of
the genera far less tolerant of waterlogging, such as *Festuca* or
Agrostis. The problem is complicated by the fact that waterlogging
and peat growth appears (see pp. 112–17) to be a common
consequence of disturbance. So some pollen groups as identified
are ambiguous in their ecological information-yield. *Calluna*, for
example, is tolerant of a wide degree of moisture in the soils on
which it grows, though it does not flourish on the very wettest.
But it could signify the growth of a heath with mor humus over
a sandy, well-drained soil, just as it might be found on seasonally
waterlogged peat at the margins of an accumulating mire. Though
it might not be found under a closed deciduous canopy, it would
be present in open birch woodland, for example. Even helpful

TABLE 3.1 Species involved in woodland recovery.

Site	Altitude	Date BP	Transition(s)	Reference
Waun Fignen Felen (SW)	480 m	~8000	Birch→hazel; high *Calluna* suggests mor humus	A. G. Smith and Cloutman 1988
Robinson's Moss (SP)	500 m	~7000	Willow→hazel then to oak and elm	Tallis and Switsur 1990
Soyland Moor D 500 cm (CP)	390 m	5820±95	*Fraxinus*, then hazel and full regeneration of ΣAP. No *Calluna* increase	C. T. Williams 1985
SM 'Second *Potentilla* peak'	390 m	~5000	Birch and ash, hawthorn→*Corylus* + full ΣAP. 'Full regeneration'	
SM 'First *Potentilla* peak'	390 m	~7150	200 years of high *Calluna* not invaded everywhere by trees and shrubs, but birch→*Corylus*	
Valley Bog (NP)	549 m	5945±50	Elm and oak; *Corylus* and alder only gradually	Chambers 1978
Bonfield Gill Head (NYM)	364 m	~5000	Birch and oak: *Calluna* and *Fraxinus* diminishing to 0. Later phase of closed woodland of mixed oak with birch and alder	Simmons and Innes 1988b
North Gill (NYM) profile 5B: *1 mm counts*	360 m	~5770	Alder, oak, birch, ash and some *Tilia* involved but recovery not complete	Innes 1989
The Dod-C (CHE)	200 m	~8000	Willow→*Corylus* (no birch recovery; more *Pinus* due to more open catchment)	Innes and Shennan 1991

investigations of recent pollen rain like that of Tinsley and Smith (1974) and Evans and Moore (1985), which suggest what pollen frequency of *Calluna* can be taken to indicate local presence, do not differentiate between habitats. On the other hand, *Pteridium* is intolerant of prolonged waterlogging and is thus an indicator of dry habitats. Yet, although high bracken-spore values can be taken as an indicator of local presence, Tinsley and Smith (1974) say that nothing can be deduced from its absence, such is its irregular pattern of spore dispersal. The further difficulty is inherent in pollen analysis, namely that identifiable taxonomic groups may share the Poaceae problem discussed above but for different plant communities. A group like Ranunculaceae, for example, will contain plants of open and broken ground as well as water plants, and so estimates as to the most probable referent have to be made in a context-laden and partly subjective way. But *Plantago lanceolata* pollen is unlikely to be from any other species, and some families like the Chenopodiaceae seem to behave in largely similar fashion.

Bearing these difficulties in mind, what does the pollen and spore evidence indicate about the flora and vegetation of areas subject to disturbance? It seems that increases in bracken, grasses, sedges or heather are common enough to allow the inference that one or more of them formed a very important element in the vegetation of an area in which disturbance had at least broken the tree canopy or had in fact removed living trees. That is, the ground vegetation of the disturbance zone was mostly covered with one of those groups or with a mosaic of one or more of them. Exactly which depended on several factors, and accounts for some of the variability in the pollen spectra. The size of the opening and the degree of canopy closure of its fringes, the acidity of the soil and the drainage of the site are probably the most significant variables; the vegetation cover need not have covered all the soil surface. So, what had been the ground layer of a woodland might become:

1. A dry grassy glade with a variable amount of bracken and/or heather. Herbs which are intolerant of shade but do not require high soils of high base status are found: *Melampyrum*, *Ranunculus* spp and *Potentilla* are examples.
2. A dry heathy glade with accumulating mor humus and a dominance of *Calluna vulgaris*. If burned, one of the pioneers would be *Rumex acetosella*.
3. A damp grassy glade, with wet-tolerant grasses such

as *Molinia* or tussock-forming *Deschampsia* spp as dominants. Herbs might include *Filipendula ulmaria* and
Succisa. The common nettle (*Urtica dioica*) might be
found as a natural component of base-rich areas of
this kind.

4. A glade in which there was a carpet of wet-tolerant,
   peat-forming plants such as *Sphagnum* moss or a sedge-
   like cotton-grass (*Eriophorum*). *Potentilla erecta* is one of
   the rather restricted suite of herbs, as is the insectivorous
   Drosera.

5. An opening like numbers 3 or 4 but with pools of
   open water in it. These might have as causes partial
   deforestation, for example, or wallowing by large mammals. Water plants and acid mire plants are all likely
   colonists.

Each of these types might have associated flora which were associated with the dominant conditions (for example, a damp grassy
area would be the most likely of these five categories to contain
Filipendula), or there might be (category 6) overriding conditions
such as the creation of broken ground (e.g. by a group of wild
pigs seeking soil invertebrates to eat, or red deer wallowing) or
a seventh category of open, puddled soil (caused by a group of
ungulates adjacent to open water coming regularly to drink), or
rapid inundation if a family of beaver had built a new dam not
far downslope. Assignment of the herbaceous taxa recognised in
pollen analysis to these habitat categories is not an exact process.
The whole body of evidence must be considered, as must the
supposition that the vegetation was probably not in any kind of
equilibrium and was therefore liable to autogenic change as well
as open to renewed disturbance.

Nevertheless, a good picture of the possibilities can be obtained, to which further detail can be added from stratigraphic
and topographic information. Some of these openings, hence,
were streamside or lakeside glades, not randomly scattered.
Addition of chronological detail from FRPA studies (Chapter 2)
allows a time dimension to be added to the longevity of the
post-disturbance vegetation.

4. PALUDIFICATION

In the uplands, peat initiation during the Holocene is reported by
many studies, excellently reviewed by Moore (1972, 1988). Two
main topographic situations are implicated:

1. Water-receiving sites which are the recipients of natural drainage, such as dry basins, basins with small lakes, channels and poorly-drained cols between stream-heads.
2. Water-shedding sites, of which the convex slopes of low angle which form the majority of the upland terrain to-day are the major category. Complex slopes with convex segments are also included. Such terrain underlies much of the blanket bog characteristic of higher ground today, but this type of peat has also overgrown sites of type 1 as at Waun Fignen Felen (sw).

In the case of category 1, relations with water input/output are reasonably direct: an increase in water input from climatic change or from beaver-dam construction will usually have a direct effect on the flora (Coles and Orme 1983). In the latter case, the existing vegetation will be swamped and replaced by an aquatic flora; in the former, the type of vegetation will reflect the nutrient status of the run-off as well as of the substrate available to any new taxa which have immigrated. So it would seem intuitively correct that climatic change towards increased precipitation would result in waterlogging and thence the growth of peat. If run-off into basins increased because less water was being lost to the atmosphere via evaporation and transpiration from plants, then the response in basins would also have been immediate. Yet the observations recorded in Chapter 2 show that in many water-shedding sites during Flandrian II, the stratigraphy records the onset of the growth of blanket peat. This is basically a mire of the type classified as *ombrogenous* since the nutrition sources of the plants are either the recycled remains of their immediate predecessors or the mineral content of rainfall. Blanket peat, today of various depths, surface vegetation types and degrees of erosion, is found on many of the uplands of England and Wales where the angle of slope, though low, is sufficient for the topographic situation to be called water-shedding. Since the inception of this kind of peat took place mostly within Flandrian II and III, it happened in the presence of humans.

The dates of onset of blanket peat in a number of upland sites have been collected by Tallis (1991); he demonstrates that any time between 9000 and 1000 BP might have seen an episode of onset of such growth. No altitudinal nor topographic control appears to be at work. In the South Pennines, for example, peat began to form on convex slopes of up to 7° in the later part of Fl II, but areas abutting steeper slopes and on summits remained free of peat until after the elm decline. In the Berwyn Mountains (NW), there was some local peat on the high cols between 6500 and 4200 BP, but the main spread of peat over gentler slopes was after 2500 BP (Bostock 1980). Thereafter, the rates of growth were faster than in the southern Pennines, suggesting that climate was permissive in the growth of blanket peat but was not necessarily responsible for its initiation. Nevertheless, if inception happened shortly after a major climatic shift to wetter conditions, such as is postulated for the British Isles around 7500–7000 BP, then the role of climatic factors must be suspected.

Biostratigraphic analysis allows some insight into the ecology of peat inception. The base of blanket peat is usually one of the following:

1. a greasy amorphous 'graphite-like' mor humus with an admixture of mineral matter and, often, small charcoal fragments. Its depth is highly variable. It may overlie a thin mineral soil which may either be unstratified or have the characteristics of a thin podsol.
2. a peat in which there are wood fragments, mixed with charcoal which is of a size to indicate a local origin. The wood may be, exceptionally, in the mineral soil or, more often, in the basal layers of the peat or at the soil/peat interface.

The pollen spectra of no. 1 are often dominated by *Calluna*, and the inference is then made that the plant community from which the basal mor is derived was heathy and probably had a podsolic soil. In the case of the wood peats, *Corylus* pollen is usually abundant even though the wood remains may be referred to other genera, along with some *Calluna*, Poaceae, *Rumex* and *Potentilla*. In both cases, the establishment of an ombrogenous peat is marked by more Cyperaceae pollen and the decline of heather pollen values. At one of the WFF profiles, the seeds of rushes (*Juncus* spp) were common in this second phase (Chambers 1982b, 1983; Tallis and Switsur 1983, 1990; A. G. Smith and Cloutman 1988; Tallis 1991; Wiltshire and Moore 1983; Taylor and Smith 1980; Moore 1973, 1975, 1986; Jacobi et al. 1976). Both the heathy mor and the scrub woodland origins appear to converge in a sedge-dominated ombrogenous peat. The rate of accumulation of this peat would have been affected both by available moisture and by the decay rates of the plant community which comprised it: sedge peats have been found to have a low rate of decay (Coulson and Butterfield 1978).

The evidence for fire is also germane to any study of the origin of ombrogenous peat. In the case of the heath formation, a number of studies make the point that the evidence only begins in the mid-Flandrian when the peat forms, and so the heath may have been formed earlier and fire may have played a role in keeping it free from encroachment by trees. Bostock (1980) emphasised the role of fire in removing trees from the uplands, and showed also that there was a period of nutrient enrichment after fire, detectable in some peat profiles by remains of the moss *Drepanocladus*, a species of flushed mires. However, the long-term effect of fire is to lower the total nutrient reserves and to make plant communities dependent upon inputs from rainfall for additions to the capital stocks. Another ecological effect of fire is to block the pores in the surface layers of soil with fine charcoal and thus to reduce its permeability to water and hence to increase the amount of water on the soil surface which is dependent upon evaporation for transport (Mallik et al. 1984). The accumulation of water is enhanced in the woodland case by the removal (by any means) of trees. Deciduous trees act as a shelter layer, intercepting precipitation and re-evaporating it from the canopy and trunk, and as water-pumps, removing water from the soils via their root systems and transpiration mechanisms. Experiments have shown that run-off increases by as much as 40 per cent after clear felling of deciduous forest. At the site scale, observations in Finland and Denmark on beech woods with heavy moraine soils showed that swamping soon took place when 75-year-old stands were clear-cut or even thinned. The forest is invaded by *Deschampsia caespitosa, Carex* and *Juncus* spp. The remaining trees often wilt and become stag-headed, and attacks by wood-boring insects are frequent (Holstener-Jorgensen 1967). Inspection of some of the pollen diagrams cited in Chapter 2 shows that disturbance phases may be accompanied by small quantities of aquatic taxa. A good example is the phase SMD 500 cm at Soyland Moor zone D (C. T. Williams 1985), where cereals are found at 5825±95 BP: these are accompanied by rises in Cyperaceae and *Sphagnum*, damp ground plants such as *Filipendula, Caltha* and *Lysimachia* and water-plants like *Potamogeton* and *Ranunculus* (cf. *tricophyllum*). At other sites, *Menyanthes* often joins the suite, and occasionally *Nymphaea*. A considerable and year-round rise in water-table would be needed to allow such taxa to grow. The pathways to peat accumulation are to some extent more complicated than allowed in this brief description: Figure 3.1 shows some of the complexities, but prior to them all is the removal of woodland and/or the presence of fire leading to waterlogging. Once waterlogging has started, then the sequence of biochemical mechanisms is initiated which will usually lead to peat formation (Moore 1993). Some amplification of these generalisations is made possible by the analyses from Pinswell on Dartmoor (Caseldine and Hatton 1993) which allow the reconstruction of the various stages through which vegetation communities passed on the way to a true bog community with *Calluna, Sphagnum, Narthecium, Potentilla* and *Drosera* (Figure 3.2). Some studies have emphasised that a rushy stage is important as a pivotal phase in the turn from grassland to bog; on Dartmoor an extended acid grassland phase (probably not detected in most other uplands) is more important than any direct transition from open hazel woodland to heather dominance.

It is also important to ask whether the process is irreversible and how widespread it was during the later Mesolithic. The possibility of the former is shown when wood layers are found in peat stratigraphy. These indicate that the peat was thin and dry enough to permit recolonisation by trees: birch and pine are common species, for example both at Lady Clough Moor (SP; Tallis 1975) and birch at Bonfield Gill Head (NYM; Simmons and Innes 1981). Generally, colonisation coincides with lower levels of all types of charcoal in the peat, suggesting that fire as well as (or rather than) any climatic shifts was a factor in the regrowth of trees. Fire frequencies often diminish after the elm decline, as evidence for agriculture strengthens.

Few studies have encompassed enough profiles to allow the construction of maps of blanket bog distribution during Flandrian II. The work of Tallis (1991) on the Snake Pass area of the southern Pennines is an exception, and his map of a 1 km² area (Figure 3.3) shows where peat had been initiated during Flandrian II. The area was chosen precisely because there was a great deal of peat, but it looks by no means atypical of upland England. So, in areas where peat started in Flandrian II, then a large portion of the terrain might have carried mire vegetation. However, it must be remembered that the Southern Pennines appear to have been peat-clad rather earlier than some other uplands, and also that regions like the North York Moors have only a small area of blanket peat, on the highest ground. To the populations of the later Mesolithic, though, heather moors accumulating mor humus and becoming seasonally waterlogged (with underlying soils undergoing gleying) and invaded by wet-tolerant sedges and *Sphagnum,*

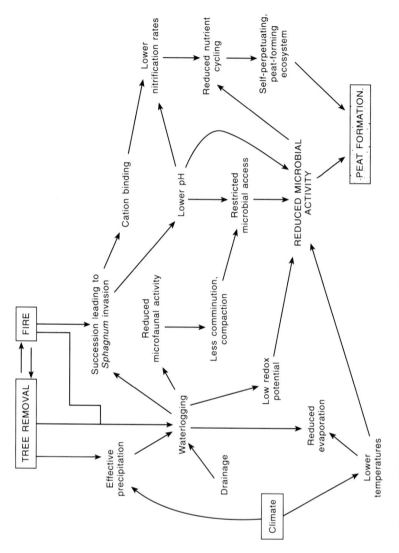

Figure 3.1   Pathways to peat accumulation, with major functions
in boxes and the equifinal state of peat accumulation
in the shaded box. The reciprocal relations between
tree removal and fire imply that either one may
precede the other. In upland Britain, it is most likely
that fire came after tree removal except at the upper
edge of woodland.

Source: adapted and amended from several diagrams
by P. D. Moore.

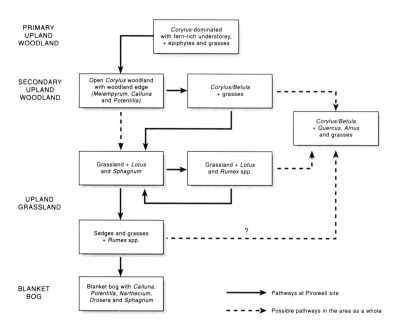

Figure 3.2   The formation of blanket bog in the Pinswell area
of northern Dartmoor, indicated by solid lines.
The pecked lines suggest other ways in which the
vegetation might have altered in the same area.

Source: C. Caseldine and J. Hatton (1993), 'The
development of high moorland on Dartmoor: fire
and the influence of Mesolithic activity on vegetation
change', in F. M. Chambers (ed.), *Climate Change and
Human Impact on the Landscape*, London: Chapman
and Hall, 119–31.

cotton-sedge mires which were wet year-round, *Sphagnum* bogs,
open hazel and birch scrub with a variety of wet-tolerant ground
flora species and a high proportion of dead trees,[1] as well as wet
mires in water-collecting sites, must have been a familiar part of
the landscape.

5. THE INCIDENCE OF FIRE

The primary source of evidence for the burning of vegetation
during Flandrian II is the presence of charcoal in organic deposits
and at the soil/peat interface. Most often, the visible carbonised
material forms a layer in or at the base of peats which is
recorded in the stratigraphy of the analysed monolith or borer
core; a few studies have traced layers laterally in exposed faces,

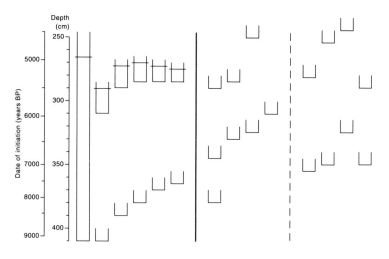

Figure 3.3   Dates of peat initiation in the South Pennines. The
              left-hand scales relate to a long profile at Robinson's
              Moss and its radiocarbon time-scale. Cross-bars
              indicate the *Ulmus* decline. All the profiles left of the
              solid line are from other Robinson's Moss profiles;
              the rest come from a variety of profiles in the region.

              Source: J. H. Tallis (1991), 'Forest and moorland in
              the South Pennine uplands in the mid-Flandrian
              period. III. The spread of moorland – local, regional
              and national' *J. Ecol.* 79, 401–15.

and very few (as in Innes 1981) have mapped coherent layers
spatially.

Classification

The classes of fragments have been variously defined, but are
commonly divided into three: large (>3 mm); small (180μ-3 mm);
and micro (<180μ). The two larger classes are usually interpreted
to mean either that there was burning on the actual sampling site
or very close to it, or that there was fire nearby with subsequent
water transport into the sampled profile. The smaller class is
usually called micro-charcoal or microscopic charcoal, though
in some literature the term 'soot' has been used. It is treated
analytically more like a very big pollen grain in the assumption
that it will have undergone wind transport before 'rainout' onto
the sampled area. If any fire creates all size classes, then a local
fire will leave simultaneous peaks of all size classes in sampled
profiles. If only micro-charcoal is present in a sampled profile,

however, then it is inferred that the fire was at a distance, and a steady curve suggests constant burning within the catchment area, though not necessarily of the same patch of ground. Peaks in micro-charcoal only suggest an intermediate situation where individual but extra-local fires are being recorded.

Identification of charcoal is very patchy in the literature. Larger fragments, especially of tree species, are normally identified, but smaller material of all kinds is rarely tracked down, though the woody stems of *Calluna* are from time to time recorded. More systematic treatment might be a useful exercise, since it is vital to know whether a local fire has in fact removed peat or mor and created a hiatus in any profile. The pollen curves are a help here, but knowledge of just which species are being burned would also be useful.

Distribution in Profiles

The coincidence of large (LA) charcoal with other disturbance indicators is good; with micro (MI) size it is less so at times of forested catchments where the contributing area is, by analogy with pollen, small. As forests recede and catchments open out, then both pollen and MI come from larger areas and may show simultaneous peaks. Some pollen appear to relate to the incidence of fire especially closely: *Melampyrum* is one of these and indeed has been characterised as a species which flowers especially well when a forest canopy has been opened and the ground layer fired. The aptly-named fireweed (*Chamerion angustifolium* = *Epilobium angustifolium* or *Chamaenerion angustifolium* in many accounts and diagrams) is a definite fire-follower in wooded environments, and its pollen, although not frequently found, is highly characteristic. The current regeneration patterns of *Pinus sylvestris* suggest that fire is an initiator of patch regeneration, and pine pollen often rises at times of charcoal incidence. This is, however, attributed by some workers to the opening-out of catchment areas at such times to higher frequencies of pine pollen, which is especially prone to long-distance transport.

The frequency of fire episodes in peat and lake profiles needs to be calculated with care, since, for earlier work at least, no size classes of charcoal may be distinguished. Careful analysis of profiles such as those of the South Pennines undertaken by J. H. Tallis at Robinson's Moss showing, for example, at least five episodes of high levels of MA, which by extrapolation from the radiocarbon dates would have happened at ~8900, ~7675, ~6210, ~5880 and ~4950 BP. (The intervals are thus 1225–1465–330–930 yr.) Frequencies above the elm decline (4875±60 BP) are no lower than before it. There are virtually no gaps in the MI record. At Bonfield Gill (NYM), LA occurs in two layers (~5670 and ~5170 BP, with an interval of 500 yr; there are no gaps in the MI record (which peaks along with the LA incidence) until the elm decline, after which MI is absent for perhaps 200–300 years. The evidence of the combined North Gill profiles was discussed in Chapter 2, which used both LA and MI peaks. Profiles 5B and 8 each have three LA layers dated by extrapolation from radiocarbon assays: 5B has 5450, 5760 and 6469, against 4685, 5790 and 6500 for 8. The latest at either profile differ by 765 yr, but the earlier two show considerable similarity, considering the limitations of the dating method and the estimation involved thereafter. (They also avoid the 'pluvial' period of 6250–5000 BP.) The intervals are 709 yr and 310 yr in profile 5B; 710 yr and 790 yr in profile 8. These are of the same order as Bonfield Gill and the later part of Robinson's Moss.

Few other profiles yield the requisite detail for further examples: WFF does not chronicle the incidence of charcoal in a form that allows vertical comparability; Bodmin Moor examples come either from an unwooded environment or are unreliable stratigraphically; many earlier studies do not record microscopic charcoal at all. What many of them remark upon, however, is the presence of carbonised material at the base of blanket peat profiles in water-shedding situations. Often, though not always, the charcoal is present in the remains of an amorphous greasy mor humus. The presumably slow accumulation rate of such a deposit may mean that a heathy vegetation may have been present for a long period before the initiation of a peat whose plants were nourished largely from rainwater. So the presence of heath (dominated by Ericaceous shrubs like *Calluna*) is not inevitably the signal for the onset of peat growth: another trigger (of which increased climatic wetness is the most obvious) is needed to initiate the new system. But mor humus can form under woodland, and if it is converted to open vegetation during a permissive climatic period then blanket peat growth will begin straight away. There is general agreement that the soils of upland Britain would have undergone progressive leaching, podsolisation and gleying during the Holocene no matter what their cover. So disturbance episodes may be superimposed, as it were, upon a much longer-term set of processes. Although burning may produce an initial flush of nutrients at the soil surface, its long-term effect is to reduce the quantity of nutrients (especially nitrogen) available for circulation in the local ecosystem.

As a footnote to this discussion, it can be recalled that evidence of fire in organic profiles is not confined to Flandrian II, and that several investigations show its presence in the landscape during Fl I, when the deciduous forest has become established, in the preceding woodlands when pine was an important component of the vegetation, and indeed in the heathy vegetation (often dominated by *Empetrum*) that was present before there was any woodland at all away from sheltered valleys. There is not enough evidence to give any estimates of frequency: it looks random in space and time.

Spatial Distribution of Fires

Few investigations have analysed enough profiles within the same locality to allow more than guesses at how large an individual fire event might have been. The evidence from the North Gill set of profiles (see Figure 2.5) seems to show that, subject to the inaccuracies inherent in the dating), few of the fire episodes recorded as LA are synchronous; adding the peaks of MI does not increase the incidence a great deal. These data imply that any one fire was confined to the immediate area of the profile and so is to be measured in tens of metres rather than anything larger. There is a possible exception if we compare the adjacent profiles NG2 and NG4: the latter has high levels of LA and MI dated in contiguous samples to 5250±45 and 5315±45 BP, and NG2 has an LA layer with an MI peak at 5220±75 BP. Separate but coincidental fires are possible, as is one which stretched over both since they are only 25 m apart. If the pollen spectra are compared, then there is remarkable similarity over the 2–3 + 1 cm samples which delineate the phase in both profiles. In particular, they both show a sudden decrease in ΣAP by ca 20 per cent, to 30 per cent at NG4 and 20 per cent at NG2. There are a few differences: at NG4, the occurrences of *Lonicera* and *Hedera* make them look like relics of the earlier phase of canopy opening (without fire) discussed on pp. 129–34. At NG2, though, those two woody climbers are suddenly present; and NG2 only has the ruderal group Chenopodiaceae and *Plantago lanceolata*, which often seems to be an indicator of intensity of disturbance. In a largely qualitative way, it looks as if the NG2 phase represents the bigger fire, but unless the charcoal layer were traced through the peats laterally and found to be coherent, there is no way of telling whether there was in fact only the one fire. Since there are no 1 mm counts at NG2, the prior episode of canopy-opening at NG4 cannot be investigated at NG2. It may be noted that at ~5220 at NG8 (the next profile downstream from NG2), there

IS NO LA, and MI is in a frequency trough. At NG5, 70 m upstream from NG4, at an extrapolated ~5200 BP horizon (at 54 cm), there is no LA and a small peak in MI. The herbs are high, and it looks as if a disturbance phase is about one third under way which may have begun with fire but in which that is no longer an autochthonous influence. The slight peak in MI could well be extra-local, that is, the reflection of the events downstream.

What Was Being Burnt?

There is not a huge quantity of positive identifications of carbonised plant remains from upland sections. However, a combination of identifications and recent ecological observations will allow some degree of informed discussion of what was being consumed by fire in the mid-Holocene uplands.

GROUND VEGETATION

The most common record is probably that of the twigs of *Calluna vulgaris*, and this is no surprise since current observations show heather to be readily inflammable in many stages of its growth and under most likely weather conditions. What applies to heather is probably also equally true of *Vaccinium* and *Empetrum*, which appear to be under-represented in pollen diagrams.

Burning of dry ground layers depends for its success upon a supply of fuel and in particular dead leafy matter not yet humified as an initial supply of flammable material. A hot ground fire may then extend to humic material and dry peats, but it is unlikely to be initiated thus. So, dry deciduous grasses like *Molinia caerulea* today provide fuel, as do upland sedges such as *Eriophorum* spp. Few positive identifications of such species from burned fragments exist, though the correlation between charcoal (in lakes at any rate) and *Calluna* pollen is high (Odgaard 1992). Given a start by a critical density of dry dead plant material, then many leafy herbaceous species and ferns will burn: autumn and late spring would seem, intuitively, to be the times when ignition was most likely.

SHRUBS

More records of this group are found than any other: birch and willow are the most frequent. Alder should probably be included since it is likely to have been part of a wetland or streamside community and thus more like a shrub than a forest tree. That willow and alder are found is entirely consonant with their growing near wetter areas, though *a priori* the probability of fires on wetlands is lower than on dry soils. But peats (especially if shallow) will burn. Birch is easily fired and also grows as a colonist of shallow peats. Burned hazel, usually as nutshells, is most often recognised at archaeological excavations rather than in organic profiles (Malham Tarn seems to be an exception). There are few records of its wood in peats or lake profiles. A proportion of MI charcoal could have come from shrubs, but that plant-size category is not normally identified by investigators.

TREES

In any sampling of recognisable carbonised remains of forest species, there is likely to be a bias against taxa that eschew wet sites, a factor emphasised by Tallis (1975) and by Tallis and Switsur (1983). Thus, in detailed lists of tree remains from fifty-three sites in the peats of the Southern Pennines, the latter paper reports the dominance of finds of pine and willow. Alder remains are not found above 425 m in that region. Oak is the commonest find after pine and willow but is found only locally above 500 m. No remains of *Corylus* are recorded. In spite of numerous finds of charcoal in the associated peat profiles, Tallis and Switsur (1983) do not indicate that any of the major remains show evidence of being burned. The same was true of birch and oak trunks and roots at Bonfield Gill Head (Simmons and Innes 1988b). So, it may tentatively be concluded that fires during Fl II in the woodlands and scrub of the uplands were more frequent in the ground layer and in scrub than in true forest; even fire-prone woodlands dominated by *Pinus sylvestris* seem to have left no marks upon the tree-trunks: Tallis (1975) reports one profile (500 m ASL) where the quantity of MI was lower in samples with high pine-pollen values than immediately before and after.

COMPARISONS

If all the charcoal layers of various kinds had been subject to close identification protocols, then there might be a better corpus of evidence as to what plants were providing fuels for upland fires in Fl II. (Given the necessary labour inputs, of course, there might not be evidence for anything else.) Hence any comparative findings must be highly provisional. It looks, though, as if:

- Closed-canopy forests dominated by mixed-oak species were not affected by fires unless these were confined

to the ground layer or undershrubs. Woodland dominated by pine was more fire-prone, and a crown fire
is not totally inconceivable in such forests. However,
the evidence for the burning of pine (see above) is not
plentiful.

- Scrub dominated by birch or willow was fire-prone; that
dominated by hazel was probably in the same category,
but the evidence is less well preserved since *Corylus* does
not grow on peaty substrates. If fired, these communities
were more likely than the mixed-oak woodlands to suffer
death of the aerial parts because of the thin bark of most
of the species.

- Ecotones, such as between the oak woods and the
streamside alderwoods, were prone to firing, which
tended to extend some of the characteristics of the first
further into the second, until the area was taken over by
blanket peats.

- Openings in the woodland or open ground beyond the
woodlands' upper edge were prone to more frequent
firing. Heathy vegetation in particular has left strong
traces, but it seems likely that several other species
would, at particular times of year, have provided potential material for fires. Grasses are key members of such
a group.

- Diversity of species provided for natural fire-breaks. Fire
at the edge of, or within, tree-clad areas would have been
small in area, with outside dimensions of 200 × 200 m
deduced from WFF and 60 × 40 m deduced from North
Gill; in heath or moor vegetation, they could well have
covered larger areas.

The ability of fire to run through heath and moorland habitats
is not in doubt. Nor is there any uncertainty about the fire-
prone nature of largely coniferous forests. The fire-characteristics
of deciduous forest are more difficult to elucidate, since most
analogous woodlands in continental Europe are intensively
managed and those in North America are, likewise, carefully
guarded against fire or are largely secondary woodland rather
than mature communities. There is more discussion of this in
the next section, but the general finding here is that since fire
damage to trees tends to be a function of bark thickness (E. A.
Johnson 1992), then the smaller tree species and the saplings of
trees of the mature forest are the most vulnerable to damage

and/or death. This recent work in Boreal forests puts forward only one stand type of interest in this study: an aspen (*Populus* spp) woodland with a well-developed shrub layer. The principal fuels are deciduous leaf litter and dried-out herbaceous material. Such stands will burn in the spring before the leaves come out on the aspen, though that fire will be less intense than an autumn fire since the litter layer is still too wet to burn. In autumn, the stand will burn after the ground and shrub layers have died back, consuming some of the litter and humus layers as well. These studies come from the North American continent, and due allowance must be made for differences in climate and weather patterns between Kenora, Ontario and Lady Clough Moor.

So, deciduous forests can experience fire, though directly applicable evidence is decidedly exiguous. Whether they will burn as a result of natural causes or only in response to opportune human intervention is discussed in section 7.

6. INFERENCES FROM THE PALAEOECOLOGICAL DATA

Discussion is long-standing about whether Mesolithic cultures possessed the means to 'clear' forest in ways that their Neolithic successors clearly did. Any argument hinges on the nature of the disturbances examined in some detail above, and comes down to discussion of the basic issue: 'were these disturbances most probably caused by natural factors (such as lightning fires, with perhaps additional charcoal from domestic fires), or were they the products (accidental or deliberate) of human activity?' In the same way, it can asked whether peat inception on water-shedding sites was only a result of changes in natural factors (such as soil maturation processes and climatic change) or whether, again, human use of the land could have produced (surely accidentally this time) conditions in which peat could accumulate. The accumulation of valley aggradations during mesolithic time in valleys of the NYM (Richards 1981, Richards et al. 1987) can of itself be attributed to neither influence.

For any of these topics, of course, it is essential to consider the possibility that neither natural nor human-led factors were solely responsible for the changes investigated, but some complex interaction of the two. It would be hypothetically possible, or example, to have a clearing created by lightning fire which was then maintained in an open condition by a hunting group until, after a climatic deterioration, it became so wet that human use of it was abandoned and peat growth proceeded apace. This section

will see if it is possible to tease out the kind of evidence which
such a sequence would leave.

Natural Possibilities

Under this heading, the possible ways of interpreting the disturbances in terms of natural phenomena will be discussed. Each
possible process will be addressed in the light of the actual
ecological changes which are indicated by the palaeoecological
evidence. Additional evidence from near-recent and current
analogues will also be brought in whenever possible.

THE POST-GLACIAL SUCCESSION

The earlier parts of Mesolithic time passed in the context of
the assembly of the tree species which eventually comprised the
dominant woodland types of the mid-Holocene and hence the
later Mesolithic. The forest cover was never complete since apart
from normal dynamic processes of death and renewal there were
habitats which were unsuitable for tree growth, as at the coasts,
on river shingle, on unstable slopes and on hydroseres not subject
to successional drying-out. The progress of species' immigration
community assembly has been charted for the British Isles by
Birks (1989) and by Huntley (1990).

A discussion of some relevance to this book has been the
early abundance and spread of hazel (*Corylus avellana*). A. G.
Smith (1970) proposed the radical hypothesis that the spread had
been much aided by fire of human origins, mostly in the early
Mesolithic. This suggestion also aided the acceptance of the idea
of human management of vegetation to provide greater hazel
abundance in the later Mesolithic (Mellars 1976b). If true for the
earlier period, then it is interesting that the later culture lived in
an environment that was already at least partially humanised. The
whole question has been re-evaluated by Huntley, who examines
no fewer than seven alternative hypotheses. He concludes that
the 'unique combination of climate conditions during the early
Holocene, perhaps along with the high fire frequency that resulted
from these conditions, favoured the early and rapid expansion of
Corylus' (Huntley 1993: 215).

More studies of fire frequency in Boreal vegetation types in
the British Isles and their analogues elsewhere are clearly needed
to affirm this finding; one previous result of the discussion has
been the contribution of Rackham (1988) who submits that *Corylus
avellana*, unlike its North American co-generics *C. cornuta* and *C.
americana*, is not fire-tolerant and unlikely to stump-sprout after

fire, which has been a cornerstone of both early spread and later management hypotheses. There has been a similar discussion about the spread of alder (*Alnus glutinosa*) in the British Isles. As with hazel, this was often rapid, though there are exceptions to that pattern. A combination of hydroseral events, flood-plain development and rare weather events allowing enhanced reproduction is at the heart of the sequence advanced by Bennett and Birks (1990); possible involvement of mesolithic communities is promoted by Chambers and Elliot (1989) on account of the charcoal which so often accompanies phases of alder expansion. In upland Ardudwy (NW), the earliest upland alder carr in Britain is established on burned wetland ~8465 BP (Chambers et al. 1988). In general, the alder story has been of lesser interest to archaeologists since that tree was not, so far as is known, of any particular significance to human communities.

LIGHTNING FIRE

Among the various natural possibilities of forest disturbance, this must rank as the most likely. It is known that most ecosystems in the world will in some season burn if struck by lightning. The question becomes: are the mid-Holocene woodlands of upland EW exempt from this generality; and, if not, what are the likely temporal and spatial results? Though the present climate is not especially prone to the convectional storms that are the most frequent sources of lightning strike, it is known that the uplands are subject to the phenomenon. Walkers are hit from time to time, and D. A. Thompson (1971) records twenty-three lightning-caused fires in the Galloway Hills (SW Scotland) during a two-day period in June 1970. These fires were in coniferous woodland and so only marginally germane to the present discussion, though it is interesting that in only nine cases did rain extinguish the fire started by the electrical storms, all of which struck between 12:00 and 17:30 hr. No data seem to exist on recent fires in deciduous woodland in England and Wales, so parallel information from abroad must be sought. The best source is North America, which has a long history of fire and fire control. However, many regions are not useful analogues. The Boreal forest, scene of most work, is too heavily coniferous to be useful, as are some of the other forests of the eastern seaboard. New England and northern Appalachia, which have many mixed hardwood forests, are the best parallels. A major caution, nevertheless, is that in no sense are these forests pristine ecosystems: work done in 'mature' and 'old-growth' forests generally means stands of dominants about 70 years old.

Such forests exist in a climate which experiences year-round rainfall, though temperatures are more like a continental climate than that of the British Isles, and in summer this may produce periods of intense drought from year to year. The weather is especially conducive to burning in coastal and hill-top districts. In these regions, not only dead material but also living plants such as Ericaceae contribute to the fuel potential, but the fine fuels (litter and humus) and their moisture content are most important in determining the outbreaks of fire. The water content of these fine fuels drops sharply in the early spring at a time when there is a strong enough sun to exert a drying effect but before the leaves are out enough to shade the forest floor. In these woodlands, most of the fires are ground burns only (Patterson and Sassaman 1988). There is no evidence, though, that lightning fires are topographically selective on a smaller scale, and certainly none that streamsides and lakesides, for example, are more prone to natural than human-caused fire. At present, there seems little doubt that most fires have a human cause. Data from Acadia National Park (on the coast of Maine) show that of 209 fires recorded after 1937, only five were ignited by lightning and none was >0.25 acre (0.1 ha). The woodlands of Cape Cod had no lightning fires between 1974 and 1983 but 112 human-caused fires. Both places are coastal, and the summer storms are renowned for the amount of rain that they dump.

Inland, work by Lorimer (1989) suggests that all types of disturbance produce a woodland with ~1 per cent of its area as gaps at any one time, with an average gap size of 280–375 m². This average results from the presence of small gaps of <25 m² to ~0.1 ha through to large examples of < 1.0–3000 ha. The small gaps are the commonest and are often caused by the loss of one tree only. One lesson from this work is that any forest in upland Britain during later Fl I and in Fl II will have had gaps in it from natural processes. Most of these are likely to have been small (375 m² is just under 20 × 20 m), but the possibility of larger areas resulting from extreme events (most likely from windthrow in the UK context) exists. The smaller gaps, however, will be subsumed in the 'normal' pollen rain from an apparently undisturbed mixed deciduous woodland whose history is chronicled from nearby peat or lake deposits. Only close sampling of, for example, deep humus pockets which had been within the woodland (see work by Aaby 1983; Andersen 1988; Mitchell 1988; Stockmarr 1975) might reveal minor events. Parallel work from recent times in Europe is hard to find. Long-established forests such as the Białowieza

Forest in eastern Poland appear to have no published fire history. In their summary, Chandler et al. (1983) assert that in Europe there are severe fires only in periods of exceptional drought; the normal fire season is bimodal in spring and autumn and the average fire size is 0.97 ha, which is a patch ~200 × 50 m (0.5 ha in intensively-managed forests) with a return period of >6000 years.

Observation of today's deciduous woodlands, especially in upland EW, tends to consider them as likely to burst into flame as a load of wet football socks. But a lightning strike which hit after a noticeably dry period in spring or autumn might kill a tree and also ignite the fine fuels of the forest floor or such as a thick but dry tangle of bramble. Any resulting fire would however be confined in area and would at most kill a few saplings and perhaps a few birch or aspens. It might well not be detectable in 1 cm sampling of peat or lake profiles for microfossil analysis.

WINDTHROW AND SENESCENCE

Discussion of this undoubted source of disturbance (to which could be added the loss of trees from ice-glaze during certain winter conditions) tends to be conflated with fire in much of the literature. Combined estimates of disturbance are often given, as in the previous paragraphs. Again, the best work comes from the Boreal forests of North America and Scandinavia, where quite refined estimates of the area under disturbance at any one time and the return period of disturbances such as storm and fire can be made. One study from a mixed deciduous-hemlock forest in New Hampshire (Foster 1988) accounted windstorms the greatest influence upon the vegetation, ahead of fire. Between 1635 and 1938, twelve storms were recorded, with the autumn remnants of tropical hurricanes likely to do the most damage. Fires recorded in the study area (Pisgah Forest) numbered ten in the 1778–1928 period, and Foster noted an interaction with windthrow where areas of downed trees contributed potentially high fuel densities.

As with fire, therefore, upland forests in EW would have been potentially subject to this form of disturbance, and the probabilities of gaps from this source would seem to be higher than those for fire. Twelve storms in 300 years in an area prone to remnant hurricanes is not a high frequency, and seems likely to have been exceeded in the cyclonic climate of the British Isles. Thus the assembling forests of the mid-Holocene would have been subject to such an influence, with the possibility of large areas being felled (and thus possibly being recorded on pollen diagrams) as well as single trees. Windstorms have the potential to wreak very extreme disturbance if accompanied by intense rainfall: soils can then be lost to erosion, and landslides may remove the entire ecosystem over a small to medium-sized area.

BEAVER

The lifeways of the beaver (*Castor fiber*) are well known in the sense that they fell trees to make dams which then inundate areas of woodland, killing the stands adjoining the pond which they have created. They eat aspen, birch and willow as well as aquatic plants; one effect might be to create a kind of natural coppice from stump-sprouting (Coles 1992). They aggregate in lodges of 5–12 animals per lodge, with an overall density (as judged by North American evidence) of 40–90 per 1000 ha (Tilley 1979). The lakes and wetlands thus created are possible aids in the spread of species like *Alnus glutinosa* in Britain (Chambers and Elliott 1989). The size and duration of beaver clearings is very variable, and it is difficult to estimate the area of Fl II forest that might be subject to forest disturbance at any one time; as Coles and Orme (1983) point out, filled-in pools would create grassy clearings even after the beaver had left. But at say 65 animals per 1000 ha at 8 per lodge (derived from data above), then there would be 8 lodges per 1000 ha, that is, a block of country ca 3 × 3 km. If that block had 10 km of suitable streams, then there would be a lodge every 1.25 km; only 6 km of streams would place one every 0.75 km, which seems a little close. Keene (1981) adds the idea of a pond of average size of 2.43 ha and suggests that in Missouri the historic density has been 7–20 beaver/ha, not all of which constructed lodges: some lived in burrows in river banks. He points out that they were not cyclic in abundance; in the case of the Montagnais of the lower St Lawrence River region, this meant that they were hunted if any other species failed or was likely to fail. Beaver distribution might then influence the hunting localities visited at any one time (Gadacz 1975). It seems very likely that beaver were present in Mesolithic England (Coles 1992).

Detection of beaver activity from palaeoecological evidence has never been claimed. Inundation of a forest floor would presumably leave the humus intact and then overlay it with lake muds and/or silt which would then either turn into a raised bog or dry out and be colonised with pioneer trees. Possible sequences have been identified in published work (summarised in Coles 1992). How a beaver dam and pool might appear in a pollen diagram from some tens of metres away is more difficult to estimate since the aquatic pollen would be unlikely to show up. So it is probable that many reconstructions of the Fl II have underestimated the effects of beaver, though if a disturbance event has fire associated with it, then the probabilities of it being beaver-created are rather lower since their abilities do not extend to eating so fast that they set the trees on fire.

GRAZING

At this time in the Holocene, there is no suggestion that domestic animals were part of the Mesolithic culture, and so the question is whether the wild fauna could create and/or maintain openings in forest that might be detectable in conventional pollen analysis. The topic has been reviewed by Buckland and Edwards (1984), who discussed the possibilities of grazing animals (principally of the domestic kind) keeping cleared areas open, and also, to a lesser extent, the roles of wild animals in preventing the growth of trees. If aurochs (*Bos primigenus*) indeed spent the year in groups of at least 4–6 (Tilley 1979), then some impact on vegetation can be imagined. C. Turner (1970a, b), in work on the Hoxnian Interglacial, put forward the notion that the open-vegetation phase in zone IIc at Hoxne and Mark's Tey was the work of wild herbivores. A. Smith (1970) also advanced the notion that some pre-Neolithic clearings were created by indigenous herbivores and affirmed this possibility at WFF (A. Smith and Cloutman 1988: 168):

> The [flora revealed by pollen analysis] gives the impression of a damp, grassy, somewhat disturbed area such as might have been quite intensively grazed by wild herbivores. In these circumstances it could have been kept open since early Flandrian times. Alternatively a clearing may have been created by prevention of woodland regeneration.

On Exmoor at the Mesolithic–Neolithic transition, a drop in *Corylus* pollen without any subsequent closure of forest is attributed to grazing, though there is no certainty about whether wild or domestic animals were involved. The absence of cereal and *Plantago* pollen suggests that farming had not at that time (6710–5130 BP) been established (Francis and Slater 1990).

It is therefore necessary to consider whether natural populations of aurochs and red and roe deer, together with wild boar, could either keep open a clearing established by some other form of disturbance or actually create the opening in the first place. Of the former, there seems no doubt, provided that some critical level of intensity of grazing and browsing is achieved by the wild creatures. No really applicable studies have been done recently, since animal populations and their habitats are now so often managed; but many studies have shown that regeneration can be prevented by a concentration of ungulate herbivores, especially if predator numbers are for some reason low. To allow that some mix of deer, aurochs and wild pigs actually turned woodland into grassy glades and/or heath is a different proposition. This could happen if all seedlings of tree species were consumed and so there was no replacement of senescent or diseased trees. It would, however, take a long time in mature woodland ecosystems since the dominants are long-lived. A faster version would be to combine a lack of regeneration with actually killing mature trees. The most likely way of accomplishing that would be a high concentration of animals into a small area in which they ate the bark and underlying growth tissues of the trees, in effect ring-barking them. This can be seen in winter-feed areas of Rocky Mountain populations of wapiti (the same species as red deer) in North American National Parks. Such concentrations would be most probably be brought about by very bad weather and be most frequent on relatively low ground. The phenomenon has been noted for many populations of *Cervus elephas* and is particularly evident in the deep or crusted snow on which red deer can scarcely move. A winter aggregation of animals (called 'yarding') allows them to dig collectively through the snow to reach dry grasses and herbs. In winter, nevertheless, browse and bark are essential foods for red deer, and presumably concentrations of them in especially bad years may lead to ring-barking of trees whose bark is especially favoured. Straus (1981) emphasises the eclectic nature of red-deer feeding, though most European literature suggests that in forested environments the deer depend more upon browse than on the ground layer's resources; bark appears to be compulsory rather than simply a famine food.

This second scenario would scarcely be detectable by normal pollen analysis: assuming that no fire was involved, then it would appear no different from a windthrow event or the onset of a disease episode as is sometimes postulated for the elm decline. This is not to deny that it could have happened in prehistory, only that its specific detection as a discrete process is at present unlikely. The first might be detected if an opening was identified and then it was kept open beyond the time when regrowth of woody genera would be normally expected, but no extraneous influences were implied by the pollen spectra. Evidence for the preferred (as distinct from the necessitated) habitats of deer, pig and aurochs in mid-Holocene Denmark (Bay-Petersen 1978) suggest that they all favour open woodland with glades and a plentiful ground cover rather than a closed-canopy forest. The optimum zone is between the forest edge and open water. If this is so, then any effects exerted upon vegetation by the animals might appear in pollen diagrams from lakes.

One small fact to be considered is the differential attraction of wild mammals to springs with high mineral concentrations in the water. In Canada, for example, moose and white-tailed deer were attracted to natural salt licks in the form of springs where the water is rich in $NaCl$, $NaHCO_3$ and Na_2SO_4, but not K, Ca or Mg. These licks were fed by slow-seeping springs and each comprised an open area 100–300 m² in size with animal tracks, disturbed mud and puddles. They were most frequently used in May and June (Fraser and Reardon 1980). In Poland, the rooting and wallowing of both wild pig and red deer produced small hollows with standing water and an acid-tolerant flora which included the cotton-sedge *Eriophorum vaginatum* and the insectivorous *Drosera rotundifolia* (Falinski 1986).

The influence of wild animals is therefore a subject on which an open mind must be kept, bearing in mind that any palaeoecological evidence is likely to give equivocal signals and that using the recent past brings the danger of drawing parallels between animal communities which are now distinctly different.

PALUDIFICATION

During the Holocene, there is no doubt that climatic change led to peat accumulation in water-collecting sites. The incised melt water channels of the NYM (Jones 1978; Simmons 1969) started to amass peats at the Boreal–Atlantic Transition (BAT) to a wetter climate. An even earlier example (10250±100 BP) is quoted by R. T. Smith and Taylor (1989) for a basin site in Wensleydale (NP). An overwiew of the dates of all types of peat inception in the South Pennines is given by Tallis (1991). It is also clear that in some places these peats acted as the focal locations for subsequent lateral spread onto water-collecting sites. Some of these, argues Honeyman (1985), may have prevented the spread of alder into habitats otherwise suitable for it. Many occasions of such spread were, however, connected with episodes of disturbance. Whether, then, they were due to natural causes depends on the origins of the disturbances themselves. But there is no doubt of the role of climate in the sense that it was conducive to peat accumulation at all times after the BAT and probably at most times before that as well since there are examples of peat accumulation in the 10,000–7800 BP era. Blanket peat on water-shedding sites seems to have been initiated at almost any time between the BAT and Roman times, and so it seems likely that non-climatic factors are dominant within the general 'permissiveness' of climate: soil deterioration processes and deforestation are the most likely candidates (see Plate 6). Neither need be attributed solely to natural causes. The ecological and biochemical processes involved in blanket peat development are discussed in a series of papers by P. D. Moore (1973, 1986, 1991), with a special accent on human involvement in Moore et al. (1986) and Moore (1993).

It remains to note that paludification was in some places revers-ible. The finding of tree remains over a variable depth of peat (e.g. at Bonfield Gill (NYM) and several sites in the Pennines (Tallis and Switsur 1983)) confirms that birch especially, but also willow and pine, will grow back over 'thin' blanket peat (60 cm at Bonfield Gill) if conditions change. At Bonfield Gill, the obvious change is the cessation of charcoal particles in the profile suggesting that fire was no longer a strong influence, confirming the possibility raised by Jacobi, Tallis and Mellars (1976). At around 5000 BP, there is no suggestion of a radical shift towards a drier climate, though it may have been less wet than in any 'pluvial' period ending in ~5800 BP. Overall, therefore, in water-collecting sites it is largely under the control of natural factors. Once onto water-shedding sites it becomes tied up with disturbance, the cause or causes of which need some more discussion.

The Possible Role of Humans

In the above account, there are places where the natural processes appear to fail to give satisfactory explanations of the phenomena inferred from the palaeoecological evidence. It is time, therefore, to turn to human societies as possible forcers of change in eco-systems. It is clear from the archaeological discussion (Chapter 1) that the Later Mesolithic people had no very advanced technology with which to manipulate their environment. The visible tools are not massive, for example, nor are they highly honed as with the Neolithic polished stone axes which have been shown to be so effective in cutting trees. It has to be assumed that fire could be used and controlled away from the hearth and that devices such as pits and nets could be constructed. So the tool-kit in essence consisted of fire, the means to capture and/or kill animals up

Plate 6   Post-forest blanket bog at Cauldron Snout in Upper Teesdale
(North Pennines). The cleaned section is ca 2.5 m high.

to the size of *Bos primigenus*, coupled with ways of gathering
plant material. The archaeological data give no indication of the
relative proportions of subsistence items while the people were
living in the uplands, nor indeed of the population size. If it is
desired to infer some of these levels from the nature of the inferred
environmental impact of the Later Mesolithic groups, then it is

equally essential to avoid circular arguments. As with the natural causes, each will be evaluated against the palaeoenvironmental evidence separately, but here especially the possibilities of multiple simultaneous causation are strong and will be difficult to disentangle.

DIRECT CLEARANCE OF WOODLAND

Inspired by the example of Neolithic communities, it can be asked whether the tool-kit of the later Mesolithic communities allowed them to fell trees of a substantial size. Assuming that the oaks whose pollen falls in disturbance phases were mature trees, then a tree typically 36 m high with a single straight trunk that had little branching below 25 m would have to have been tackled. Roughly the same would be true of lime, elm and pine trees; most specimens of birch, ash and alder would have had thinner bark and more slender trunks than the oaks and limes. It seems unlikely that any stone axe found in Later Mesolithic contexts (or indeed any other) would have made much impression on mature forest trees, and it would not have been very effective against smaller individuals. Where relatively small tools (though not as small as the microlith category) might have been effective was in ring-barking. If a complete circle of bark is removed, then it takes with it the tissues responsible for water and nutrient conduction as well as the live tissue adding wood each year to the trunk. Ring-barking a group of oaks would in due course cause their death. The trees would be left standing but there would be no summer canopy to deter shade-intolerant species of the forest floor or shrub layer. It is also possible to kill and fell large trees by lighting fires around their bases and stoking these fires until they burn through the trunk: African examples have been observed (Shaw 1969). A last possibility is that the trees were not cleared at all but prevented from flowering, so that their pollen was not shed onto the collecting surface eventually subject to analysis. This would involve the cutting of branches before the flowering season (see Table 3.2) and would have been on a large scale if it was to produce the sharp drops in, for example, oak and alder pollen observed in some of the disturbance phases chronicled in Chapter 2. Lopping, its variants and its effects is discussed further below under the topic of relations between humans and wild animals.

There is no unequivocal evidence for log-boats of Mesolithic age in the British Isles (C. Smith 1992a), but a number of examples exist in continental Europe, including one Danish example hollowed out from a single lime-tree trunk. Even given the relative paucity

TABLE 3.2 Detailed pollen fluctuations at NG4.

A. Fluctuations in tree pollen

mm	Be	Ul	Qu	Ti	Fr	Al	Co	Cal	Shrubs	Years
695	high	low	low	high>	high	low>	high	low	Prunus; Hedera	5–6
696	high	low	low	high	high	low>	low	low	Prunus; Crataegus	3–4
697	high	high	low	low	v. low	low	high	high		0–2
698	low	high	high	low	low	high	high	high		
699	low	high	high	low	zero	high	high	high		

B. Fluctuations in non-tree pollen

mm	Rosaceae undiff.	Potentilla (+ Ranunculaceae)	Rumex	Melamp	Pteridium	Micro-charcoal	Years
695	high<	present	single	peak	medium <	low	5–6
696	high<	zero (+)	3 grains	zero	medium <	low	3–4
697	high	present	single	present	medium <	medium	0–2
698	low	low	single	present	low	low	
699	low	low	single	zero	low	low	

Notes: Each column gives values relative to itself only; < = falling from last sample, > rising from last sample. Years start after the stable woodland phase.
Abbreviations: Be = *Betula*; Ul = *Ulmus*; Qu = *Quercus*; Ti = *Tilia*; Fr = *Fraxinus*; Al = *Alnus*; Co = *Corylus*; Cal = *Calluna*; Melamp = *Melampyrum*.

of axes in the British Isles, it seems probable that at some time large trees would have been tackled for that purpose if no other, and that although the canoes might well not have found their way into the uplands, the tree-felling technology would have been easily transferable. More evidence is awaited.

THE USE OF FIRE

It is time to consider the possibility that some or all of the use of fire in the woodlands of Flandrian II is human-induced. It is undisputed that Mesolithic people would have used domestic fire. The spreads of charcoal allied to stone materials found in the uplands imply that such fire was a feature of whatever type of settlement these remains represent. Such a use of fire would contribute a cascade (possibly seasonal) of fine charcoal to the atmosphere, some of which would no doubt rain out onto nearby vegetation. Detailed studies of peats during Flandrian II show that a low level of MI rainout is almost always present, and it seems likely that one of the sources of this 'background' level of fine charcoal is domestic fires (Bennett et al. 1990). An indication of the refinements possible in future work on charcoal fall-out is given in the study by Wein et al. (1987) on the Acadian Forest of eastern Canada.

Here, is it also useful to wonder whether fire is being used at a landscape scale, as a modifier of vegetation (accidental or deliberate) or as a hunting aid. In order to differentiate such occurrences from lightning fire, the temporal frequency revealed by the eleven profiles at North Gill is a help (see Figure 2.5). It seems reasonable to treat the 350-m section as a single landscape element and to be able to recognise various charcoal peaks as separate entities given their dating. It then becomes apparent that these fires would have had a return period far below what would be expected for deciduous forest. In the case of North Gill, the streamside concentration again makes lightning an unlikely cause for all of them. The probability that the fires are not only domestic is increased by the finding of layers of charcoal in peats, with different sizes of charcoal being present. Nothing in these sources of evidence suggests that human-induced fire might not be used as a modifier of vegetation or as a hunting aid. The tilt towards connecting the charcoal frequencies with deliberate human use of fire is the knowledge that these ecosystems would not have burned easily and that human-directed choice of the exact time when sufficient dry fuels were present would have increased the frequency of fires leaving some trace for the palaeoecological record.

So, without denying that (a) lightning fire might have been

an influence on vegetation (particularly coniferous woodlands or heathy vegetation), especially during any period of more continental climate; or (b) continuous human presence would have been a constant source of microcharcoal which will appear in peats as background rainout, landscape-scale fire is still a high probability, though it must be noted that a small ground fire in a forest clearing will not be an enormous source of charcoal. Discussion needs now to centre on the evidence for how such fire might be used.

To Clear Forest?

An attempt to gauge the extent to which fire might have been used by human communities to clear forest may be made by inspecting the 1 mm counts at North Gill to see if zones of SM that coincide with peaks in MI are also times of loss of ΣAP (Simmons and Innes 1996b). The lesson of these data seems to be that there is no obvious relationship between the incidence of charcoal (and hence the presence of fire) and the loss of tree pollen during the years of the disturbance, which is typically 2–3 years per 1 mm horizon. So in 10–20-year time-slices, the burning is apparently not affecting tree populations. This is borne out by another profile from North Gill, NG9A, part of which (900–990 mm; older than ~6260 BP) is counted at 5 mm intervals, and the 90 mm sector is probably at least 450 years long, maybe more. SM and MI are high for the whole of this time, but there is ± no change in the ΣAP and SP pollen totals. This is perhaps not surprising: how might a ground fire actually clear deciduous woodland unless the trees were already dead? In the long term, there might be some weakening effect on tree growth if, for example, the fire vaporised nutrients or consumed seedlings. But on the time-scale of 10–20 years, this is less probable and so the conclusion is tenable that fire did not of itself remove the trees.

To Increase the Quantity of Hazel?

Embedded in the literature on Flandrian II is the idea that fire was used to increase the quantity of hazel as a food for animals or humans. One suitable place to look for such effects might be at the ecotones: between scrub and heath for example, or between woodland and scrub. Two examples can be seen in the North Gill sequence: (a) NG9 (363 m) between 80 and 90 cm where ΣAP is constant but low at ~20 per cent and there is about 50 per cent *Corylus* pollen, and (b) North Gill Head (NGH: 365 m) in the basal 25 cm, where ΣAP is about 20 per cent but irregular and there is ca 50 per cent hazel pollen. Both have 1 cm counts.

At NG9, there is a fire maximum at 86, 87 and 88 cm, with silt, LA and SM in each sample, and an MI peak at 86. The pollen curves at 88 cm show low birch, high oak, grasses and sedges, and a small weedy flora but which includes *Plantago lanceolata* and Cruciferae. In the two succeeding samples, oak drops and is replaced by birch, with willow. Sedges are down but *Calluna* rises and falls; in sample 86 the herbs include *Mercurialis*, *Silene* and *Valeriana*. Throughout this phase (no bracketing radiocarbon dates exist: it is probably a minimum of 50 yr and a maximum of 150 yr), the hazel pollen shifts very little.

At NGH, there is a charcoal layer (LA + SM) at 162–163 cm which improves the *Corylus* frequency but does not raise it to levels seen in the basal samples. The phase of recovery after this fire is centred upon *Betula* and *Calluna*, with subsidiary rises in lime and ash, grasses, Rosaceae, *Pteridium* and *Sphagnum*. Hazel does not feature in this response. There are no radiocarbon dates from this profile; as above, 50–150 years would bracket the episode.

What these both show is that at the apparent boundary between a mixed community and one dominated by hazel, there was no shifting of the vegetation towards a higher representation of hazel in association with episodes of fire, in this stream section. The conclusion should not be universalised: this is not, for example, the tree-line where scrub gives way to heath, as far as can be seen from the grass and heather values, which are both modest. Further, if there was already a lot of hazel, the perceived need to increase the amount of it might be less. Elsewhere at this site, in profile NG5B, there is a conventional disturbance phase (70–75 cm; 5750±90 BP) where ΣAP falls from 80 to 20 per cent but there is a large increase in *Corylus*. It is accompanied by increases in birch, pine, willow, *Calluna*, Poaceae, Rosaceae, Filicales, *Pteridium* and *Melampyrum*. This is an example of the pattern for EW reported in Chapter 2, where hazel increased its frequency in 62 per cent of the disturbance phases in which its values altered (it went down in 15 per cent).

Much closer analysis of both existing data and more carefully sited profiles will probably permit explanations of the differences between these two trends. At Robinson's Moss (CP), for example, Tallis and Switsur (1990) point to a loss of hazel at ~8200 BP which they attribute to repeated burning at the upper edge of *Corylus* scrub at ca 500 m ASL. There is a similar phase at 5470±60 BP, with the first appearance of *Plantago lanceolata*. The course of soil change in a particular locality is probably important: Smith and Cloutman (1988) draw attention to the probable loss of hazel as mor humus ('black with charcoal': 169) began to accumulate, as a precursor to peat formation.

Only tentative conclusions can be drawn from this collection of material. The Chapter 2 finding (p. 60) that hazel sometimes diminishes at disturbance episodes is confirmed by FRPA as a phenomenon, but this does not lead very far in the direction of any explanation involving humans. The loss of hazel at some places may have been acceptable; elsewhere, fire intended for another purpose may have accidentally removed it. Yet again, the maintenance of open areas may have allowed hazel to flower more abundantly without increasing the actual number of plants, or to allow its pollen to travel further. Nevertheless, the pollen frequencies encountered at most Fl II increases in *Corylus* suggest that it was growing very close to the sampled profile, for values of >30 per cent ΣLP only occur within hazel woodland (Goddard 1971). So while the currently accepted story that the production of extra hazel was a purpose of Mesolithic vegetation manipulation is certainly not disproved, there are a number of fuzzinesses which need further investigation, since other circumstances could produce the same kind of palaeoecological results as a push towards more hazel for wild animal browse.

To Manipulate the Floor of an Opening?

In considering relationships with animals, the detailed evidence of disturbances like those of NG7 (see pp. 93–8) can be re-examined. If it is accepted for the moment that some of the MI charcoal might be local (from the burning of fine fuels), then some patterns can be seen to emerge even before the onset of the disturbance phase beginning at 812 mm (pp. 95–6 and Table 2.11).

Sub-phase	Charcoal	Pollen and spores
820–819–818 mm	MI peak at 818	± no bracken
817–816–815–814–813–812 mm	MI low but peak at 815	High grasses 816–815–814; high Rosaceae 818–817–816
812–797		See Table 2.11

In fact, the pattern whereby the presence of SM in the profile is followed in the subsequent sample by a fall in grass-pollen frequency but then by a rise can be detected through this disturbance phase (i.e. to 797 mm). Not quite so clear, but detectable more than once is the pattern seen at 818–813 mm for bracken spores which are wiped out immediately after the charcoal at 818 mm (at 817 and 816 mm), then have increased frequencies for 1 sample and are then wiped out again at 814 and 813 mm, after the minor MI peak at 815 mm. This allows an interpretation of a fire which burns off grasses that do not recover much in the next year but then have 5–6 years of better growth and which also keeps bracken down for about 3 years before it comes back. In the samples in which the charcoal appears, the levels for grasses and (less often) bracken are high but fall in the next horizon, a pattern which could be explained by a fire after the year's pollen or spores had been deposited. *Corylus* pollen peaks both at and between charcoal peaks and so is probably not affected by the burning. Following E. A. Johnson (1992) on aspen woodland, it seems unlikely that leaf-litter and cured herbaceous material would be dry enough to burn in spring. Hence, a late summer or autumn incidence of fire is most likely.

A recognisably similar pattern can be seen at NG5B within the 730–700 mm 1 mm count zone of Table 2.8. Here the calculations imply that each sample is ~3 years' pollen rain, and so the configuration is not so apparent. But at a time when there is both SM and MI in the profile, bracken is highest when the fire frequency is lowest, in a sequence which would run in chronological order: 7 samples × 3 years = 21 years (no bracken); 7 samples × 3 years = 21 years (build-up of bracken); 3 samples × 3 years = 9 years (diminution to zero level).

There is some expansion of hazel during the last 9 years. In the same samples, high fire incidence equals low grass frequencies, but the grass reaches higher frequencies when the fire intensity (as measured by the levels and presence of SM and MI) drops, as at profile NG7. At NG4, where interpolation in the upper part of the section would suggest 1.8 years/sample, the grass is knocked out at the onset of high MI levels at 729 mm; it then rises but diminishes after 709 mm, when there is no charcoal; a further rise is then succeeded by a sharp fall with the high levels of MI at 692 mm. The onset of SM at 689 seems to aid recovery and also brings in *Artemisia* about 5–6 years after the burning started. Bracken is knocked out by the high fire levels of 729–719 mm (= 18–20 years) and builds up during the low fire years. It is high during a later fire period (SM = MI) but diminishes suddenly at the end of the SM incidence at 682 mm (as does *Melampyrum*) and looks as if it is being shaded by birch, hazel and perhaps willow.

Comparisons between these profiles are inevitably subjective to some extent, but there seem to be enough common features to suggest that burning is taking place in the openings and affecting grass and bracken frequencies. Fire seems to be deleterious to bracken and to keep it down for periods of 3–20 years. Grasses are quickly killed off by the fire but come back soon and stay high. They will diminish if there is no more fire, partly because this may well be the end of the disturbance phase and shading by woody species takes place. Grasses will under certain circumstances compete successfully with heather: the accumulation of nutrients (especially nitrogen) is one circumstance. Another is trampling and grazing by large mammals, which will lead towards the replacement of *Calluna* by grasses such as *Deschampsia flexuosa*. Heather will also disappear under conditions of continuous waterlogging, though not of merely seasonal quagginess (Gimingham 1989; Moss 1989).

To Drive or Hunt Game?

The essential distinction here is between the human use of fire on the occasion of the hunt, and its use to prepare the terrain for the hunt so as to make the hunters' task easier. Evidence from a number of near-recent groups makes it clear that fire may be used to drive animals: towards groups of hidden hunters, into water, towards nets or pitfalls or over cliffs, for example (Anell 1969).

It is difficult to see what kind of evidence so far examined would yield any evidence about fire drives. None of the investigations, for good reasons, has covered a wide enough area to be able to plot the remains of a fire front advancing through scrub, for example, or a circular fire in underbrush which corrals prey animals, even supposing that such fires left enough traces and were incorporated into mor or peats in proper stratigraphic order. So there is no palaeoecological evidence one way or the other. On the other hand, any repeated use of fire to rid a woodland of the layer of vegetation which interrupted sight-lines for bowmen (assuming that technology to be indicated by the presence of microliths) might produce taxonomic shifts that could be revealed by pollen analysis. The fires might have removed shrubby plants like hawthorn, holly and bramble (both probably unpopular with hunters) and any understorey trees like birch, hazel and alder; ash too if it was present. Given the thin bark of this group, a reasonably hot ground fire would probably kill the species involved, but such an action assumes that the damage to the woodland *per se* was not counter-productive. The loss on this basis of birch or hazel woodland, or of alder, would not be distinguishable in pollen diagrams from its loss from any other causes. Any species still presenting obstacles from low branches could be lopped, though this would be very labour-intensive and in any case forest dominants probably did not branch until high off the ground. Probably all that can usefully be said is that the diminution of hazel and alder pollen at times of fire should have this possible cause listed among the others about which speculation is taking place. As for bramble and holly, pollen referable to the *Rubus* group containing the brambles is only rarely recognised in pollen diagrams, and *Ilex* pollen is similarly relatively rare: a continuous curve is virtually unknown in profiles from upland Britain. At NG1A, one of the disturbance phases with fire (720–750 mm) turns up a near-continuous curve for *Crataegus*. This is coincident with the fire and with the other disturbance pollens and so seems to have been favoured rather than eradicated.

THE WILD ANIMAL RESOURCE

From around the world, near-recent evidence shows that hunters often tried to minimise their own energy input into that process. Any means that improved the ratio of meat taken to distance run was generally welcome. Sedentary resources like marine molluscs are one possibility, but mobile game are always desirable, not only for food. Traps, nets, poison, concentration on choke-points during migration (such as narrow valleys or rivers), energy-efficient technology like the bow and arrow, and social-settlement mobility (like the temporary detachment of single hunters or a small group of men) have all been in the repertoire. Few of them have left traces in the upland Mesolithic of EW, but a few inferences can be made about the use of wild animals as a resource from the archaeological and palaeoecological evidence. More elaborate statements need the use of modelling, discussed later.

The evidence of microliths suggests that wild animals were hunted from bases in the uplands. Was this a simple chase, or were there attempts to improve the hunters' chances of making a kill? The possible use of fire to improve sight-lines has already been mentioned. But the management of open areas (and especially those near water) to attract wild animals may have had a wider context. Humans might seek to attract game to sites where killing was relatively easy. Such a site, in this context, would have one or both of the following characteristics: it would be open and attractive to wild animals by virtue of providing food and/or water; and it would possess good cover for the hunters from more than one side, to take account of varying wind directions.

To provide such conditions, human groups might try to manipulate the vegetation so as to improve the attractiveness of the fodder for game species, in terms of species available and quantity; this might attempt to compensate for seasonal deficiencies or extend a seasonal resource. Human groups might also intervene in the flow of water should it be possible to improve its appeal to the animals; or they might manipulate the surrounding vegetation to provide cover and/or good sight-lines (which sounds contradictory) for the benefit of the hunters. It seems unlikely that the second of these will leave any trace in the types of evidence currently available. The first and last, however, might be hypotheses that could be tested against the palaeoecological evidence.

Thinking about the attractiveness of vegetation to potential game species involves first some consideration of their dietary preferences. (Tilley (1979) and Jochim (1976) give concise accounts.) The spectrum of species (wild pig, roe and red deer, aurochs for their meat; wolf, beaver, fox, badger, wild cat and marten for fur) that are mobile are of primary importance. (Beaver may have been taken in autumn and winter when their fat content is 30–40 per cent of live weight and their pelts are in prime condition, but it seems unlikely that practical attempts to improve their habitat would have been deliberately made. *Per contra*, they were hunted in North America by tapping their dams.) The capture of wolves presumably requires either the taking and raising of their young or the use of a decoy animal, and neither would have a palaeoecological profile. So the search needs to be narrowed to the food and habitat choices of the bigger herbivores. In common, there seems to be an ability to flourish best in wooded areas dominated by deciduous species. Relatively open canopies allow ground flora to flourish in spring and summer and provide enough light for some shrub growth. The presence of open water and adjacent marshy areas is an added attraction. None of these species is an animal of large herds in woodland conditions except for possible seasonal aggregations at times of rut or for 'yarding' in very bad snow conditions. The food preferences of pig include soil invertebrates, most often found in soft ground with grassy vegetation. Roe deer were probably least favoured by Flandrian II forests since they are mostly browsers (indeed, Coy (1982) says that they need high-quality browse of the kind provided by large amounts of hazel), and so trees that only branched at over 25 m from the ground were of little use to them. Aurochs are generally thought to have been primarily grazers, using browse when grassy areas were depleted or unavailable, at times of drought or deep snow, for example. Red deer were to some extent opposite in behaviour, preferring browse and bark but using herbaceous vegetation seasonally.

If these preferences are accepted, then human-induced manipulation of vegetation to attract the larger species would have been focused on improving the grass and herb content of the forest floor. (Heather is also eaten by deer, but not bracken.) Three potential practices immediately come to mind: maintain any existing openings free from the encroachment of woody vegetation or indeed any species not eaten by the game animals; create openings with the same purpose in view; attract animals with fodder, as leaves are an obvious source, and seasons lacking browse resources for chiefly browsing animals (red and roe deer especially) are a possible purpose.

Evaluation of the first of these against the evidence is difficult since, as suggested above, normal pollen analysis is unlikely to detect a natural opening of the commonest kind, involving only a few trees at once. The opening will more likely show up if it is maintained, since it will last long enough to be detected by 1 cm sampling. It may well be indistinguishable from a deliberately-created opening. Only if the beginning of the disturbance is sampled by FRPA is it likely that the two can be separated out. Foddering will show in detailed sampling if the canopy-tree frequencies diminish, but there is no other immediate response.

CANOPIES AND CLEARINGS

An example of canopy opening may be seen at NG4, in the 690–700 mm horizons, counted at 1 mm intervals, each representing 1.8–2.0 years. At 69 cm, the date is 5315±45 BP. At 690 mm there is a disturbance phase with fire, but in the 9 mm below this there is, as pointed out by Innes (1989), a different sequence, which can be interpreted as canopy manipulation. The horizons involved are: 690 mm and above: disturbance phase with fire; 691–694 mm: selective regrowth of woody species; 695–697 mm: canopy manipulation; 698–699 mm: stable woodland.

The two lowest samples (699 and 698 mm) can be designated as stable woodland, which has recovered from an earlier disturbance: ΣAP is at 45 per cent and ΣAP+s is at 70 per cent. The woodland is of oak and elm, hazel and alder, but no pollen of ash is getting to the collecting site. The low herb values and especially low *Pteridium* suggest that the canopy was largely closed. The low values for MI and absence of other sizes suggest that fire was extra-local.

The next three samples are taken as indicative of an opening in the canopy. At 697 mm, the pollen frequencies of oak and alder fall, whereas those of birch and elm rise and *Corylus* becomes high. The Rosaceae rise and there is a little ash (*Fraxinus*). There is some *Melampyrum* (though not more than in the previous sample) and a few herbs; the bracken count rises. After two years, in the 696 mm sample, oak and alder are still low and elm is depressed, as is hazel from its former frequency. The same applies to *Calluna*. Higher values are seen in *Tilia* (lime), birch, the Rosaceae and *Pteridium*. Notably, ash rises. There is no *Melampyrum* nor *Potentilla*, but Ranunculaceae are present and there is a sharp peak of *Rumex*. Then, after four years (695 mm sample), low values stay for oak, elm, alder and hazel; the Rosaceae are high but lower than the previous sample, and bracken values are falling. The presence of ivy (*Hedera*) and *Prunus* may be noted, and there are high levels of *Fraxinus* and *Melampyrum*. Levels 694–691 mm look like a selective recovery. Higher values are found for elm, oak, alder and hazel. Ash, birch and lime all dip, and most of the shrub taxa disappear. The spores of bracken dip to lower values, whereas those of the grasses and sedges rise.

The vegetational sequence is therefore dominated by six years of selective opening of the canopy in which there is no local fire but when some shrubs flower rather better and there is a temporally non-patterned response of the ground flora. Since the affected grow back quickly in the recovery years of 694–691 mm, it is unlikely that trees were being killed. The notion of the selective lopping of branches of oak, alder, elm and hazel must be considered (Simmons and Innes 1996c). This would allow the pollen of poor producers like ash and lime to be spread more widely and call forth a modest response from the ground flora, especially bracken fern. Thereafter there is a recovery phase for about sixteen years before a much more radical disturbance phase, with local fire, is detectable. Purpose has to be assumed, and foddering of animals is the most likely. At ~5300 BP,[2] however, this could be early Neolithic in date and hence for domesticated rather than wild animals.

The sequences of burning with higher grass values and lower bracken (discussed above under human-induced fire) would also benefit wild animals and indeed, given some apparent preferences for grassy fodder, are likely to have been a more important

cause of manipulation than foddering. It is not surprising, therefore, to find evidence which fits that model rather more often than
the foddering details; however, detecting the onset of foddering
as at NG4 in 1 cm (or greater interval) diagrams would be difficult.
So, empirical data about the frequency of the two uses await
additional detailed studies.

CORRALS

The pollen analyses from Soyland Moor (CP) include a phase
of disturbance without fire (~7900–7150 BP) which is interpreted
by C. T. Williams (1985) as evidence of confined herds. The
pollen sequences which lead to this inference revolve around the
following:

- An initial fire, denoted by *Melampyrum* at an early stage;
- Low *Corylus* regeneration suggests heavy grazing pres-
  sure;
- Smooth profiles of all the clearance indicators suggest one
  long period of disturbance;
- The grass sward is a late development in the episode;
- There are ± constant *Hedera* values, which might indicate ring-barking. (This would produce dead but
  standing trees.)

The notion of 'over 600 years' of maintaining either a fenced corral
for, or otherwise confining, wild species in the early part of the
later Mesolithic is striking, but no strong challenge to Williams'
suggestion has been published. The chief difficulty of managing
such a production system would probably be getting the balance
between the numbers of animals and the available fodder within a
confined space. However, the Soyland interpretation is predicated
upon wild mammal herbivores preferring browse to grassy areas.
Pott (1989) invokes the first creation of wood pasture out of the
clearings of Mesolithic times in North Germany.

THE WILD PLANT RESOURCE

In 1976, D. L. Clarke suggested that too much attention had been
directed towards the relationship of Mesolithic cultures with animals and not enough to the use of plants which, by analogy with
most near-recent hunter-gatherer groups, formed an important
element in their diet. Apart from the frequent finds of hazel nuts in
Mesolithic contexts, very little evidence of what might have been
any kind of resource has accumulated for the British Isles: finds

of small-seeded plants such as *Chenopodium* and the remains of wetland genera like *Menyanthes*, *Phragmites* and *Nymphaea*, whose tubers are edible, have added to the list a little, and remains of pear have been found in Ireland. No over-stretching of the speculative facility is needed to consider that edible fruits, nuts, seeds and possibly tubers were in fact eaten and that some tools (e.g. antler mattocks) might relate to such procurement. Oil-rich seeds must have had special attractions. (Table 4.1 offers some examples of plants of potential economic value in the mid-Holocene.)

The questions for the present context are: was the vegetation actively managed to enhance the productivity of such plants? Would other forms of management incidentally produce such higher levels? To these can be answered, unhelpfully, 'maybe' and 'quite possibly'. The reward for Mesolithic people and the bane of current investigation is that several processes might produce the same type of result. If the seeds of *Chenopodium* were useful to eat, then attracting wild animals which broke the soil and allowed the ruderal to grow would serve both processes. Encouragement of hazel for winter browse for deer (for example, by opening the canopy of the forest dominants) might increase the number of shoots bearing nuts. Openings mean lots of 'edge', which helps the production and gathering of blackberries. Grassy clearings for animal feed might produce small-seeded grasses which may have had a culinary role. In most British discussions, little mention is made of acorns as a possible food, though in many cultures world-wide they are so used, both with and without processing. If hazel nuts turn up archaeologically, it might be expected that acorn cups might do so as well, though ethnological practices resulting in such an absence are never totally convincing. *Quercus robur* and *Q. petraea* acorns would both need processing before they were comestible, however: they are unlikely to be 'snack' foods to be eaten on the move away from a base.

Here as in other sections, it seems prudent not to rule out any such possibilities but to note that the evidence is still tenuous. But there seems little doubt that a landscape with a mosaic of forest, scrub and edge, together with open water and wetland, would attract and carry the highest densities of most edible plants as well as game animals.

The Scale of Disturbance

This has two dimensions: how frequent were disturbances attributable to human activity, and what kind of area did they cover? From these two dimensions, an idea can be gained of the amount to which a largely natural landscape was being turned into a cultural landscape, apparently by the use of active management practices.

TEMPORAL SCALE

In section 5, the run of disturbances at various localities was plotted and discussed, though without any attribution of cause. If it is now seen as likely that human activities were the origin of these ecological changes, then certain other conclusions can be drawn. From the normal run of palaeoecological data, with pollen analysis at 1 cm or greater intervals, the interventions look as if they are well spaced (by hundreds of years, occasionally longer: see pp. 118–19) and long-lasting, of the order of decades certainly and centuries here and there. What FRPA has shown is that some at least of these episodes are composite phenomena and that a combination of distance from pollen collection site and integration of several years' pollen rain into a single sample give a rather coarse picture. The forest openings at NG5B, NG7 and NG4, for instance, show a much more subtle picture, with canopy opening and fire, and possibly continued canopy or branch utilisation, being used to produce a desired vegetation pattern. So a site was chosen, and it was managed according to some culturally-set pattern until the vegetation was allowed to undergo an unmanaged succession. Why management stopped is not entirely evident directly from the palaeoecological data, but it looks as if at some sites, paludification set in and this presumably changed the ground flora beyond the point of usefulness (i.e. it become too wet), and as the change to a food-producing economy took place in the fifth millennium BP, the need to burn became less and so unmanaged successions occurred.

The background rain-out of fine charcoal present at many upland sites (see the diagrams for the South and Central Pennines in the various papers of J. H. Tallis, for example) suggests that there was a constant recourse to burning. Given the very low population densities which modelling will suggest (see below) that the area supported, this is not likely all to have come from domestic fires, and the various spreads of charcoal show that indeed that was not so. A golden eagle in the years 8000–5000 BP would at some time of the year have looked down on a landscape with a number of fires burning in gaps in the forest.

7. THE MESOLITHIC–NEOLITHIC TRANSITION

One of the great transitions in the history of humanity has been that of the adoption of agriculture: the replacement of food-collecting with food production. Its introduction to the British Isles is of no less interest since it is a long way in time and space from the zones of Western Asia where the relevant domestications were made. In crude terms, this distance has led to some conflict between explanations about the circumstances of the introduction of agriculture to Britain. On the one hand there is the possibility that it came as part of an immigrant package in which the indigenous Mesolithic people were swamped by new groups of people with an economy based on domesticated cereals and beasts. The alternative view is that Mesolithic groups acquired the new technology by some diffusive mechanism such as trade and gradually converted to the different ways. Nor is it impossible to imagine mixtures of both processes.

Palaeoecological Evidence

The first solid evidence in Britain usually comes in the form of forest disturbances at or just before the elm decline which are accompanied by cereal pollen. Such disturbances are often more intense than their predecessors and indeed sometimes bear the first occurrence in a profile of the pollen of *Plantago lanceolata*. The question as to whether the large grass pollens are without doubt attributable to domesticated grasses (and especially in the case of upland EW whether they are wheat, *Triticum* spp) and the whole relationship of the new economy to the elm decline is complex and has been the subject of much evaluation (see for example Edwards and Hirons 1984; Edwards 1988, 1989). The discussion is complicated by negative evidence: cereal pollen is not widely dispersed, so that profiles quite close together may have cereal pollen in one and not the other (e.g. at Soyland Moor); further, the cereal pollen may only receive such minor dispersal when the tree canopy is opened up. Absence of cereal pollen during a disturbance phase shortly before, at, or just after an elm decline does not necessarily mean that there were no cereals. But after all the caveats, it seems quite possible that cereals were being grown in openings in woodland in upland EW from about 5800 BP onwards, and this includes some instances of this phenomenon preceding any local elm decline. But it is premature to assign every case of forest disturbance between 5800 and 5300 BP to a desire to grow cereals. Palaeoecological evidence of leaf-foddering in the Neolithic has been well documented in continental Europe (Austad 1988; Rasmussen 1989, 1990a, 1990b). The investigations

make the points that a considerable degree of woodland management is needed to provide the necessary amounts of leaf fodder
(especially for cattle), and that pollen diagrams are not necessarily
the best guides to the degree and selectivity of the canopy
and branch management. All round, therefore, the congruence
between pollen diagrams and early Neolithic agriculture is likely
to be poor.

Chronology and Archaeology

Applying very strict criteria of pollen recognition and of radiocarbon date acceptability, E. Williams (1989) notes that only
Soyland Moor (C. Williams 1985) and an Irish site are acceptable as pre-elm-decline cereal locations, but she further denotes
a batch of Mesolithic dates in Britain between 5900 and 5400
BP. Also on archaeological grounds, she marks the Neolithic
sites as 5300–4800 BP, with one early exception at 5440 BP.
The full suite of Neolithic site types and stone artefact types
only seems to appear after the initial technological change,
however.

Models of Change

One of the most creative ways of modelling this change has
been that of Zvelebil and Rowley-Conwy (1984: 104–5), in which,
as they put it, 'the merits of farming should be understood in
terms relative to those of indigenous foraging: its productivity,
its organization and its vulnerability.' They thus distinguish
three phases: *availability, substitution* and *consolidation*. In the first
of these, farming is known to the foraging (= hunter-gatherer)
groups and there is an interchange of materials and information.
Farming is not however adopted until the end of this phase,
when some elements enter the economy of the foragers or some
agriculturalists settle in among or alongside the hunter-gatherers.
The substitution phase sees the transition to a farming *genre de
vie*, though it is assumed that hunting and gathering remain
important activities. Consolidation implies that there is now
dependence upon farming and that this practice will be both extended and intensified. Hunting and gathering will doubtless not
be absent but are distinctly secondary operations. In areas where
this model has been applied (e.g. Zvelebil and Dolukhanov 1991),
there is far more evidence against which to test this model than
in upland EW. Nevertheless, it will be useful to have it in mind
when constructing (section 8) models of the end of the Mesolithic
period.

SPATIAL SCALE

How big were such burned-over gaps, and how many at one time, were in a given area? The second question cannot be addressed from this kind of evidence; only deductive modelling can suggest the probable values. As to the first, spreads of charcoal at for example North Gill suggest a maximum size of ca 400 × 70 metres, and a minimum size (based on the notion of separate pollen catchments for each profile) of a radius of 20 metres. The variation in area is thus about 20 times, but to expect uniformity seems unreasonable. It may well be, though, that some parts of a landscape are less prone to management (of any kind) than others, with water being a definite focus for managed areas. If indeed streamsides, lakes and springs were focal points, then there may have been large segments of the land which were not changed in any way by human activity. To suggest that the land was aflame more or less continuously for 3000 years is a gross exaggeration: small-scale alterations with a medium-length time-span were the rule. Though much of the landscape at any one time was not being managed, it would have shown to an informed observer the traits of having been altered by previous periods of management: areas of mire growth, for example, resulting from paludification of deforested areas; secondary woodland not yet dominated by tall, unbranched, shade-intolerant trees like oak; remnant patches of nitrophile plants (such as the common nettle, *Urtica dioica*) marking a now abandoned settlement. In a number of ways, the upland landscape of the terminal later Mesolithic would have exhibited the marks of humanisation of ecosystems and landscapes.

8. CHAPTER SUMMARY

Humanisation notwithstanding, the natural world was still a profound influence in the life of groups of hunter-gatherers. Hence, it is reasonable to postulate a sequence of events leading to ecological change in which both natural and human-directed processes have important roles. A possible progression might be:

1. A mixed oak forest on the uplands, covering almost all the terrain, though broken where there was open water and mire accumulation in water-receiving sites. The upper edge of woody vegetation was marked by a hazel scrub. The forest underwent normal processes of death and renewal, which included gaps of various sizes caused by windthrow. The lower edge near streams underwent a sharp transition to an alder wood with other deciduous species, including elm.

2. Openings in the forest with a ground cover of grasses and herbs attracted mammal herbivores differentially on a seasonal basis. This had two consequences:

   a) The concentration of animals made regeneration of the woodland less likely;

   b) Humans noticed the concentration of animals and wished to maintain and/or enhance it.

3. Humans thus took over some of the existing openings and maintained them, using fire to keep a grassy sward rather than allow bracken to cover the ground in the early years. Heather grew as well and was burned, though it too attracted grazing animals. Attempts to extend the virtues of a grass-herb sward to the alder woodland were also made.

4. During this time, climatic change and soil maturation brought about the accumulation of mor humus over podsolic and gleyed soils. This predisposed scrub to turn to a heathy vegetation.

5. Increasing human populations (or more resource-hungry groups) wanted to try to create extra openings in the woodlands or at their ecotones. They did this by killing trees using ring-barking and by opening the canopy by breaking off leafy branches, which were also useful in attracting animals to feed, especially in winter; their merits did not entirely depend upon human presence and they could be left behind as a general encouragement, for instance, rather than be immediate bait.

6. Some of the openings underwent rises in water-table and became invaded by rushes; thereafter, peat accumulation began to get under way even on ground which was water-shedding rather than water-collecting in a micro-topographic sense.

7. None of the human-induced processes totally replaced natural events: natural openings continued to be formed by natural processes.

Notes

1. This need not have been a very lengthy process. There is an eighteenth-century description of part of Scotland (Lochbrun) in which the author tells of the transformation of a 'Firr' wood into a bog:

   In the year 1651 . . . This little plain was at that time covered over with a firm standing wood; which was so very Old that the trees had no green leaves but the Bark was totally thrown off . . . the outside of these standing white Trees, and for the space of one Inch inward, was dead white Timber; but what was within that, was good solid timber, even to the very Pith, and as full of Rozin as it could stand in the wood. Some Fifteen years after . . . there was not so much as a Tree . . . but in place whereof . . . was all over a plain green ground, covered with a plain green Moss . . . the green Moss (there in the *British* language called Fog) had overgrown the whole timber; . . . and they said none could pass over it, because the scurf of the Fog would not support them. I would needs try it; and accordingly I fell in to the Arm-Pits . . . (George, Earl of Cromertie, FRS, 'An account of the mosses in Scotland' (1711), *Phil. Trans. Roy. Soc. Lond.* 27, 296–301. Most of the spelling has been modernised.)

2. The calibration of 5300 BP for 1σ is cal. BC 4228 (4219, 4197, 4148, 4113, 4099) 4043, and the probability distributions for 1σ are:

4226–4212	0.10
4207–4178	0.20
4165–4131	0.23
4130–4078	0.38
4059–4046	0.09

For 2σ, they are:

4250–4032	0.94
4026–3997	0.05

CHAPTER FOUR

Analogies from Past and Near-Recent Times

The topic of this chapter is that of trying to add to the archaeological and the palaeoecological evidence in order to build models
of the cultural ecology of the terminal Mesolithic in upland EW.
The new inputs to these models will consist of analogous evidence from other parts of the British Isles and Europe, followed
by ethnographic parallels which might have relevance to these
prehistoric hunter-gatherers. Some examples are also given of
integrated subsistence models.

1. MODELLING THE LATER MESOLITHIC

The empirical evidence produces frustration. There is some
archaeological material, and a lot of palaeoecology. Both are
sometimes imprecise in what can be read from them. The classic
procedure is then to fill in the gaps by importing information
from other sources, with the aim of reconstructing a plausible (if
provisional and tentative) set of lifeways which connect elements
like economy, ecology and society. In the case of the later
Mesolithic, two principal sources of additional data are mostly
brought in.

Empirical data for the Mesolithic of other regions encompass
the rest of the British Isles, obviously, but also continental Europe
and in particular the North European Plain and Scandinavia. It
is assumed that even after the insulation of Britain in the mid-
Holocene, there is enough cultural similarity with the occupants
of lands to the east across the sea to make transfer of information a reasonably scholarly act, while taking care to inform
the reader exactly what is being done with it. These data are
reviewed below.

Ethnographic data also exist from hunter-gatherers of the
near-recent past and from the further past if well documented.
In general, the better fit is likely to be obtained from similar
environments; unhappily, the hunter-gatherers of temperate deciduous forests are mostly long gone. But early travellers' and

colonial accounts of the Indians of north-eastern North America (from, say, Washington DC to Newfoundland in today's terms) are of interest, as are cultures like the Ainu of Hokkaido, who were little affected by Japanese culture until the nineteenth century.

There some extant models which try to bring cultural and ecological material together.

The Mesolithic in Other Parts of the British Isles

The chronology adapted for EW (see Chapter 1) does not necessarily transfer wholesale to Scotland and Ireland. In the former, the division by types of industry is probably similar to that of England but not so precise (Morrison and Bonsall 1989), with a broad-blade industry up to 9000 BP and a later Mesolithic narrow-blade industry between that date and 5200 BP, after which sites contain evidence of post-mesolithic cultures. In Ireland, the period 8950–5650 BP has been designated as Mesolithic, with a division between early and later at 7950 BP (S. W. Green and Zvelebil 1990). Scotland has provided some additional climatic evidence: in the Cairngorms, measurement of stable isotopes of deuterium in pine stumps (Dubois and Ferguson 1985; Bridge et al. 1990) has suggested the existence of periods of very heavy rainfall or 'pluvials'. These are dated about 7300, 6200–5800, 4200–3940 and about 3300 BP, and have been referred to in earlier sections. However, part of the time of the Mesolithic occupation of Oronsay (ca 6100–5400 BP) seems to have been a period of lower storm frequencies, if the evidence of the relationship between shape and wave-exposure parameters in the dog-whelk (*Nucella lapillus*) is accepted (Mellars 1987).

In Ireland (as with England), an early Mesolithic site gives the best evidence of settlement and economy. In the Irish Midlands, at Lough Boora (ninth millennium BP), the summer killing of wild pig, eels and brown trout seem to have provided the subsistence base (van Wijngaarden-Bakker 1989). Mount Sandel on the River Bann (occupied 9100–8500 and 8100–7650 BP) has evidence of circular huts with central hearths (Woodman 1985). Wear studies on microliths showed that a variety of subsistence activities were pursued, not just the fishing which yielded the dominant sets of remains, namely 80 per cent of all the bones. Occupation was concentrated in late summer and autumn, and there are good indications of oval shelters. At Newferry, A. G. Smith (1984) draws attention to the creation of open areas eventually colonised by hazel as a kind of secondary maximum, and the strong rise of the alder pollen curve at the end of a well-defined zone with very high grass-pollen values together with *Plantago lanceolata* and *Artemisia*. A possible explanation for these trends is seen in the development of open areas maintained by grazing following the removal of hazel scrub. Other contemporary sites in northern Ireland have the appearance of being exploitation sites for small groups. No equivalent site to Mount Sandel has been found for the later Mesolithic; indeed, Woodman and Andersen (1990: 381) say that 'Virtually every Later Mesolithic site which has been investigated has produced indications that they were occupied for a limited time and perhaps with a limited set of intentions'.

In Scotland, it was for many years the received wisdom that all mesolithic was coastal, but later work has shown that inland occupation took place. The uplands of south-west Scotland are an especially good example, and some detailed pollen analyses exist for this region (Edwards 1989). In Scotland, Edwards (1985, 1990) has maintained that although vegetation disturbance allied to fire took place during the relevant years, there is no way of linking it to human activities. He has argued that it was small-scale and in no way connected with larger species shifts such as the hazel maximum of Flandrian I. Alder is more ambiguous, and some possibility of causal connection is mooted in a later paper (Edwards 1990) and confirmed for the Kinloch area of the Isle of Rum, where its temporary demise (~5950–4950 BP) is also attributed to human activity. The behaviour of the *Alnus* and *Corylus* curves is such that the existence of managed coppice is mooted (Hirons and Edwards 1990). Similar depredations into woodland or scrub have been noted for South Uist and the Isle of Lewis. The antiquity of *Calluna* heath on South Uist is traced back to the use of fire during the Mesolithic (Edwards et al. 1995).

The economy–ecology relations for both countries do not take away many of the uncertainties of the EW picture. No part of Scotland or Ireland has received the detailed treatment experienced by some areas of EW; on the other hand, Mesolithic specialists such as K. J. Edwards and A. G. Smith have worked in those two countries. The outcome, combined with archaeological data, does not differ enormously from the material for EW, with the possible exception of the emphasis on fish and on pig as prey at Irish sites. Fl II interferences with the vegetation take place in both sets of localities, and in Scotland in particular the interpretation of background levels of microscopic charcoal is uncertain: Edwards often reminds readers of its possible provenance in domestic contexts rather than as a landscape management factor.

The Mesolithic in Continental Europe

To summarise the variety of findings from the continent of Europe (displayed in its variety in for example Bonsall (1989) as well as Vermeersch and van Peer (1990)) is not possible here. A few recent detailed inquiries will be reviewed, however, in order to try and plug gaps in the material from EW where the continental studies give an idea of what could be expected to the west. Scandinavia is a fruitful source, as is Germany, since both contain either higher land or areas of highly siliceous soils. Although the Early/Later division of Britain is not recognised in all parts of Europe, there is nevertheless a tendency towards a typology-based partition with two major portions divided by the time-zone 7500–8000 BP. In the first period, there appear to be 8–10 distinct 'social units' across the North European Plain; in the second, Atlantic, period, the number has increased to 15 or more, which is interpreted by T. D. Price (1981) as meaning smaller social territories with higher population densities. Gendel (1984) postulated that the territories were visible after 9000 BP and that their intensification was due to population growth and the loss of some land from rising sea-levels.

As so often, a caution is needed. The British Isles need not be like the rest of Europe, the more so since insulation meant that after the separation of the mid-seventh millennium BP, an insular culture might develop even in the absence of any significant environmental differences. So, simple transfer of information from Scandinavia or Switzerland to fill in gaps is not likely to be acceptable. The density of evidence from mainland Europe and Scandinavia does however allow the reminder (issued by Newell and Constandse-Westermann 1984) that complex models can be attempted and that simple cause–effect relationships can begin to be replaced by more intricate associations between technology, population density and environment.

SETTLEMENT

Compared with later periods, the Mesolithic has yielded rather little evidence of structures which comprise settlements, or of the pattern of settlements. Often, both have been inferred from the distribution of lithic artifacts or organic remains. In countries like Denmark, Norway and Poland, where actual 'structures' can be detected, then a small size is common: tent areas are inferred from rows of stones that held down the covering, for example; areas cleared of stones are likewise thought to be living floors under some kind of shelter (especially if flints are present, though hearths may not) perhaps 2–2.5 × 3.5–4 m in size. Post-holes or the footings of sod walls are also found, up to 8.8 × 3.5 m, with the possibility of a tunnel entrance. Pit dwellings are also postulated, of a rectangular shape 12 × 15 m and 10–15 cm deep; shallow small circular depressions are also noted but might well be the remains of tree-root systems (Rajala and Westergren 1990). An unusual find is that of a probable one-person sleeping-floor at Duvensee (south of Lübeck) where a mat of birch bark had been cut in a single strip 1.3 × 0.88 m and placed alongside a fireplace of two pine logs. The person had a snack of a few (uncharred) hazel nuts to hand and had evidently made a few unretouched flint tools *in situ* (Bokelmann 1986). Evidence of more specialised structures is rare. Larsson (1988) describes an early Ertbølle structure in Denmark which is interpreted as having had ceremonial use.

The settlement patterns that emerge from hundreds of such studies have been described by T. D. Price (1981). In chronological terms, for instance, there seems to be a shift to larger and more permanent settlements as the Mesolithic progresses. He further makes the point that where there are environmental contrasts (in topography or seasonality), then there is a differentiation between the settlement pattern in the two zones: the British material classified by Mellars (1978), and reviewed on pp. 30, is one example. In Denmark, there appears to be good evidence for larger settlements, but size cannot be equated with season. There are inevitably questions of the seasonality of settlement and resource use, and the population units to be found at any settlement type at a particular season: were groups sedentary or mobile, or both? The material for discussing these questions is mostly economic or environmental and is reviewed under that heading below. However, all of the theory, the settlements excavated and the lithic material come together in the suggestion that for Europe as a whole (not excluding the British Isles) there were two basic classes of settlement, following Binford (1980).

Maintenance or base camps involve general purpose activities: food processing and preparation, manufacture of tools, and social activities. These camps are the most likely to leave archaeological traces of shelter and be the largest elements in any given system. It is usually assumed that most of the people of a given group live in this settlement for most of the time. If this camp is moved, then the process is called *residential mobility*.

Extraction camps are special-purpose settlement sites such as hunting camps, kill sites, quarries or gathering places for other purposes. They exist for the garnering of specific resources from the environment and are likely to be smaller than the base camps and possibly occupied for only a limited part of the year. A key question is whether only a limited number of the people went to them. Movement of this type is called *logistic mobility*.

Given that this classification seems to be pan-European, then it may well be a classification worth building upon in any synthesis or modelling for upland Britain.

POPULATION AND TERRITORY

A number of attempts have been made to estimate the population density of Mesolithic Europe. One basis is generally modelling based on data for presumed biological productivity (i.e. how many people could the available resources have supported at adequate levels of nutrition?) or, more frequently, analogy with near-recent populations of hunter-gatherers, such as the $0.17/km^2$ for temperate North America. Broadly summarised for Europe, the range would be $0.01–0.1$ people per km^2 with an average of $0.03/km^2$. A group of 500 people (the size calculated to provide for an adequate number of mates and thus ensure reproductive viability) would then need just under 17,000 km^2 in which to live, or a circular area with a diameter of 146 km (Price 1981). For the North European Plain from the British Isles to eastern Poland and southern Scandinavia to northern France, there would be fifty-four different regional territories. Higher estimates have come from Rozoy (1978) for France, of $0.9/km^2$, and from Bogucki (1987) for the North European Plain as a whole, of $1.0/km^2$. Where empirical data have been used to make such calculations away from the coasts, then these data fall within the expected limits. A possible exception is south-western Germany, where the later Mesolithic shows many signs of resource-use intensification accompanied by a change in settlement organisation. As Jochim (1979: 190) says, the region does not show the same trends as the 'familiar record of population growth in Northern Europe'. A sign of attachment to territory in this region is the presence of cemeteries which appear to be a symbol of permanence – but not necessarily of isolation, since the Upper Danube region received shells and fossil shells, presumably by trade or exchange, from areas between 200 and 600 km away.

It is highly likely, however, that any resource-rich zones would have higher densities of population, and the coastlines of Europe are the outstanding example of such a belt. In Denmark and southern Sweden, for populations known to have had access to the coasts, empirical data have produced estimates in which the density for shore-using groups might be three times that for inland people (Rowley-Conwy 1983). Local groups of flake axe types on the eastern side of Zealand during the late Ertbølle allowed Petersen (1984) to suggest that these represented defended territories which were basically sedentary, though no specific evidence is adduced for this. Comparison (sixty people) with the estimated population of the Vedbæk inlet itself implies that the population of each of these territories might be 500 people (Figure 4.1).

ECOLOGY AND ECONOMY

Of all the types of human economy, that of the hunter-gatherer is in the closest relationship to natural ecosystems. There must indeed be many direct links between them, but a simple determinism would be misplaced. Subsistence is still a matter of cultural choice except in the most extreme circumstances, and so buffers between ecology and economy can be found. Food storage (an elusive trait in terms of archaeological and palaeoenvironmental visibility) is one such possibility: there may be no animals to hunt in the winter at a particular spot, but if the huts are full of smoked meat, nuts in the shell and dried berries, then having to fill the stomach with bracken rhizomes might be bearable. It was presumably a cultural choice that Rozoy (1978) had in mind when he averred that Mesolithic hunter-gatherers in France ate well on 3–4 hours' work per day, including preparation.

The evidence as presented usually comes without the cultural framework, and so it is often overlooked. When the use of the natural environment is not discussed, that dimension must be implicit in the discussions, hovering as it were just out of sight. It comes into view almost immediately in the discussion of alterations through time in the types of mesolithic arrow-heads found in Scandinavia (Friis-Hansen 1990). Experiments showed that all the different types were effective in killing wild animals and so the change in time was likely to be non-functional in origin, bringing to mind the axe types recognised as territorial markers by Petersen (see above). Bearing in mind, therefore, that what looks like a materialistic list of plants and animals used for food and materials has been filtered through Mesolithic cultural choice, post-Mesolithic taphonomy and twentieth century scholarly narrative, the use of the environment in Mesolithic Europe can be summarised in extreme brevity. Plants are the most difficult to assess: a list (see

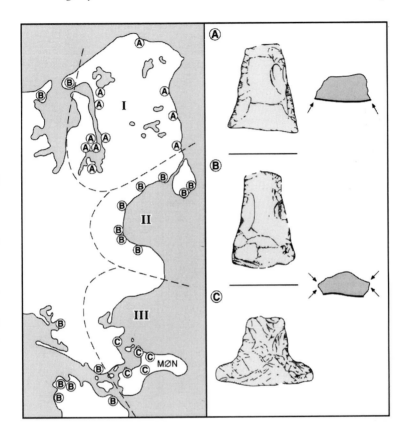

Figure 4.1   The eastern side of Zealand in Denmark, showing
different types of tool shape in the late Ertbølle
phase of the Mesolithic which can be used to infer
the presence of territories.

Source: P. V. Petersen (1984), 'Chronological and
regional variation in the Late Mesolithic of eastern
Denmark', *J. Danish Archaeol.* 3, 7–18.

Table 4.1) of plants known to be of value for food and possibly
fodder for wild ungulates is illuminated by only a few remains
at archaeological sites and ambiguous pollen and macrofossil
records. Only the virtually ubiquitous hazel, as charred and non-
charred nuts as well as pollen, is well documented. Water plants
such as *Phragmites communis* are often found forming mire peats,
but the only trace of their use as human food comes from wear
analysis of flint blades (Göransson 1988). Soft plant foods such
as bracken rhizome (which is 8 per cent protein and ~50 per cent

TABLE 4.1 Plants of potential economic value in the Mesolithic of
north-west Europe.

Scientific name	Common name	Product(s)
Corylus avellana	Hazel	nuts, forage,
Fagus sylvatica	Beech	nuts, forage
*Juglans regia	Walnut	nuts, forage
Quercus spp	Oak	acorns, bark
Trapa natans	Water chestnut	nuts
Potentilla anserina	Silverweed	roots
Stachys palustris	Woundwort	roots
Nymphaea alba	White water lily	tubers and seeds
Pteridium aquilinum	Bracken	rhizomes
Alisma plantago-aquatica	Water plantain	rhizomes
Menyanthes trifoliata	Bogbean	rhizomes
Phragmites communis	Reed	rhizomes
Typha latifolia	Bulrush	rhizomes
Atriplex spp	Orache	seeds
Chenopodium spp	Goosefoot	seeds
Poaceae (Gramineae)	Grasses	seeds
Nuphar luteum	Yellow water-lily	seeds
Polygonum spp	Knotweed	seeds
Vicia spp	Vetch	seeds
Crataegus spp	Hawthorn	leaves and fruit
Fragaria vesca	Wild strawberry	leaves and fruit
Malus spp	Crab apple	fruit
Prunus avium	Wild cherry	fruit
Pyrus spp	Wild pear	fruit
Ribes nigrum	Blackcurrant	fruit
Rosa spp	Wild rose	fruit
Sambucus nigra	Elderflower	fruit
Rubus spp	Bramble, wild raspberry, cloudberry	fruit
Vaccinium spp	Bilberry	fruit
Empetrum nigrum	Crowberry	leaves
Chamerion angustifolium	Willowherb	leaves
Galeopsis tetrahit	Common hemp-nettle	leaves
Polygonum bistorta	Bistort	leaves
Rumex crispa	Curled dock	leaves
Urtica dioica	Common nettle	leaves, fibre
Stellaria media	Chickweed	leaves

Source: T. D. Price 1989, with amendments and additions. Plants
marked* were not in the British flora in Mesolithic times.

starch) are unlikely to be preserved, even though it would have been possible to harvest 200–500 kg/ha from unforested habitats.

The animals comprise the normal suite for the mid-Holocene, but greater quantities of remains than in most of the British Isles force a reminder that not only the large mammals, but also many smaller mammals (hedgehog, badger, mustelids, squirrels) came into contact with humans, as did many species of birds. Analysis of bone fragments for the later Mesolithic in Denmark, for example, suggests that wild pig has consistently been demoted as a member of the resource base; at a time of high deciduous forest it might have adapted better than deer, for instance. This emphasises the importance of edge habitat in providing food for deer and probably aurochs; such zones would have harboured many edible plants as well, like wild apples and pears and berry-bearers like wild rose, blackberry and wild raspberry. Indeed, it might be useful to add *'woodland edge'* to the list of 'resource spaces' categorised by Paludan-Müller (1978):

Estuaries	Closed forest
Freshwater systems	*Woodland edge*
Islands	*Mires*
Outer peninsulas	*Heaths*
Narrow straits	
Exposed coasts	

Such a list brings to the fore the importance once again of the coast in regions like Scandinavia; but, as detailed work in south-western Germany shows, inland regions can support Mesolithic populations even if not of the same density (Jochim 1976). In neither case, however, does the total archaeozoological fauna necessarily reflect dietary preferences: at Skateholm in southern Scania, isotope analysis of human bone suggested that terrestrial fauna, freshwater fish and saltwater fish had an equal importance in the diet (Göransson 1988). Here, it was too brackish for oysters. The possible complexities of interpreting shellfish remains in a period of changing climate and sea-level are demonstrated for New England's Late Archaic–Middle Woodland cultures (third and fourth millennia BP) by Braun (1974).

Only occasionally does the evidence demonstrate seasonality with any great force. For the early Mesolithic, for example, dog skeletons found inland at Star Carr and Kongemose showed isotope levels that resulted from being fed largely on sea-fish; the inference is that they lived mostly by the coast but died while on hunting trips inland (Clutton-Brock and Noe-Nygaard 1990). Skateholm's plenty perhaps meant year-round occupation, though Rowley-Conwy (personal communication) thinks that the evidence is insecure. A combination of remains of animals and geomorphic criteria, however, allowed Jochim (1976) to assign seasons of occupation to four caves and thence by extrapolation to the regions in which they formed part of a seasonally-differentiated resource procurement. Many other studies, however, derive their seasonal assignations from expectations based on modelling rather than local evidence. Work on bones at Ertbølle and Maglemosian sites in Denmark has led Rowley-Conwy (1993) to argue that Mesolithic settlements cannot be understood simply from their site locations.

One implication of all these (and many more) pieces of information is that Mesolithic populations must have had some impact upon wild populations of plants and animals even if only seasonal and temporary. In her study of foraging upon birds, Grigson (1989) points out that some wholesale slaughter, presumably by driving birds into nets or by taking large numbers of eggs or nestlings, must have taken place. Yet no extinctions occurred, even though some of the foraging was very specialised, with concentration upon *inter alia* swans, great auks and eagles. The equivalent of the net-hunt in the world of vegetation is perhaps the fire, and Welinder (1989) has summarised some of the occurrences of fire in Scandinavia before the Neolithic. He gives examples of fires in deciduous forests in the years 9000–5000 BP and singles out the presence of SM and MI charcoal and maxima of *Populus, Betula, Corylus, Pteridium, Melampyrum, Rumex, Urtica, Vicia* and Poaceae as characteristic of disturbance phases. He also notes that settlement sites and pollen-analysis sites are not necessarily contiguous, and thus attributing cause is made more difficult. Changes in the values of *Populus* associated with disturbance are not normally found in the British Isles; in Poland, this genus has been shown to exhibit short-time complex fluctuations within disturbance phases (Ralska-Jasiewiczowa and van Geel 1992) which are tracked by annual laminations in Lake Gościaż dated to 5990–5600 BP.

Fires in oak forests in part of the Mesolithic (~7250–5750 BP) of south-western Germany occurred at 250-year intervals, and the expected succession of colonising trees occurred. Here, fire appears to have played a role in the transition from hazel to mixed-oak forest (after ~7350 BP) but not in the early establishment of *Corylus*. Specialised use of the forest is noted for the

Jura lakes of Switzerland by the coincidence of deforestation and large quantities (40 per cent) of *Hedera* pollen at 7000 BP (J.S. Clark et al. 1989; Sakellaridis 1979). At certain times, northern forests have undergone catastrophic transformation as the result of disturbances which are usually attributed to natural fire. In Sweden, mixed deciduous forest appears to have been replaced by conifers after disturbance (Bradshaw and Hannon 1992). Paludification in upland Britain seems like an analogue of this. At the closely-investigated site of Skateholm, Göransson (1988) claimed to be able to identify the transformation of part of the high forest to 'coppice wood'. This was accomplished by girdling the trees (for which there is no direct evidence) and causing them to sprout at the base from suckers and basal sprouts. The death of the crowns (conifers and aspen would die completely) would open up the forest, but pollen concentrations would rise for a few years since girdling makes trees flower and fruit abundantly for a short while. Certainly, management of trees for leaf-fodder is well documented for the Swiss Neolithic (Rasmussen 1989) and for recent times (Austad 1988; Rasmussen 1990a, b). It is tempting to extend consideration of the practice of leaf-foddering backwards to pre-agricultural economies and to speculate that deer, for example, might have been subject to husbandry in some way (Jarman 1972), although White (1989 proposes that there is no evidence for herding in France before the Neolithic.

The total picture of ecology and economy is linked by the notion of resource scheduling, derived by modelling near-recent hunter-gatherers. Evidence for the actual historical pattern of time-schedules is largely lacking except for seasonal exploitation patterns postulated for some biological resources. But it seems reasonable to suppose that it encompasses both totally sedentary groups and largely mobile people: in mesolithic Norway, Mikkelsen (1978) detects a yearly round of up to 400 km between coast, forest and highland.

Ecological and Ethnographic Analogy

As with the use of archaeological analogy, this category can provide material for models in the absence of reliable information from local palaeoecology. As with those other sources, it has to be recalled that exact replicas no longer exist in either vegetation type or human communities. The woodlands that may be studied as sources of likely parallel to the forests of Flandrian II in EW have been subject to 5000 years of climatic change together with management, clearance and replenishment. The near-recent hunter-gatherers were often people living at the margins, social and ecological, and unlikely to be unaltered from the time when there were only hunters in the world. Few of them were occupying mixed deciduous woodland by the time detailed accounts were compiled; even the seventeenth century accounts of the Indians of north-eastern North America can be suspected of having a political purpose as well as any descriptive objective. Nevertheless, such material can be useful, at least in showing the probable limits of the values of various processes, whether these be natural like lightning fires, or human-directed, such as food procurement patterns.

WOODLAND ECOLOGY

Probably the best analogy to the mixed deciduous woodlands of Fl II in Britain is the deciduous woodlands of north-east North America (roughly from the Great Lakes to Maine, from Nova Scotia to Virginia), already mentioned in connection with the incidence of lightning fire. Because they have been written about even since Europeans entered the region, and have also attracted a good density of scientific work, their structure and processes are well known. There are significant differences in climate, for example, with the frequency of high winds (from the tail-ends of Atlantic coast hurricanes) being much higher than in the British Isles, and summer temperatures being reliably higher with a more rapid warm-up in the spring. The woodlands are dominated by deciduous species, though the Eastern Hemlock is often present, perhaps like pine in parts of Fl II in Britain. Much of the area currently covered by forest has been managed in various ways: the term 'old growth' usually means dominants of ca 70 years of age. Closer to home, there is a good body of work on the deciduous and mixed-coniferous forests of the ancient forest of Białowieza in eastern Poland which combines both plant-community dynamics with detailed investigation on the large mammals (Falinski 1986, 1988). These include the European Bison (*Bison bonasus*), which is as near as it is possible to get to a living analogue of *Bos primigenus*.

Structure

Knowledge of the woodlands arrays itself around the fact of their dynamics and in particular the patchiness of the forests. The very assembly of the forests under the changing climate of the Holocene may have been partly in patches, with some tree species extending their range by the establishment of small populations which later expanded their ranges because of environmental changes. This may have had its importance for resource diversity and differential human colonisation, the more so since isopoll maps suggest that steep ecotones occurred (Gaudreau 1988). (The British history of *Alnus* may well have been similar in its patchiness.) The woodlands contained many species which were intolerant of fire: even the larger trees were not fire-resistant, with the exception of some of the pines. Ash and maple, birches and aspens were all very sensitive. Most, however, had rapid-recovery strategies, utilising closed cones, wind-transported seeds or spores, storage of seeds in humus or soil, or vegetative reproduction to re-establish themselves. The result seems to have been that in the seventeenth century there was a lot of open woodland free of shrubs, seedlings and saplings and with a lot of edge. Impenetrable forest was confined to cold, wet slopes and damp hollows (D. Q. Thompson and R. H. Smith 1977). Whether, however, such open woodlands were 'virgin' or were 'managed' forests needs re-examination after considering the possibility of the latter.

European forests which have been little managed in recent times can contribute a little to this background. Białowieza forest, for example, is noted for its limes and oaks which reach over 35 m before branching: there are thus few lateral branches, and the crowns are shallow. Since most European forests have been strongly manipulated very recently, the North American examples are usually better indicators of the spatial and temporal dimensions of natural disturbance in analogous areas. But some of the actual species of Fl II (plant and animal) are present in the Polish lowlands today; and two plant communities are of special interest.

There are mesophilic oak forests which might in some ways be like the Fl II mixed oak forests. Here, they contain spruce, beech and aspen, with an understorey of lime and hornbeam (*Carpinus betulus*). There is a lower layer of *Prunus padus*, *Euonymus*, *Corylus*, *Ribes*, *Cornus sanguineus* and *Lonicera*. The herbs include *Vaccinium*, *Calamagrostis* and the fern *Pteridium*; in its most thermophilous form, *Melampyrum nemorosum* is found and in its wettest, *Molinia* and *Lysimachia*. So here is an acid-soil oak forest with one coniferous tree which is not too different from the Fl II forests into whose openings *Calluna* and *Melampyrum* spread. The commonest deciduous forests in the region, however, are dominated by lime and hornbeam and are hence less relevant to upland Britain. The only reference to fire in these forests suggests that when spruce is present, any burning produces a very wet ground surface.

Given the importance of the waterside locations of disturbances noted in Chapter 3, the ecology of woodland near streams is of particular interest. Patches of both alder-ash and ash-elm forest have survived along some of the streams, with the former being the more common. The vegetation is sporadically inundated and spruce is often present, but the dampness means that oak and lime are absent. The under-layer has in it *Prunus padus, Corylus, Fraxinus, Alnus, Euonymus* and *Ribes*. The ground flora undergoes a great deal of seasonal change with a 1-m high layer of perennial herbs in summer, including *Filipendula, Cirsium oleraceum* and the fern *Athyrium felix-femina*; a lower layer of herbs includes *Caltha palustris*. The ash-elm forest is drier: it is more like the oak-hornbeam-lime forests of drier areas though with the constant presence of single individuals of the elms *Ulmus glabra* and *U. minor*. The herbs include *Allium, Mercurialis* and species of *Ranunculus*. Dutch elm disease has apparently produced single-species stands of alder.

The Białowieza Forest: Animal Behaviour

This forest has wild populations of bison, deer and pig, whose behaviour is of interest in this book. Neither the plant nor the animal communities, however, are 'natural': in the last 150 years, both have been subject to a great deal of exploitation as well as more conservation-minded management.

Since *Bison bonasus* may, with reservations, be used as a 'marker' for mesolithic *Bos*, its behaviour merits some comment. At times when there is no snow, it forms herds of (a) 10–11 animals of both sexes and (b) 2–15 bulls. A few solitary bulls are also found. In winter, larger groups gather, but these are influenced by artificial feeding, as no doubt is the density of animals, which ranges from 1.7–7.0 beasts per sq km. The animals spend some 90 per cent of their time in the dry *Tilia*-dominated forests and the pine-oak woods; they find the alder woodlands too wet, too phenologically late to be useful, and too full of insects. The lime, oak and hornbeam woods, on the other hand, contain many of the plants which constitute their preferred diet. A small (ca 30 per cent) but indispensable component of this is woody; of this, 80 per cent is from bark (the order of preference is oak→hornbeam→ash) and the rest from shoots and leaves (in the order hornbeam→ash→willow→blackberry). The rest is herbaceous, mostly grasses and sedges. The bison grass 'żubrówka' (*Hierochloë odorata*) is a favourite food. (This is a coastal grass of Scotland and Northern Ireland only in the British Isles today: the nearest equivalent would probably be the common *Anthoxanthum odoratum*.)

Also taken are *Milium, Melica, Deschampsia caespitosa* and species of *Carex*. Among the herbs, *Aegopodium, Urtica dioica* and species of *Ranunculus* and *Cirsium* are featured. If bison form larger herds in winter, then a ruderal nitrophile community may spring up in heavily manured patches, with species of *Rumex, Urtica, Arctium, Torilis, Chelidonum* and *Elsholtzia*. The overall conclusion seems to be that *Bison* is adaptable, since it will take some foods in proportion to their abundance but others are sought out even if they are in low abundance: in this latter category are found *Salix caprea, Betula pubescens, Ulmus glabra, Ranunculus ficaria, Stachys sylvatica* and *Digitalis purpurea*, for instance. Some plants are avoided entirely, including most mosses and lichens. So the European bison gets 67 per cent of its food in the snow-free season from grasses, sedges and herbs, and the rest from trees and shrubs, yet prefers the drier woods as feeding sites (Borowski and Kossak 1972).

Comparable work has been done on deer, though the differentiation between red and roe is not always clear. Both species are highly managed, and also affected by the length of winter snow-lie and depth, which affect their survival. Red deer are affected by depth of >80 cm, roe by >50 cm and both by snow-lie beyond the average length of 92 days/year. In normal conditions, red deer are often found in herds of 10 animals, with the largest groups being >21 individuals; the smaller groups are rare in April–October according to Dzięciołowski (1979). The red deer spend about 90 per cent of their time in the dry *Tilia-Carpinus-Quercus* forests but are able to penetrate the riverside alder woods, for the remaining 10 per cent of their time. (Roe deer do not enter the riverside alderwoods at all.) In winter, two-thirds at least of red-deer food is derived from trees, with grasses dominating the non-tree component (Gębczyńska 1980). Bark is an essential element of the diet, and this becomes intensive in March. Overall, the species preferred are, in order, hornbeam, ash, oak and spruce. In areas where there are a number of species, as in the *Pinus-Quercus* woodlands, hazel accounted for 1.5 per cent of the food intake, but in the riverside alder communities, hazel was third in importance, with 11.5 per cent of the intake, ash being the most selected species. Herb and grass usage by red deer depends upon phenology: in the oak woods, May–September marks the season of their availability, with a peak of feeding upon them in May-June and August. The chief species eaten are *Ranunculus lanuginosum, Urtica diocia* and *Filipendula ulmaria*. In the alder woods, few or no herbs are taken in December-April, but between May and November, a nearly constant 60–70 per cent of the diet is herbs and grasses when the

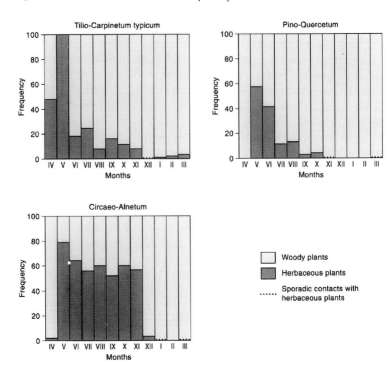

Figure 4.2   Three different types of woodland in the Białowieza
Forest, showing the proportions of different types
of food taken by red and roe deer in the months of
the year. The vegetation types are the mesic *Tilia-
Carpinus* forest; *Pinus-Quercus* woodland, and the
wetter *Alnus* woodland of streamsides. Note that
the months run from April to March, so that the
late winter months are at the right-hand end of each
block. Note the importance of woody plants at those
times of year.

Source: S. Borowski and S. Kossak (1975), 'The food
habits of deer in the Białowieza primeval forest',
Acta Theriologica 20, 463–506.

deer are in the alder woods (Borowski and Kossak 1975; see also
Figure 4.2). The findings about winter diet being dominated by
browse and bark have been confirmed for the Polish Carpathians
and for Hungary (Jamrozy 1980; Mátrai and Kabai 1989). In the
latter study, willow was the most popular browse plant and
Corylus was ranked 10th with about 15 per cent of the value of
willow species. In other Polish forests, Dzięciołowski (1969) has

reported on the importance of *Melampyrum pratense* in the diet of red deer in spring, summer and autumn.

Falinski (1986) also remarks upon the habits of wild boar (*Sus scrofa*). This finds most food in the mesic forests. It will penetrate the riverside woodlands, though not for long periods; pig are most often found there in late April to early June, with a peak in May. In the *Tilia* forests, the major season is much the same but with a peak in June; in the *Pinus-Quercus* woods, the boar are found more or less evenly through the year but with a peak in autumn, presumably for the acorns. Pig tend to make short but repeated visits to feeding locations, and 66 per cent of the above-ground biomass of all the plants selected are eaten. In the flood-plain ecosystems, rooting (for earthworms and molluscs) is deep, up to 22 cm. The turnover of the soil encourages plants such as *Urtica dioica, Impatiens noli-tangere* and brambles (*Rubus* spp).

The relevance of these findings for upland palaeoecological interpretation may be summarised as follows:

- *Bison* prefer herbaceous vegetation; red deer prefer browse, but both are adaptable: the success of red deer in Scotland attests to that fact.
- Both species spend most of their time in the mesic forests, but red deer will visit the streamside alder woodlands to feed on ground vegetation during the summer, up to the end of November. When they do so, the herbs rather than the grasses are the most palatable.
- The herb vegetation (especially the grasses) of the alder woods is attractive to *Bison*, but other factors (penetrability, insects) make it less appealing to them.
- The rooting, wallowing and debarking activities of red deer and wild pig give them a potential to affect the growth of trees, their regeneration and the detail of the ground flora pattern.

Using these data as analogues for Flandrian II in the uplands makes it possible to fill in certain details of the ecology–economy models which are proposed in Chapter 5.

Disturbance Dynamics

An overview for North American forests is given by Oliver (1981), and this is amplified by current thinking which focuses on the process of replacement of dead trees by patches of new vegetation. A patch is a discrete spatial pattern without constraints of size, discreteness or internal homogeneity, with no implication of an equilibrium. It results from a disturbance which is itself a relatively discrete event in time that disrupts an ecosystem, community or population structure and so changes the resources, substrate availability or physical environment. The parameters whose values need to be specified in each case include the distribution in space at any one time; frequency (number of events per time period or as a decimal probability for one year); return interval (mean time between disturbances, minus the reciprocal of the frequency); rotation period (the mean time to disturb all the study area); predictability; area (often given as the percentage of the total area disturbed); intensity (the physical force such as heat released per unit area/unit time); severity (the impact upon organisms, communities or ecosystems); and synergisms, as when for example drought leads to fire or insect damage and thence to windthrow of affected trees (Pickett and White 1985). Whereas earlier theories portrayed succession as a steady procession of replacement taxa, patch dynamics centres on a Markov chain of replacement processes deriving from the life-history strategies of plants, the residual propagules (seeds, spores, bulbs and cysts, for example), along with the residual chemical and physical properties of the disturbed area. Species early into the opened area are highly mobile or highly proximate. Later species, less mobile and less proximate, may need more time for a statistical chance to get established. The pattern, however, of spatial organisation of an edge once created (either by natural or human-initiated factors) shows persistence for a long time, up to 55 years being recorded in Pennsylvania and Delaware, USA (Matlack 1994).

The physical environment of the gap is different from the closed forest: temperatures are both higher and lower, for instance, and soil moisture increased by up to 20 per cent. But at the same time the top 2.5 cm may be drier because of the raising of the temperature. These changes will exert effects upon herb phenology, biomass, leaf morphology and bulb weight. A dense herb layer is competitive, and so there is a lower biomass of each species than if there were few species. Some of the competition may be diminished by seasonal and shade scheduling since there are herbs which are, just as with trees, shade-intolerant as well those which are flexible (e.g. adjusting their flowering periods to light availability) or entirely shade-tolerant (Collins et al. 1985). After fire, herbs from the seed banks in the soil and humus layers proliferate for 4–8 years and then disappear; mosses and liverworts flourish in the 1–6-year period; burning of a mossy layer will eliminate *Sphagnum* and *Dicranum* (Heinselman 1981).

The regional success of these and other colonising plants depends upon the supply of disturbed areas. A great deal of work has been done on disturbances in the Boreal forests of North America, though less on the hardwood-dominated areas. The kinds of data which emerge chronicle some of the parameters listed above:

- In southern Appalachian mixed hardwoods, six lightning fires/yr/400,000 ha exceeds the (unspecified) number for the north-east USA but is less than that for the south-east pine forests at 20+/yr/400,000 ha. The median fire size is 0.8 ha (a square 90 × 90 m; a circle of radius = 50 m; an elongate rectangle 50 × 160 m or 20 × 400 m), and 90 per cent of the fires occur between April and August; over half started on the top third of the slope; and none developed into a crown fire or started spot fires elsewhere (Barden and Woods 1974).
- In temperate-zone 'old' hardwoods, gaps cover 1 per cent of the land area, with a gap size of 280–375 m², and if there is neither fire nor storms then small gaps equivalent to one tree-fall are the commonest. In these there may be no new trees but rather the lateral extension of existing growth, so that the forest is not composed of obvious mosaics (Oliver and Stephens 1977; Lorimer 1989; Frelich and Lorimer 1991).
- In New Hampshire, Bormann and Likens (1979) suggest that the forests are resistant to fire but highly suscep-tible to windthrow; a possible synergism is that high levels of windthrow make the forests more susceptible to fire, though low depths of humus and litter make it less likely. They suggest that the fire-rotation period in New Brunswick (Canada) hardwoods is of the order of 650–2000 years. A rotation time for hardwoods in Maine and New Hampshire of 625 years is postulated by Fahey and Reiners (1981).
- Reviewing eastern forests of North America, Runkle (1985) calculated an average rate of disturbance (defined by him as a force that kills at least one canopy tree) as ~1 per cent per annum, with a range of 0.5–2.0 per cent per annum. The natural return interval was 50–200 years. Small gaps might elicit two types of response:
  a) Growth of bordering trees by lateral extension at an average of 4–14 cm/yr and proportionally more important in the smaller gaps.

    b) The growth of saplings at 25–50 mm/yr in height. After 5 years this is especially important in closing gaps ≥100 m² in size.

- In mature forests with hemlock in southern Appalachia, fires are uncommon but occur on south-west-facing slopes near ridge tops. Tree-fall converts to gap 0.5–2.0 per cent each year, with an average of 1.5 per cent per annum. Most of the gaps are small but a few are large: the average size is 31 m², the largest 1490 m². About 1 per cent of the land area is in gaps of >400 m². Here, the gaps are often the foci for further tree loss: only in 112 out of 275 did this not occur; as in other studies, lateral growth was an important method of filling the smaller gaps. Further north, in the Allegheny forests of Pennsylvania, fires were rare or absent on the moister uplands but windthrow was important. However, the loss of a single tree here and there was still the most important gap-former. The disturbance rate was 0.05 per cent p.a. since the area was dominated by very long-lived species.

- Studies of the Pisgah Forest, New Hampshire, have chronicled disturbance history since European settlement. The forest types included stands dominated by hardwoods and events such as a fire that killed beech, oak and chestnut trees in 1830 could be mapped. The main finding, however, is that windstorms, especially hurricanes, are the main source of disturbances, at a frequency of about 5–10 per century. Fire was the second most frequent event, with the fire season in spring and autumn; interaction of these two processes comes in the form of increased fire risk after windthrow in coniferous woodlands but not in hardwood tracts. Overall, the forest has many even-aged stands within which competition between tree species occurs.

- Work has concentrated on the disappearance and regeneration of tree species rather than the vegetation of the cleared areas. Niering et al. (1970) describe experiments on controlled burning in New Hampshire which had an especially beneficial effect upon bluestem (*Andropogon* sp.) grasses, making them more vigorous, taller and floriferous. Stem-kill of certain smaller trees and shrubs was common, but root-kill happened only to the smaller size-classes of the more fire-sensitive tree species. Woody shrubs were also favoured by firing.

Two further aspects of North American forests are of interest, concerning the resources which they offer to foraging economies. The edible plant resources are high (nuts, bush fruit, tree fruit, tubers, greens, tree sap and seeds). The gathering of acorns from many species of oak was practised by human groups without resorting to management, though Keene (1981) notes that oaks at the edge of stands and whose branches had access to light were the more productive. For modelling purposes, however, he calculates that even in a good acorn year, the competition for the crop is such that only about 10 per cent of it might be available to human communities. Part of the competition comes from wild pig, whose rooting can reduce the cover afforded by the ground layer to (5 per cent of its expected value and produce smaller and non-flowering individuals. Following disturbance (especially fire), white-tailed deer populations (the white-tailed deer, *Odocoileus virginianus*) may be dense enough to affect the regeneration of trees and indeed to affect stand structure and composition. The populations of deer in the hardwoods of the south-east Ozarks were also consumers of acorns, and their populations might be affected by the availability of the oak mast since it was an important food for them in autumn and winter. For the autumn rut, the deer concentrate in the oak-hickory woods of the uplands and stay there for the winter. During the rut, the males are less wary than normal and so are easier to hunt. Early in the year, stream bottoms are a favourite feeding ground since emerging grasses and sedges are found there. Such seasonality of behaviour is also found in *Cervus canadensis* ('elk' in North America): normally non-migratory and with a low population density, it will 'yard' in groups of about 10 animals in late winter. Indians of this region also took mustelids, racoon, squirrel, birds, turtle, fish and freshwater mussels. Many of these were stored by drying in the summer sun, a facility presumably less reliably available in upland EW even at a time of temperatures which averaged 2–3°C higher than today. Presumably, though, bears were also present in EW: in the Ozarks they were hunted by the Indians in the late autumn or early winter when their fat content was high and mobility low. Systematic hunting may not have been practised, however, since one informant reckoned that a hunt lasted eight days.

CULTURAL ECOLOGY OF NORTH AMERICAN WOODLANDS

Happily, a number of accounts of Indian practices in the north-eastern woodlands have survived. To these can be added the increasing volume of palaeoecological work which acknowledges the aboriginal population's influence on the ecology, and some near-recent accounts from more remote parts of the continent.

Hunting Techniques

The collections of descriptions of game hunting on land are diffuse in their conclusions to the extent that no one technique seems to have been favoured over others. The continent-wide survey by Anell (1969) has most emphasis on Eskimo (sic) groups and buffalo drivers of the west, but techniques used by those groups seem to have been found in other regions as well. Driving into water was very widespread and was found in Great Lakes Indians; fire drives were used in the western third of the continent and in the eastern woodlands. Anell suggests that the eastern woodlands were virtually free of running down on foot as a practice, but Cronon (1983) somewhat contradicts this in his account of the northern New England communities. He suggests that there was great variation: lone hunters with bow and arrow might be part of a spectrum with 200–300 men together at the other end. Traps might be set for a single species; equally, specially-planted hedges were set as drive lanes perhaps 1.5 km long to steer animals towards waiting hunters. No mention is made of whether traps were baited with foods preferred by the deer, but among the Algonkians trapping was the commonest form of taking deer (Cox 1973). Baiting with preferred foods (hazel and ivy might be considered in the British context) could have improved the efficiency. On the other hand, Rozoy (1978) claims evidence for the use of nets. Hunting was especially the work of the men, and they might detach themselves from any other settlement unit for periods of up to 10 days to go hunting or fishing, especially in the autumn when food had to be gathered and stored against the winter. The meat which the men gathered might form about half the calorie intake of their group; deer and bear were especially important. Moving camp and varying group size to maximise the chances of resource acquisition was very important, but camp might also be moved because of war, death or fleas. Rozoy (1978: vol. II, 1166) thinks that men also moved 'for the fun of the thing'.

Fire Management

This material concentrates largely upon the purposes of fire management in North America, though it also describes what little seems to have been written about the methods of burning. The existence of controversy about the scale of burning is mentioned, and there is a epilogue of material from places other than North America.

The purposes of management are well detailed in the summary accounts of New England at contact time and soon after, and in statements given relatively recently of the practices of Cree Indians in the Boreal forests of Alberta around 1910 (for New England: Thompson and Smith 1977; Cronon 1983; Russell 1983; Patterson and Sassaman 1988; for Alberta: Lewis 1977, 1982; Lewis and Ferguson 1988). It is summed up for the first region in a nineteenth-century account by a visitor: 'the object of these conflagrations [Indian-set fires] was to produce fresh and sweet pasture for the purpose of alluring the deer to the spots on which they had been kindled'; and the effects in the seventeenth century were, for east-central Massachusetts:

> The Salvages are accustomed ... to burn it, twice a year, vixe, at the Spring, and at the fall of the leafe ... The burning of the grasse destroys the under-woods, and so scorcheth the elder trees, that it shrinks them, and hinders their growth very much: So that he that will look to find large trees ... must seeke for them in the lower grounds where the grounds are wet when the country is fired. (quoted in Maxwell 1910)

This was the common practice, it seems, in southern New England. The firing brought about a forest of large, well-spaced trees, few shrubs and much grass and other herbage, and this in turn increased the populations of elk, deer, beaver, hare, porcupine, turkey, quail and ruffed grouse as well as their predators, which were often fur-bearers. Mostly ground fires were employed, and these might be used to drive game, especially by encircling the animals. Otherwise, the fire cleared away underbrush and also consumed twigs and other crackly litter which gave away hunters. The negative effects were upon the provision of firewood and on the mast of oak and beech; in the long term, the size of oaks decreased and their mortality increased. Fire at 20-year intervals apparently improved oak regeneration but at 1–5-year intervals over an 8–9-year period was negative in effect from the viewpoint of a twentieth-century ecologist; the Indians might have thought differently.

In northern New England, the situation was different. Though coastal forests were burned, there is less evidence for it inland, though a recurrence of data allowed Patterson and Sassaman

(1988) to wonder if it had been practised by aboriginal groups without access to the coast who were trying to improve their habitat. They note, however, that contact with the fur trade was a form of resource specialisation which brought about intensification of land use, which itself might have meant the use of fire in hitherto fire-free areas.

In Alberta, Lewis distinguishes two desirable products of burning the vegetation. These he calls 'fire yards' and 'fire corridors'. The first produced areas of grass- and sedge-dominated vegetation among the trees which could be called 'hay' meadows, smaller open areas ('swales') and grassy lakeshores. The second produced grassy fringes to streams, and mires, open areas along ridges, and by trails. Both kinds were collecting and traversing places for game animals. For instance, the burning of brush near water encouraged moose in the autumn, the firing of areas near water produced good trapline conditions and around water helped to provide food for ducks. Early grass in the meadows was an attraction to several species of game. If small mammals were encouraged, then not only might they be edible but their predators were also higher in numbers. Mires ('sloughs') were also burned over at the edges to improve the quantities of aspen and birch, the principal food for beavers. In the woods, there was the added advantage that natural fires were seen as dangerous and uncontrollable; these latter might start also in deadfall areas, and so these openings were converted to swales by being burned every spring or burned for two years to get rid of the high fuel loads and then allowed to return to forest. So, the human-induced fires existed alongside a natural mosaic, but there were differences in terms of seasonality, frequency and intensity.

The methods of fire management are not well documented for New England. One account suggests that burning took place twice per year, in spring and fall, but a counter-argument points to the difficulty of burning deciduous forests (especially oak) twice per year since there is not enough litter production. This might apply with less force if it was abundantly-growing grasses that were being burned. In Alberta, spring and fall were the seasons for burning, with some emphasis on the spring since the remaining moisture made fire easier to control. Summer was avoided. Indeed, the question of control of fire was very important: both natural and human-made fire-breaks were used, and fire was only set in the meadows when surrounding conditions were moist enough to ensure that there was no uncontrolled spread. Topography was also used as a regulator: fires were set to run uphill for intensive fires, downhill for lighter burns, and towards water as a natural fire-break. Fire was, though, never used to run animals.

Some of these interpretations have been challenged by Russell (1983), who asserts that since only six of the thirty-five relevant records refer to the burning of forests, then the case is made only for domestic use of fire. But since the actual accounts are so graphic and detailed, both Myers and Perni (1983) as well as Patterson and Sassaman (1988) are happy with the landscape-forming interpretations.

Other parts of the world which have experienced sophisticated fire management by hunter-gatherers are chronicled by Lewis (1982). They include regions with heavily pronounced dry seasons such as California and western Washington and the dry zone of Australia's Northern Territory. But also included are Tasmania and New South Wales, where burning focused on waterholes and creeks, producing strips and circular areas of grass among the bush. For Tasmania, Hiatt (1967) documents closely her initial statement that 'Very early descriptions of Tasmania give the impression that the island was one slowly burning mass'.

A general finding of many of these studies is the relationship between fire and water. The intermediate factor may be the type of soils, the behaviour of animals, or safety, but the spatial link is often there. As with the other details, these prove nothing for the upland Mesolithic in EW, but they do open up a range of possible behavioural inputs into modelling, extending the lines of thought so fruitfully opened up by Mellars (1976b). If any modification of that thinking is needed as a result of further evidence of the type just outlined, then it is probably in the direction of more emphasis on grasses and herbs than on shrubs.

Settlement Analogies

There is a very large literature in both archaeology and anthropology on this topic, and no attempt to review it all will be made here. Among the selection of sources, the global review of Hayden (1981) is especially helpful.

An assumption is often made that hunter-gatherer societies are 'nomadic', that is, that their settlements are moved from time to time, usually on a yearly cycle determined by the availability of subsistence resources. Since aggregations of people are likely to increase the intensity of their environmental impact, a closer look at this concept may well be useful. The basic information which it would be valuable to have concerns the number of people who move, and how often and at what times of year. Since the Mesolithic has chronological depth, the possibilities of long-term transitions (e.g. from mobility to sedentarism, from gathering to farming) of the kind modelled by Harris (1990) are also germane. The question of territory is relevant as well, since no near-recent groups have had an unlimited spatial area from which to garner resources: there are always limits imposed by the nature of the environment or the proximity of other human groups. Thus a key question is that of ownership and defence, since only if a territory is established can planned movements to predictable resources take place. The probable situation is well summarised by M. T. Mulholland (1988: 146):

> mobile foragers defend a multiresource territory that re-
> quires exclusive control of a large geographic area . . . This
> large 'sufficient resource' territory should encompass many
> biotic zones but would be most intensively utilized in the
> coastal and riverine zones, where maximum clustering of
> nutritionally important resources would occur. The upland
> interior, especially in areas with high lake and wetland
> intensities, was also occupied, but territories would be
> larger because nutritionally important resources are of
> lower density, and the distance between areas of predict-
> able subsistence resources is frequently greater than in the
> lowlands.

From this follows the probability of groups and/or sub-groups moving in response to resource yields of high predictability and availability. Other factors, such as water, shelter and firewood, may also play a role in some regions. In terms of environmental impact, the location and duration of all types of settlement are an important input into any modelling. Long-term possession of rights over territory may also lead, as in Australia, to phenomena such as cemeteries (Pardoe 1988). This emphasises the idea that several cultural factors may probably have affected the archaeological visibility of any foraging culture. Near-recent anthropology suggests that, for instance, the rules governing who may consume certain animals may have an impact on subsistence strategies: women were often forbidden certain foods. Likewise, the butchering of some species had to be done away from a settlement because it could not be done in the presence of women. The remains of a temporary settlement might be much diminished because of rules about cleaning up the site. Illness and death were both powerful reasons for moving, since they betokened the breaking of a taboo which was place-related.

RESIDENTIAL MOBILITY

This refers to the movement of all the members of a group, often with their shelters and normally with all their possessions. It contrasts with logistic mobility when a sub-group goes in search of a predicted resource, usually for a limited period of time. The question begged by such statements is what number of people comprises different groups and sub-groups. The first is usually called a *band*, and near-recent examples in northern forest environments are of the order of 50–200 people. The terrain involved is of the order of a 16-km radius circle for winter hunting and trapping territories for the Cree (Jochim 1976). Surveys show a great variety in the amount of movement. At one extreme, Cronon (1983) relays how whole Indian villages in New England were moved, with wooden houses being taken apart; such people were however poor at estimating how much food they needed to store for the winter, and so were often hungry towards the oncoming of spring. In Western Australia, however, several groups lived in permanent or semi-permanent settlements (E. Williams 1987), as did the Ainu of Hokkaido, where river-basins were the territorial focus for permanent settlements (Watanabe 1972). In general, it seems as if residential camps would be sited near secure resources; logistical camps were established to tap more mobile but probably high-prestige foods.

LOGISTIC MOBILITY

In this phase, a sub-group of the band moves to what are often called 'hunting camps'. The amount of movement is the minimum necessary to procure resources of the predicted proportions. Jochim (1976) gives examples from many parts of the world and notes that in addition to the presence of the resources, shelter and a view (for the observation of game and strangers) are necessities. The Ainu are a good example of groups going out from a permanent settlement for hunting higher in the river valleys in spring and autumn, but similar budding-off behaviour is reported from, for example, Cree groups in Canada. In most such cases, it is adult males that form these logistical groups. The Cree groups are 3–5 men strong, while the Ainu groups comprise the adult males from three houses. On the Arctic shores of Canada, Inuit hunting groups have been any size from 1-n but with a mean coastal size of 1.5–10.3 men; inland caribou hunts required a mean size of 4 men.

Cooperative hunting in Chipewyan bands meant male groups of 9–41 individuals. (A recent review of temporary group size by Dunbar (1992) suggested a range of 30–50 individuals, which seems large.) The hunting trips last between one and several days, and trapping trips in the Boreal forests between 7 and 10 days. Distances are usually limited if foot travel is the only available means: for plants a maximum distance of 8 km will be traversed, for animals 16–24 km. The nature of the terrain and of the prey may mean that 'hunting camp' is a simplification, with different kinds of trek and hunting camps being used for different lengths of time at different seasons and each leaving certain kinds of traces, many of which would not be archaeologically visible.

COASTAL SETTLEMENTS

The ethnographic literature emphasises the richness of coastal zones as habitats for hunter-gatherers. Fish provided up to 50 per cent of the yearly calories of such groups in the latitudes 50–70° N, according to Hayden (1981: 358). Fish, too, are only one of the food sources at coasts, and some of the other animals have the convenient habit of being sessile. The upshot has been two-fold: coastal groups suffered far less nutritional stress than inland groups, and were able to maintain higher population densities. Yesner (1980) puts forward the figure of 6 persons/km as an average density in temperate latitudes. Many of the animals taken are migratory, and so there are seasonal variations in the avail-ability of food sources, with possibly the sessile molluscs 'filling in' when other taxa are scarce. Hence there has always been a greater degree of sedentarism among coastal groups, especially in temperate latitudes. Indeed, it is possible to link the degree of sedentarism at coasts to the diversity of the resources. Equally, a society experiencing rapid population growth might expand into less productive areas on a seasonal basis (Fitzhugh 1975). In all ways, therefore, coasts are a highly favourable environment (technological requirements are not high once sea-mammals and deep-water fish can be taken safely), and it seems axiomatic that any hunter-gatherer culture, near- or far-recent, would utilise them whenever possible.

The variability in the role of marine resources has been categorised by Fitzhugh (1975) for what he calls 'Northern Mari-time Adaptation types'. In the context of upland EW, two groups come closest to the likely Mesolithic situation, albeit recalling that no near-recent group is likely to be a perfect analogue of the mid-Holocene. 'Modified Interior' groups have a dual economy with seasonal subsistence on both coast and interior, and generalised interior-type technology without specialisation for intensive maritime hunting and fishing. 'Interior-Maritime' groups have a dual economy with seasonal subsistence on interior and coast, but with a more intensive maritime economy with technological specialisation such as toggling harpoon, and a generalised interior economy. The first type is tied to the Montagnais and the second to the Sea of Okhotsk; in very crude terms the Okhotsk type looks more like the early Mesolithic just as the Montagnais type more resembles the later Mesolithic.

COMPARISONS

An assumption of environmental determinism is all too easy in these discussions. The movement of settlement is no doubt influenced strongly by the pull of resource availability: the examples of North Americans being compelled to disperse in search of game in winter is one instance. Movement is however mediated through the push of cultural factors as well, and these may introduce unpredictable elements (Riches 1982). Thus, however detailed the knowledge of the resource base in the far past, it will always underdetermine the cultural pattern. The complex of increasing functional complexity, increasing population density and increased intensity of environmental utilisation presents a series of choices among which cultural determinants will be paramount.

Combined Models of Resource and Settlement Scheduling for the Mesolithic

This brings us nearer to the integrated models of economy and ecology for upland EW that are the goal of this section. The material reviewed here attempts to combine environmental, archaeological and ethnographic data to produce models which address the seasonal availability of foods to foragers in temperate latitudes, and the seasonal movement of settlements, or the lack of it. The general approach has been to erect a deductive model based on ethnographic inference and/or biological inference (productivity studies or animal behaviour, for example) and then to match this with the archaeological and palaeoecological data.

INLAND ENVIRONMENTS

All the previous material points to the fact that in Mesolithic times in temperate latitudes, the coasts were likely to have been relatively resource-rich. It seems reasonable, therefore, to separate out the models where there could have been no possibility of

TABLE 4.2 Saginaw Valley schedule.

Season	Resources used	Settlement
Spring	Spawning fish, new shoots of plants, tubers, turtles, dried venison	Logistical mobility groups; few remains at sites
Summer	Fish, turtle, beaver, dried fish, herbs and berries, deer	Residential mobility groups; leave variety of tools, hearths and pits
Fall	Intensive exploitation of deer in uplands, fruits	Logistically mobile groups, but RM camps still occupied
Winter	Beaver, deer, racoon, stored fruit, venison, fish	LM groups on ridges for deer; racks = post-holes

Source: Keene 1981.

access to shorelines from those where it was either possible or certain.

Saginaw Valley, Michigan

For this deciduous woodland environment of the Late Archaic (i.e. immediately pre-agricultural) period, Keene (1981) has construc- ted a resource-settlement schedule, in the form of an optimisation model based on calories and biological production, summarised in Table 4.2. A picture emerges of residential mobility (RM) accom- panied by logistic mobility (LM) to tap particular resources such as deer.

South-west Germany

Jochim (1976) constructs a detailed model of subsistence prob- abilities, with a seasonal resource schedule as a key stage (Table 4.3; Figure 4.3). The basis is site catchment analysis plus the inferred distribution of animals during the year. The valley of the upper Danube is a key environmental factor, as is the finding of shelter during winter excursions to higher terrain. Four base camps (RM type) are envisaged, with a winter camp along the Danube and a summer camp by lakes or the edges of the lower Danube. Intermediate spring and autumn camps are found along the river, at the mouths of tributaries. The largest aggregations of people probably occurred in the summer, with the smallest in

TABLE 4.3 Jochim's (1976) resource schedule for south-west Germany.

	Jan–Mar	April	May–August	Sept–Dec
	Pop.: 17–33	Smaller	Pop.: 54–108	Pop.: 17–33
	Deep in main valley	At tributary	Higher land	Sheltered valley
			Aurochs possible	Aurochs possible
Red deer	46	20	15	24
Roe deer	5	4	2	3
Boar	28	11	15	28
Fish	4	13	31	9
Small game	12	12	12	7
Beaver	2	0	0	1
Birds	2	6	0	3
Plants	0	30	30	23

the spring, and intermediate size groups were together in fall and winter. Also calculated are the population densities that might be supported on various levels of harvest: the fish catch is thought to be critical in enforcing a maximum human density of $0.13/\text{km}^2$, but this would largely be concentrated in the lowlands rather than the Alb heights.

The Netherlands

A model of the inland area of the Netherlands during the Boreal is presented by T. D. Price (1978), following the methods of Jochim (see above). Since it is for the Boreal, the original includes the European elk or moose. Given a change to more deciduous wood-land, then probably roe deer, wild pig and small game would fill the food niche. In this model, there are five seasonal stops, but Price does not allocate these simply to the resource seasons. The settlements contain, from the evidence of artefact density, numbers of people which range from a small single-purpose task group to as many as ten families. Possibly the most striking thing about the data as deduced here is their evenness through the year: apart from plants, there are no large fluctuations of diet, which seems logical for a lowland area like that of the Netherlands.

Lowland England

For the Fenlands of East Anglia and the adjacent drier terrains,

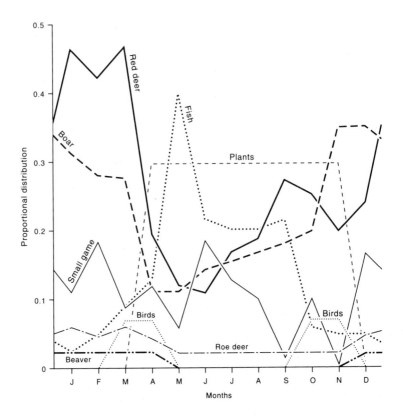

Figure 4.3   A model of the proportions of foods (by yield of edible
material) in the diet of the Mesolithic inhabitants
of south-west Germany. Birds feature in the spring
in the form of eggs and chicks rather than adult
specimens. The fish kill is related directly to the runs
of migratory fish.

Source: M. A. Jochim (1976), *Hunter-Gatherer
Subsistence and Settlement: A Predictive Model*, New
York: Academic Press.

TILLEY (1979) has used site catchment analysis combined with
inferences about animal behaviour and densities to construct a
seasonal resource schedule (Fig 4.4). This is matched against the
archaeological data, a set which *inter alia* allows the inference that
there was no population growth during the later Mesolithic. Large
sites are attributed to base camps in an RM pattern and are found
on the Breckland edge. Smaller sites are located in the Fen basin
and on 'damp woodland' terrains. The absolute number of sites

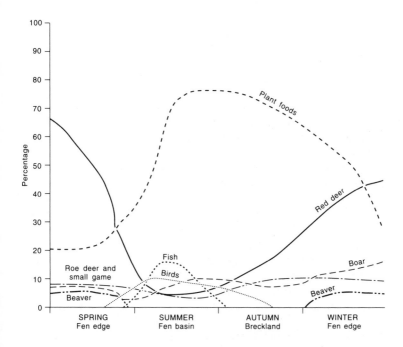

Figure 4.4   A model of the proportions of foods (by yield of edible
material) in the diet of the Mesolithic inhabitants of
the Fenland edge of East Anglia, assuming that the
group moved between the fen, its edge and the drier
Breckland during the year. During this time, the
fen was subject to marine incursions which would
presumably have increased the resource variability
of this environment.

Source: C. Y. Tilley (1979), *Post-Glacial Communities in
the Cambridge Region*, Oxford: British Archaeological
Reports British Series 66.

is highest on the fen edge, where there is the highest potential for
environmental manipulation. An RM pattern emerges in which the
fen basin is occupied in the summer and the Breckland in autumn
(hazel nuts and bracken rhizomes being major attractions), with
intermediate camps along the fen edge in winter and spring.

COASTAL ENVIRONMENTS

Here is the possibility to consider Mesolithic groups who lived
in coastal sites for at least part of the year; some of them may
however have had access to inland forests or even, in the case of
Norway, mountains above the tree-line.

The Danish Ertbølle

The richness of archaeological and palaeoecological information
for this culture has enabled very fruitful attempts at reconstruction to be made. Rowley-Conwy (1983) has combined deductive
approaches based on theoretical calculations about population
size with the resource schedules of many near-recent groups
(Fig 4.5) to round out the models based on archaeological data.
He suggests that the Ertbølle people occupied base camps on a
sedentary basis, with LM groups going out for special purposes.
The advantages of permanent sites by the sea centre around the
extension of the technological repertoire by the storage of bulky
items like big nets, the ability to watch over food stores, the ease of
transport by water for LM groups, and the fact that sheltered zones
like estuaries offer habitats for molluscs like oysters which would
have provided a food source for the lean time of late winter/early
spring. The base camp group is most likely, in this model, to have
numbered about eighty.

The later Ertbølle, as considered for north-west Zealand by
Paludan-Müller (1978), concentrates on the value of the shore
zone but allows for excursions into the interior forests. The
basis is a calculation of the distribution of known sites of later
Ertbølle age:

Islands	41%
Mainland 0–1 km from sea	25%
Mainland 1–5 km from sea	4%
Mainland 5–10 km from sea	12%
Mainland > 10 km from sea	18%

He further makes the point that inland fishing (especially at lakes)
would be good in the early spring and late autumn but poor in
winter. Based on coastal resources, he then postulates year-round
base camps on the estuaries, with a major move to the fresh waters
in spring and autumn, with perhaps some use of these areas in
winter for LM groups to hunt for furs. The islands will have been
used by LM groups for seasonal resources such as seals in winter.
Paludan-Müller makes the additional point (1978: 154) that the
earliest date for manipulation of the forest canopy should be
expected near the inland fresh waters.

Southern Sweden

The detail available from the multidisciplinary excavations at
Skateholm, facing the Øresund, has brought into focus the great

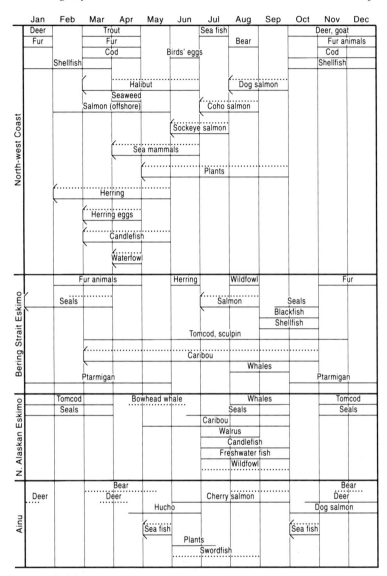

Figure 4.5   The resources available to different groups of coastal
             hunter-gathers in near-recent times. The way in
             which January and February appear often to be lean
             months is striking, though the ability to buffer that
             period with preserved food is always present.

             Source: P. Rowley-Conwy, 'Sedentary hunters:
             the Ertbølle example', in G. Bailey (ed.), *Hunter-
             Gatherer Economy in Prehistory. A European Perspective*,
             Cambridge University Press, 111–26.

range of potential foods from a lagoon+seashore+forest set of environments in close proximity (Göransson 1988). In particular, the plants can be stressed: the rootstocks of *Phragmites*, for example, along with those of bulrush; seaweeds, and the salt-tolerant plants of the Cruciferae and Chenopodiaceae families. In the forests, over 400 edible species were present, of which hazel and bracken (both of which store well) were probably the most important. An edible-matter yield for the latter of 20–50 t/km^2 is postulated. Possible exogenous change is indicated by the finding of fewer roe-deer bones as the Atlantic period (= Fl II) progresses, and more wild pig and seal, with red deer staying constant. The bone remains also indicate that animals were butchered at kill sites and the best parts brought into what was, Göransson thinks, a permanent settlement. The presence of a cemetery gives additional, though not conclusive, force to that possibility.

Migration in Norway

The environment of Norway offers a greater set of contrasts than Denmark, but the coast equally acts as a plentiful supplier of subsistence. Mikkelsen (1978) suggests that permanent base camps were set up between different ecological zones, from which small groups could be sent out to exploit other terrains. There is thus a pattern of permanent residence, though perhaps not for every nuclear family for every part of the year. The ensuing migration patterns may have been very diverse: some groups may have made long treks up rivers in summer for the hunting, others short-cycle local excursions for a particular seasonal resource. Some later work (Renouf 1984), however, admits of sedentary settlements near the coast, with task groups radiating out from there in search of particular resources.

Cumbria, England: Meals by the Esk

A series of coastal Mesolithic sites at Eskmeals in Cumbria lie near the contact between the coast and a mountainous interior. Bonsall et al. (1989) interpreted two seasonal possibilities, the first being seasonal movement between lowland and upland. But no sites that fill the role of summer camps have been found on the upland between the Duddon and the Esk, for example. They may not be there, or may simply not have been found. The second possibility is a year-round occupation of the coastal lowland, with localised shifts in resource emphasis, for example to salmon in summer, and local game in winter, together with waterfowl. These could be supplemented with plants, eggs and shellfish as available.

The latter model is considered the more probable, though Bonsall et al. comment that it may not mean permanent settlement; there might be some RM around the shoreline of an estuary. However, since the physical evolution of the coastline was dynamic during mesolithic time, the opportunities presented to occupying groups will also have changed, especially those relating to estuarine resources. This coast was occupied into Neolithic times, and elm declines are a feature of the pollen analyses from the Fl II/III boundary near the shore: Bonsall et al. (1989) think that incipient cattle foddering can be inferred.

3. CHAPTER SUMMARY

The material on both ecology and lifeways which can be brought to bear on the scattered data for the Mesolithic is very diverse. But if a brief distillation of it is made for present purposes, then it ought to include a number of findings. Most of these have been culled from the primary literature, but an excellent recent summary can be found in Peterken (1996).

1. The overall proportion of disturbed area is within the range 0.5–2.0 per cent at any one time, with the modal average value at 1 per cent. Most disturbances are small (i.e. one-tree size), but there are always a few larger examples. The size of disturbed areas varies from 31 m² for the single tree to 0.8 ha for a fire. A median size might be 280–375 m². The return period is very variable, within the range of 50–2000 years, with considerable local variation.

2. Animals can affect the herb vegetation of the disturbed area as well as the course and mixture of regenerating tree species. Humans interested in such disturbed areas would have to contend with the remains of any wind-thrown trees. It seems unlikely that the trunks of the larger specimens would be shifted by any means.

3. Burning open areas will affect the vigour with which some species grow: some negatively, others positively. Root-kill of tree species is rare. The vigour of grasses and some herbs is increased. Lightning-caused fire in forests with a high conifer component is most probable in old stands, though once a fire is under way it will burn vegetation of any age. In a transect of a valley, fire is most likely on the open watershed away from the declivity itself.

4. Attempts to draw out generalisations from the examples of cultural ecology in Europe and North America are open to the

accusation that the list is short and selective. But perhaps it is not too much of a travesty to suggest that in both coastal and inland environments there may be diversity of resource use and scheduling: cultural factors may determine the eventual pattern.

5. Accounts like these tend to be 'freeze-frames' and to under state modifications in the patterns of environment–society relations, whether these are exogenic (e.g. changes in climate or sea-level) or endogenic, as with population growth.

6. Coasts exert a very strong pull force in terms of available resources, to the point where no society would ignore them unless prevented by other human groups from gaining access to them.

7. Movement may vary from being non-existent to yearly distances of 400 km. A largely sedentary main group may bud off task groups, or the company may move *en masse*. Although movement has cultural determinants as well as resource-seeking aims, it must be assumed that Zipf's principle of least effort is not seriously contravened.

8. Certainly by the onset of the later Mesolithic, no human group would have licence to settle and seek resources anywhere it wished: territoriality of some form would have laid restrictions on the use of the land. Strict bounded territories with periphery markers, however, are not necessary to this state of territorial evolution.

With these conditions in mind, and gathering all the evidence presented so far in this book, it is time to attempt the modelling of society–environment relations in the later Mesolithic of the uplands of England and Wales.

CHAPTER FIVE

Models of Society–Environment Relations

A few statements in the previous chapter have given a hint that 'modelling' is not a single process, but that there are different types of models. They all, however, share the aim of simplifying the multivariate realities so that only the variables judged to be essential to the problem are manipulated in the search for a solution. One main class in this context is the theoretical-deductive model which would proceed from initial assumptions about, for example, biological productivity and human population density. Eventually, though, these inputs are derived from analogies or direct observations of one sort or another; they are not the same as the physicists' initial deductive models of black holes, for example. The other main group is the analogue model, derived from the kind of data relayed above. This entails difficulties in selecting appropriate variables, in plotting the interactions among diachronic variables and in avoiding circular arguments between assumptions and results (Dincauze 1981).

The different types of model used in archaeology have been categorised by Bettinger (1991), who classifies the main ones thus:

- Middle-range theory and models; these are concerned with the assignment of meaning to empirical observations about the archaeological record, with an emphasis on the processes of how once-living cultures come to form an archaeological (and for that matter palaeoecological) record.
- Optimal foraging models, which are based on human decisions to maximise the net rate of energy gain. This involves choices about diet, location of search for food, time spent on foraging, numbers of people assigned to foraging, and location of settlement.
- Marxist theories, which place total emphasis on social relations when trying to frame explanations of the past.

The social relations of production are thus the dominant element in the system, to the virtual exclusion of any other elements, those of nature included. Indeed, Marxist explanations have often denigrated environmental variables, which in the case of hunter-gatherers seems unrealistic.

- Neo-Darwinian models, which stress features like the fitness of adaptation of a culture: how it changes and thus how human–environment relations stand in terms of change and equilibrium. In the long run, adaptations must have genetic significance; models of cultural transmission which echo Darwinism's biological embodiments are also being considered.
- Post-processual models, which are concerned with explanations in terms of power, ideology and symbol, and with exposing positivist science (as wielded in some of the above models) as an agent of capitalist hegemony.

All the material so far covered has fallen into one of the first two categories: either as discussions of how various patterns of data may be interpreted in terms of socio-economic and ecological processes (or their interactions) or in terms of how groups of humans constructed a series of pathways in nature that led to continued survival. In this chapter and the next, a similar materialist approach will be taken: in essence, the attempt will be made to set out the functional relationships between inferred societies and their reconstructed environment with, it must be said, rather more being known about the latter than the former. In upland EW, conditions which have preserved the pollen, charcoal and macrofossils from the Holocene have been largely inimical to the survival of organic materials in cultural contexts. A limited number of broader meanings which may flow from these models form the core of Chapter 6, which ends this book.

1. ASSUMPTIONS

In attempting to model the upland Mesolithic, it is necessary to make clear the assumptions that can be drawn from the corpus of work summarised to this point. It has become apparent that certain 'facts' are better documented than others, and so two classes of assumption (more may be possible, but are unwieldy) are now designated.

Foundations

Subsequent discussion and constructions will assume the validity of the following statements:

- That in Flandrian II there existed a forest-scrub-heath/ bog zonation in the uplands, with only a few places totally covered in closed forest at that time.
- The biota of the environments occupied by Mesolithic people provided a set of resource-availability schedules which would have been a strong influence upon settlement and population movements, though not in the end totally determinative.
- That late winter is likely to be the critical time for the survival of human groups.
- That the overall population density inland was between 0.1 and 1.0 persons/km²; coasts could be more densely populated by a factor of three.
- That there were two basic types of settlement inland: 'base' camps, the moving of which would constitute residential mobility; and 'extraction camps', which constitute logistic mobility.
- That any patterns inferred from these and other assumptions need not have been static throughout the later Mesolithic.

LESS FIRM FOUNDATIONS

This set of assumptions is less securely based than those above, but nevertheless cannot be ignored.

- Lithics are directly related to the hunter-gatherer economy.
- 'Camps' as identified archaeologically represent the above mobility categories, at any rate inland. It is probable that logistically mobile groups would have an impact at two sites in the uplands: the actual 'camp' and the place to which animals were attracted were unlikely to have been the same.
- It is possible to envisage a territorial arrangement in which coastal bands were separate from those inland, just as it is possible to think of them as one and the same.
- Either or all of residentially mobile groups, sedentary groups or logistically mobile units may have manipulated their natural environments to increase the quantity

of food per unit area, that is, to have intensified food collection.

- This becomes more likely if population growth rates increase, but is not inevitable, since subsistence can sometimes be extended into new niches or new territories, giving more extensive food collection.
- Territory size for an exogamous population depends primarily on shape and density. To contain 500 people, a circular area needs to be:

0.01 persons/km²	50,000 km²	d = 250 km
0.1 persons/km²	5,000 km²	d = 80 km
1.0 persons/km²	500 km²	d = 25 km
10.0 persons/km²	50 km²	d = 8.0 km

However, it is likely that inland territories will be arrayed around river basins as the basic territorial/geomorphological unit.

- Hunter-gatherer groups normally exist below the maximum biological carrying capacity of their territories.

2. CONSTRUCTED MODELS

What follows is an attempt to construct a number of integrated settlement-subsistence models for the later Mesolithic in the uplands, recognising both that these people may not have occupied high ground all year, and that the coast would have been a very attractive environment and is not far from most upland areas. Thus access to the coast, or the absence thereof, can be taken as an early sorting criterion.

The input materials are summarised in Figures 5.1–2. Table 5.1 acts as a ground base to all the models since it suggests a seasonal schedule of food resources which is applicable to them all. It is derived from sources cited in the text. These are however the immediate sources of food and do not take into account any stored edible materials. Howsoever the yearly pattern of settlement movement (or lack of it) may be arranged, these are the likely dispositions of the main food sources. Important though non-material cognitions are always likely to be, it is assumed here that no culture is going to by pass entirely a good source of food only for such reasons: rational explanations of most food avoidances (like beef and pork) exist alongside the well-known religious grounds. The band sizes encompass the range put forward by various authors and evaluated by Constandse-Westermann and Newell (1989); in the end, these latter authors

TABLE 5.1 Resource scheduling in uplands and at coast.

Season	Inland	Coastal
Spring (♣)	roe, pig, plants, eggs	eggs, nestlings, fish
Summer (☼)	red deer, plants, fish, aurochs	red deer, freshwater fish, plants
Autumn (♠)	roe, pigs, fish, plants, aurochs	fish, plants
Winter (♦)	roe, pigs, red deer	seals, shellfish

These are the *fresh* sources, not the stored foods.

are sure that band sizes have been under estimated and that the basic social band averages 300 persons with an estimated density of 0.1/km² (cf Table 5.2). The number of 500 people for a mating network derives from a computer simulation by Wobst (1974).

No Access to the Coast

In this category, it is assumed that the hunter-gatherer group is confined to inland areas with no access to exclusively salt-water resources, though the group territory may contain land below 300 m as well as the higher ground. Two levels of occupation are considered, those of an overall density of 0.1/km² and of 1.0/km². The first model to be described will contain some details which are not repeated in later examples; it is emphasised in Table 5.3.

TABLE 5.2 Models for a band of 300.

	0.01 per km²	0.1 per km²	1.0 per km²
Band size = 300	Territory of ca 30,000 sq-km seems very large indeed and perhaps not practicable	Territory block of ca 60 + 60 km covers > one river valley and probably coast as well; an RM pattern with possible LM elements at stages is likely; yearly journey of 150 km possible	Very dense occupation of the land: would likely leave a higher density of archaeological remains of larger size

TABLE 5.3 Model types: inland.

		0.01 per km²	0.1 per km²	1.0 per km²
band size = 25		Territory is 83 x 30 km: the whole of two basins. RM most likely so as to avoid long absences of LM groups		
	RM sub-type		Territory 25 x 4 km; B at riverside but moves to hills in summer; sequential occupance of E1–E4	Territory 6 x 4 km; B at riverside, with E1–E4 very close; and to attract deer very strong
	LM sub-type		Territory 25 x 4 km; B at river side all year; LM groups to hill setts 1–2 hours away in ☼; E1–E2 occ during period	Territory 6 x 4 km; B moves to uplands for ☼ and keeps moving so as not to overuse. Too small a territory for all to move on?
Band size = 100		133 x 75 km: the whole of five valleys. Could be very widely spaced, and RM very likely. For 500 people, perhaps four 'provinces' in all EW	Territory 125 x 8 km or 33 x 30 km across two valleys. If river from source to sea E then B moves three times to tributary mouths: seven days' travel end to end. E1–E4 accessed from upper B stops. (500 people would occupy five major river basins)	Territory 12 x 8 km possibly two x B on each side of river; E1–E3 on each side. Too many people all to go on walkabout.

MODELS 1 AND 2: BAND SIZE 25

Models 1 and 2 both have the same band size but are divided into two types, depending upon whether a density of population of $0.1/km^2$ or $1.0/km^2$ is postulated.

Model 1: population density of $0.1/km^2$ (Figure 5.1a, upper diagram)

Using a river basin as a topographic unit, this system need only occupy a territory 25×4 km, that is, on one side of the river only. If an 8 km watershed-to-watershed slice is taken (which seems more likely), then the streamside length need only be 12.5 km. The base camp is taken to be at a confluence of a tributary and main streams, on a terrace, and is occupied all year since there are sufficient food sources to maintain the extended family group. In summer to early autumn, small sub-groups of men and possibly boys move up to logistical camps near the spring-heads in order to hunt red deer. If the weather is dry enough while they are there, moving between logistical camps, burning is carried out on the floor of forest openings and at the upper edge of the hazel scrub. The upper camps are 1–2 hours away from the base settlement and so butchered animals are brought down for processing and storage. Since the upper camps are relatively close to the main settlement, sporadic visits for other purposes (e.g. gathering hazel nuts) are possible. Manipulation of vegetation around the base settlement is inevitable even if not deliberate, with ruderal and nitrophilous plants, for example, being established permanently.

Base settlement activities comprise food-processing and storage, tool-making and social activities. Logistical camp activities comprise deer-hunting (possibly also aurochs), burning of vegetation, butchering of kill, tool repair and social activities such as rites of passage for youths.

Model 2: population density $1.0/km^2$ (Figure 5.1a, lower diagram)

This is in the same territory as the above, with a home camp by the river. In this model, the whole band moves up to the hill camps in summer-to-autumn. Movement between these camps is then likely. This model does not appear to give any period of segregation between the men and the women and would seem to yield a restricted diet during the occupation of the logistic camps should there be any resources unavailable up the hill, such as fish, some birds and any plants restricted

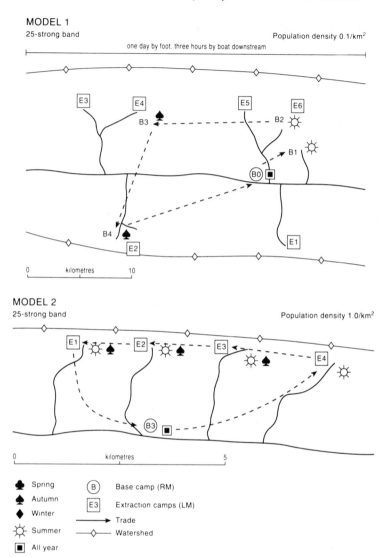

Figure 5.1a   Two models for a 25-strong band. The upper diagram envisages
a population density of 0.1/km² in a basically enclosed
territory on both sides of a river, so that 12.5 × 8 km is the
basic block. In this model, a base camp is occupied all year
and LM groups go out to the extraction camps, which are in
fact not far away. The lower diagram packs 25 people into a
small space and suggest that they would all move to the hill
camps and between each of them. It suggests that a density
of 1.0/km² in an enclosed territory is rather high in terms of
being close to the carrying capacity.

to lower altitudes. This model would represent a very dense packing.

MODEL 3: BAND SIZE 100 DENSITY 0.1/KM² (Figure 5.1b)

The territory is 125 × 8 km from interfluve to interfluve, or ca 33 × 30 km if two valleys are straddled. The former would approximately encompass a river from source to sea and so the base settlement would move perhaps three times during the year, from the upper reaches in summer towards the coast in winter, halting at the mouths of tributaries if there was no access to the coast. It would be about seven days' travel from end to end of the territory. Logistical camps would be accessed from the upper base camp in the same manner as above and processed meat for storage transported downstream by water. An exogamous marriage group would occupy perhaps five major river basins.

MODEL 4: DENSITY 1.0/KM² (Figure 5.1b)

This seems as if it would occupy too small a space to accommodate everybody on the move. The logistical equivalent would see the base settlement at the riverside with extraction camps relatively close above. But the need to move part or all of the base camp might be strong. Given the close packing, the need to *attract* deer and possibly other animals would be convincing. Providing a surplus for trade seems rather a challenge.

If it is accepted that the band sizes so far considered are too small, then a model with a density of 0.1/km² and band size (not illustrated) takes in that choice. The territory needed to enclose such a group is 3000 km², which comprises a circle of diameter 62 km, a square ~55 × 55 km. (Most oblongs based on river valleys are too long for the rivers in EW.) Such a large territory would almost certainly include some coast, and this would then be a good wintering ground, with journeys inland to places on rivers where large quantities of migratory fish could be caught with traps or at weirs and for the deer hunting, as well as any other game that could be encountered or attracted: wild pig and *Bos* are obvious examples. Within such a territory, LM strategies would require periods of absence of perhaps 2–3 weeks away from the base settlement, and so an RM stance seems the more likely, though LM camps could be added on to appropriate stages. A yearly journey of 150 km could easily be clocked up inside such a schedule. Long distances, though, might well reduce the

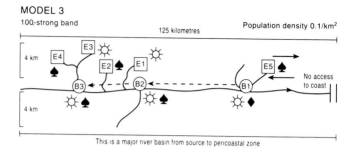

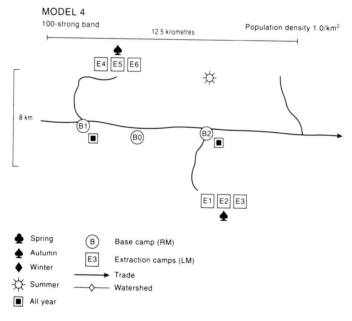

Figure 5.1b   Two models for a 100-strong band. The upper diagram (Model
             3) envisages a population density of 0.1/km² without access
             to the coast. But 125 km enclose a river basin from the source
             to the sea. Some movement of the base camp is envisaged
             during the year, using the river valley as an axis. The winter
             season would be spent at the lowest altitude. Trade with coastal
             groups is envisaged. In Model 4 (lower diagram), a territory
             of 12.5 × 8 km is needed. The main settlement is always by
             the river, and LM camps are occupied in the autumn; other
             hunting might take place sporadically at almost any time.
             The need to attract animals to the territory would likely be
             stronger than under Model 3 conditions.

TABLE 5.4 Populations of selected uplands at varying densities.

Persons/ km²	BM	DM	EX	SW	SP	CP	WT	NYM	Total
0.2	150	275	175	400	375	550	375	400	2,700
0.03	8	33	21	48	45	66	45	48	314
0.01	6	11	7	16	15	22	15	16	108

amount of stored food used since it would have to be carried between settlement stages or else left to await a return journey. (Large territories such as this are presumably the locales for 'encounter' hunting where the location of game cannot be accurately predicted, as it might have been in pre-forest times (Myers 1989). The manipulation of vegetation to attract deer can then be seen as reducing the human energy input into the process of hunting.) One coincidental feature of this size of territorial block is that it neatly encloses many of the upland blocks of EW, along with contingent coastlines in appropriate places. In this case, two such blocks would provide for the numbers quoted as necessary for exogamous populations (see Table 5.4). Populations at this density would also fulfil the assumption that most hunter-gatherer populations are at levels well below the calculated carrying capacity of the ecosystems off which they subsist. Table 5.5

TABLE 5.5 Possible sizes of detached hunting groups.

Size of party	Number of parties		
	60 hunters	120 hunters	180 hunters
5	12	24	36
10	6	12	18
20	3	6	9
30	2	4	6
40	1–2	3	4–5
50	1	2–3	3–4

Note: This table assumes a band of 300 individuals, which might supply 60–180 men and youths for detached hunting parties. The very large parties seem unrealistically large for stealth hunting, but for cooperative coercive methods such as net- or fence-driving or ring-driving (with or without fire) they are much more in line with near-recent accounts.

speculates about the sizes of detached hunting groups that might be found.

Access to the Coast

If the assumption can be made that the coast yielded organic resources more prolifically than other environments, then access to it introduces an attractive-seeming element into reconstructions of the life of a Mesolithic group. The obvious model is that of a coastal party who migrate inland in order to diversify their resource base or avoid a leaner season; or of an intermittently mobile group who include the shore in their yearly round. One other possibility must be mentioned: that of sedentary coastal groups who sequester the resources of the sea from other units inland, cutting them off from access to salt water; if the latter group are to obtain marine products (or e.g. flint from chalk cliffs), then they have to trade, fight or steal. It is of course possible that territories might be fluid in the sense of not being exclusively arrogated to one group for every extractable resource.

MODEL 5: BAND SIZE 25: 6 PERSONS/KM OF COAST (Figure 5.1c)

This also includes an inland area deemed to belong to the same territory, with an overall density of 0.1 persons/km². Assuming it to be centred on a river and its mouth, then the territory is 30 × 8 km but might be wider if the rivers are sparsely spaced along the coastline. Within the territory (see Table 5.6), there is a base settlement on the estuary, with logistical camps on the open coast to gain access to particular marine resources. LM camps inland would be on rivers or at lakes in order to access freshwater fish and deer. The base settlement would be occupied year-round, with excursions to open coast especially in winter and spring, and inland in late spring and in summer. Given a small number of people and a large terrain with the summer

TABLE 5.6 Model types: coastal.

	Six persons/km of coast
Band size=25	At 0.1/km² inland, then territory is 8 x 30 km. B at estuary, E1, E2 on open coasts, E3 inland for deer or freshwater fish in ♣ ☼
Band size = 100	Most resource use at coasts; plenty of space inland for deer, freshwater fish to 20 km inland. Estuary density limiting?

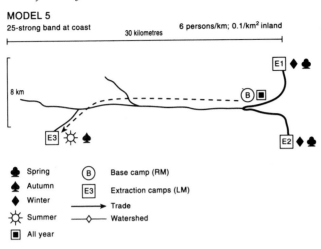

MODEL 5

25-strong band at coast

30 kilometres

6 persons/km; 0.1/km² inland

8 km

E1 ◆ ♣

B ■

E3 ☀ ♠

E2 ◆ ♠

♣ Spring	Ⓑ	Base camp (RM)
♠ Autumn	E3	Extraction camps (LM)
◆ Winter	——▶	Trade
☀ Summer	——◇——	Watershed
■ All year		

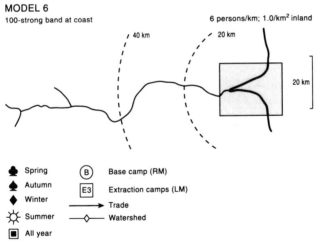

MODEL 6

100-strong band at coast

6 persons/km; 1.0/km² inland

40 km

20 km

20 km

♣ Spring	Ⓑ	Base camp (RM)
♠ Autumn	E3	Extraction camps (LM)
◆ Winter	——▶	Trade
☀ Summer	——◇——	Watershed
■ All year		

Figure 5.1c   Two models involving access to coastal resources as well as inland territory. The upper diagram (Model 5) detaches groups from a main settlement to other parts of the coast for seasonal resources as well as sending them inland. A low population density is postulated. The lower diagram (Model 6) suggests a base terrain at the coast for a 100-strong band with the suggested densities (see text) of 6 persons/km of coast, plus an inland density of 0.1/km². The packing along the coast would probably reflect the mixture of high- and low-energy coastline types.

territories of red deer probably much larger than in winter, the advantages of attracting this species to a particular place are apparent.

MODEL 6: BAND SIZE 100: 6 PERSONS / KM OF COAST (Figure 5.1c)

The key zone in this model is the productive coastline and the packing thereof: it suggests that the number and spacing of estuaries will be critical in determining population numbers, especially on high-energy coasts. If islands are not very significant, then a resource-space model derived from the coastal Ertbølle might collapse to ca 65 per cent coasts and inland 30 per cent, up to 20 km. This latter would again bring deer and freshwater fish within reach. There would be plenty of manpower for inland hunting in such an arrangement. If inland density went up to $1/km^2$, for example, then the territory would need to be extended up the river basin only a short distance; at $0.01/km^2$, the territory needed would cover more than one river basin. If these were distanced say 40 km apart, then the inland penetration would be 250 km: at least the whole length of a river system. It seems more likely that such a group would occupy perhaps 80 km of coastline with 125 km of hinterland depth.

MODEL 7: SEPARATE INLAND AND COASTAL GROUPS
   (Figure 5.1d)

Lastly, there is the possibility that there were coastal groups of one of the above types occupying, for example, the coast and an inland zone of 20 km depth. Beyond that was to be found a totally landlocked group existing at one of the probable population densities. There might then be two base settlements along the length of a river: one on the estuary and another perhaps 50 km upstream at a confluence (cf 2. model 1). The coastal group would have its own inland LM camps, and the upper-reaches group would function as in model 1 or its variants. Indeed, there might be more than one inland group along a river. Social agreements about territorial allocation at boundaries might also be the means for passing resources upstream (e.g. coastal lithic material) and downstream, when dried *Bos* or deer meat is a possible commodity.

3. GENERAL INFERENCES

A concise statement needs to be made of which of the above models look the most likely in the light of the empirical evidence;

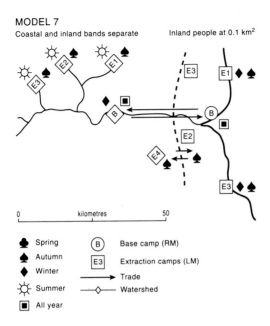

MODEL 7
Coastal and inland bands separate   Inland people at 0.1 km²

0   kilometres   50

♣   Spring   ⒷB   Base camp (RM)

♠   Autumn   ▣E3   Extraction camps (LM)

♦   Winter   ⟶   Trade

☼   Summer   ⟶◇⟶   Watershed

▣   All year

Figure 5.1d   A possible territorial arrangement for two groups,
only one of which occupied the coastal zone. In this
case, the base camps (B) belong one to each separate
group. An active trade relationship is suggested,
with interchange of materials at different places
along the 'border'. If territorial markers are needed,
then possibly fire along such zones would be one
of the means employed.

and, using all the available empirical and analogue evidence, of
the likely pattern of human–environment relations in the later
Mesolithic.

The Most Likely Model

Although many types of evidence can be used to throw light
on the likely Mesolithic situation, in the end any model has
to be consistent with the empirical evidence from upland EW.
It might be argued, though, that this evidence is radically
underdeterminative in the sense that it could, without much
distortion, be made to fit any of the above models (or indeed
several others) since it is so exiguous. Since one use of a model is to
allow the generation of hypotheses, then one will be chosen here
and used as a 'standard' in the hope that future work will either

confirm its status or undermine it and replace it with a closer set of arguments.

Which criteria cannot be ignored in the fitting of empirical evidence to models, in this instance? The following are suggested:

- The population density found overall, in both uplands and surrounding areas; there are no obvious reasons, of course, why this had to be uniform over the whole of EW. The empirical evidence is not very solid even where there are a great number of Mesolithic sites, since there is no indication of their synchronicity or lack of it.
- Whether or not bands of people have access to coasts. This immediately raises the possibility of regional differences in economy, since in the South-west, for example, all but the smallest territories might have had a coastal sector, while the inland nature of the SP would make it less likely. In his models for the early Mesolithic based on the Star Carr material, J. G. D. Clark (1972) found no difficulty in considering a movement from the Yorkshire coast to the uplands of the Pennines, a round trip of over 200 km. Firmer evidence comes from the Star Carr dogs, where isotope evidence suggests that they had fed largely on marine food and thus died on a trip inland (Clutton-Brock and Noe-Nygaard 1990). A model based on movement from the coast to the Upper Wear in Co. Durham is posited by R. Young (1987).

The empirical evidence does not allow the fitting of precise numbers to these questions, and the extension of data from elsewhere seems essential if any progress is to be made. The spatially nearest evidence to be tested against the archaeological evidence (even though there is a large analogue input from North American aboriginal data) is from continental Europe (Constandse-Westermann and Newell 1989). This involves a territory which as a block would be 60×60 km at a density of $0.1/km^2$ and could be traversed in 2–3 days. A human group would thus have the choice of either RM or LM patterns of mobility; access to a stretch of coastline might make the difference between a largely sedentary pattern and one in which intermittent movement of the entire group was essential to maintain food supplies. Given that many groups in the recent past have moved for non-material reasons, there is a credible case for suggesting that exodus from a pericoastal base camp might happen in late spring and summer, lasting, for some at least, until the autumn plant harvest and fire season in the uplands.

Environmental Relations of the Annual Cycle

The main aim of this book is to examine the plausibility of continued environmental impact by LM groups in the uplands, and so not all of a yearly subsistence round is necessarily relevant to it. It may be profitable to divide the environmental relations into two kinds:

- *usufruct relations* in which the human population crops the natural resources for year after year in accordance with socially-determined patterns which in turn do not produce any diminution in the quantity or quality of those resources which requires an adjustment of practice that shows up in the record. Environmental impact will be largely inadvertent.
- *managed relations* in which the human population attempts to maintain or enhance the flow of natural resources in the face of socially mediated perceptions of sub-optimality, such as a normally low density of prey species or a down-cycle in numbers, inimical environmental changes such as the growth of closed-canopy woodlands with little edge habitat, or climatic changes with spin-off effects into ecosystems.

The range of resources put forward by Jochim, Tilley and others (see Chapter 4 above) can be re-arrayed in this light (see Table 5.7). This suggests that most resources are taken in an unmanaged form: some more or less literally as the result of opportunist encounters, other as the result of a planned expedition, as to a shellfish bed or a nesting cliff. Thus any environmental impact is likely to have been unplanned to the point of inadvertence, and only the exhaustion of a resource would have invoked any feedback. This could have happened if for example the less common *Bos* was hunted to extinction regionally. The New England native Americans apparently moved their villages for want of firewood as often as from any other cause, and indeed thought that the Europeans had come because their own firewood was exhausted – not perhaps a transferable example to the later Mesolithic, but an instructive case.

The managed resources might have two sub-categories: those where it was possible to avoid over-culling the animals, and those

Table 5.7 Types of resource relationships in the Later Mesolithic.

Resource	Main season	Usufruct	Management
Aurochs	☼ ♠	Mostly in groups of 4–6; management not feasible	Managed via vegetable: attract deer by enhancing either grasses or browse (latter especially winter food)
Red deer	☼ ♠	Chance encounters not ignored	Edge is critical to numbers: 7 spin-off of other management processes
Roe deer	♣	10–20 per km² solitary	
Wild pig	♣ ♠ ♦	Variable density, marshes good	
Shellfish	♣ ♠ ♦	Sheltered water has highest density	
Salt-water fish	♣ ♠	Taken as and when possible	
Fresh-water fish	☼ ♠	Ease depends on water conditions	Signs of over-use could be spotted
Migratory fish	☼ ♠	Heavily seasonal and then usually super-abundant	
Beaver	♦	Fat and pelt main attractions	
Birds	♠ ♦	Eggs the easiest to obtain; also wild-fowl in flocks	Over-use could be seen; Easy to learn to leave a few eggs
Small game	♠ ♦	Encounter game; valuable furs > food	
Plants	♣ ☼	As snack food	Value of edge for many food plants as well as of open ground, e.g. for bracken rhizomes

Spring ♣
Summer ☼
Autumn ♠
Winter ♦

where some form of indirect management of the game beasts' food supplies might enhance their numbers or make them easier to hunt. (The latter is also the more likely to be visible in the empirical evidence from upland EW, and the danger of adopting it as a ruling hypothesis is thus always strong.) The maintenance or provision of edge and of the right kind of ground vegetation in openings in the mesic and streamside woodlands would be paramount aims of any such management. Here, then, is the nexus of palaeoecological, archaeological and empirical evidence in the manipulation of vegetation to improve the energy ratios of hunters using a logistical movement model of extraction. It all conforms to the idea of Mesolithic cultures as 'energy-maximising', though it throws no further light on Mithen's (1987) extension of that construct, namely that in hunting groups able to produce an energy surplus, hunting might be competitive between males, with prestige being gained from killing large animals.

This is not a new finding: it has been regularly put forward in the literature for the last twenty years. What is different here is the volume and concatenation of the evidence, the degree of precision of documentation of the processes employed and the shading which can now be given to rather general statements about human–nature relationships. The prevalent model can now be elaborated in the following ways:

- The management of clearings and forest edge was not directed solely at *Corylus* and its production of browse and nuts. In so far as a zone of hazel scrub often succeeded the mixed oak forest upslope, there was good supply of this on most uplands.
- The work at North Gill suggests that streamside woodlands with alder were manipulated in order to improve their magnetism to mammals during the herb-grass production season. A less dense canopy together with openings would lengthen this season, for example.
- Deer were encouraged to visit certain places within the oak forest by the provision of leaf-fodder, which resulted in some canopy-lightening.
- The production of edge and openings away from natural margins was carried out by ring-barking rather than fire. This process was aided by the barking propensities of concentrations of red deer, especially in severe winters.
- Fire was important for the maintenance and production of edge at the upper edge of forests advancing upslope

in response to periods of favourable climatic change; at
the hazel scrub–heath interface, where it often resulted
in a mor humus that was the precursor of paludification;
and near water bodies such as lakes and streams, to
keep open a grassy meadow in conjunction with grazing
wild animals. Where and when dry enough, alder woods
and their edges were subject to fire in order to enhance
their grass-herb flora (attractive to *Bos*) and their browse
content to interest red deer.

- Natural openings in the mesic forest canopy were maintained by suppressing regeneration with fire: an aim of
this practice was to encourage grass-herb ground vegetation as summer food for red deer; edge effect will increase
the amount of browse which is an important food for deer.
The grasses may encourage *Bos* as well.

- This burning took place in the period of the autumn when
conditions might be dry enough for a controlled ground
fire. This might not be every year. The incidence of fire
might have interacted with gathering bracken rhizomes
as a food, but this seems less likely at an LM camp (unless
other resources were scarce) than near a base settlement.
Visiting such areas for hunting might however have been
a longer season: if *Bos* was being hunted, then it might
have coincided with the ground flora production season
in the streamside woodlands; deer were also likely visitors since this is the season when they are most likely to
feed off herbaceous material. At North Gill, this type of
woodland disappeared in the sixth millennium BP, being
replaced by encroaching blanket bog.

- Although the same general locality formed the LM camps
year after year, the same exact site was not used. Multiple
spreads of charcoal and flints are probably evidence of
repeated visits. Burned areas are not necessarily the same
spots used for sleeping, tool repair and food-processing,
which seems logical: indeed, some separation of the two
would be needed to avoid scaring deer. (The filled-in pits
at Brenig (Lynch 1993) might be attempts to reduce the
traces of human presence.) The apparent lack of worked
stone immediately adjacent to the disturbed areas at
North Gill and Soyland Moor confirms this likelihood,
and the same pattern can be inferred for other localities.
Indeed, the pairs of sites noted by Stonehouse (1992) for
the early Mesolithic and the concentrations of tool types

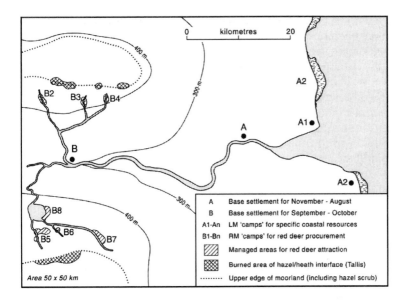

Figure 5.2   A suggestion for a 'most likely' model which assumes
that the coast was indeed part of the resource and
was used within the yearly cycle. However, it allows
that the group would like to move *in toto* during the
year, and hence there is a secondary base camp inland
from which the upland managed areas are visited,
both for hunting and for vegetation management.

which he maps (1990) for the later period have a certain
resonance here, though not one susceptible to an obvious
set of explanations.

4. A MODEL

Figure 5.2 shows a hypothetical settlement-resource schedule for
the later Mesolithic. Settlement A is assumed to be the main
locality for the group, occupied for most of the year but with
an RM scene change for the summer-to-autumn period up the
river, where fishing would be fruitful. From this camp, LM
groups would procure deer (and probably *Bos*) and engage in
management activities to improve upon the energy relations of
pure encounter hunting. Once these activities were complete, then
movement back to the coast for the winter and spring leaner times
was an obvious adaptation. LM groups would leave the main
settlement for specific resources, such as sea-bird eggs in spring,
but a sheltered location for the main settlement is most likely.

Hence it was easily submerged by any sea-level rises. There would have been hunting in the catchment area of the more permanent settlement, and more evidence is needed to determine what, if any, the impact of this might have been. It would be useful to know whether there was manipulation in this zone, or whether it was not needed, not possible or not detected. The same is to some extent true of the coastal zone itself. Given the apparent popularity of such environments, the question arises as to whether the human communities exerted any environmental impact. Animal populations can only be the subject of modelling and speculation, since the archaeozoological evidence which would make possible the more exact calculation of the human impact on the wild populations does not exist. Most workers imply however that it seems unlikely that Mesolithic groups could have affected in any long-term way the populations of fish, sea-birds or marine mammals. Molluscs attract more speculation because of the huge quantities of refuse found in shell-middens; but here again, compared with the size of shell-fish beds, even local extirpation seems unlikely.

Impact upon plant resources is even more difficult to determine. Pollen and macrofossil analysis, for example, usually detect mesolithic influence from patterns which signify openings in closed-canopy vegetation. R. L. Jones (1988) collects details of some sites where this has happened: at Lytham (Lancs), charcoal dated to 8390±105 BP came from a Fl I pollen spectrum in which declines in tree-pollen frequencies were accompanied by increases in hazel, heather, grasses and *Plantago lanceolata*. At Westward Ho! (North Devon), a mesolithic kitchen midden at sea level (6585±130 BP) was sealed by a peat of Fl II age with reduced *Quercus* levels and *Plantago lanceolata* (Balaam et al. 1987). Intertidal peat of later Mesolithic–early Neolithic age (~5000 BP) in Hartlepool Bay, Cleveland, also yielded a pollen spectrum that indicated the recession of the coastal forest and the expansion of open habitats. In a wider framework, Tooley (1978) suggests that the dunes of south-west Lancashire became unstable towards the end of Fl II as a direct result of clearance and deforestation, that is, at about the same time as the Hartlepool Bay episode. Certainly, Cowell and Innes (1994) point out, in their work from the wetlands of Merseyside, that in twelve pollen diagrams, the only disturbance from before the fifth millennium cal. BC comes from coastal areas. The indications are that mesolithic populations might have been active in changing some of the woody vegetation at the coasts, as no doubt elsewhere. On the fen edge of Cambridgeshire, A. G. Smith et al. (1989) talk of a change from dense forest to a local environment in which there was pronounced human impact for 700–1500 years before forest was re-established. A 'black band' of Mesolithic age forms the stratigraphic context (8500–6500 BP) for this interference with the woodlands.

One feature of this model is that it puts the uplands into a wider perspective and with them the practices of environmental manipulation. That is, much of the subsistence of Mesolithic groups was on a usufruct basis and only in particular localities was any positive management attempted. This could even have been done because it was possible rather than necessary (which might be labelled the Concorde syndrome) but more likely because of the desirability of the produce: plausible reasons might be for variety, for storage or for trade. No one of these need be exclusive. It is a perspective on the disequilibrium of the upland ecosystems that so little human impact might, over a long period admittedly, bring about such large-scale changes in woodland type and in the development of mires.

Two variants need to be considered: a purely inland version; and an intensified form with a higher population density. The first assumes either that it was too far to go to a coast or that the coast was already occupied by firmly-established groups. Thus the coastal contribution to nutrition is either removed or has to be acquired by trade. In either case, the manipulation of the forests and their edges for animal produce has to be intensified; this might well lead to attempts to modify forests in lowland areas as well as the uplands. The second would produce greater impact on all resources and in the uplands would be indistinguishable from the first. Either might bring about the greater intensity of disturbance which is seen shortly before ~5000 BP in some but not all localities. The second set of circumstances might in fact bring about the first.

It should be stressed that the available evidence under-determines these constructions: it is possible to suggest other models using the same inputs. What is put forward here seems the most likely in the light of all the available material of all kinds. New evidence may quite readily alter the patterns that can be reconstructed.

5. INTO THE NEOLITHIC

Before the appearance of the full panoply of Neolithic monuments and settlements (not that plentiful in the upland areas), there is often a period of intensified environmental impact, sometimes accompanied by cereal pollen and usually preceding an decline in *Ulmus* pollen. (The elm declines are not usually synchronous when several are measured over a small area.) A number of explanations are possible:

- Population growth is necessitating an intensified impact upon the vegetation, for example via more densely-occupied and packed territories;
- A new economy has become widespread but only part of its ecosystemic relations is visible in the palaeoecological evidence: cereal growing is one possibility, herding and feeding of domesticated animals (most likely cattle) is another; there is no apparent evidence for specialised husbandry (Layton et al. 1991);
- Though a hunting-gathering economy persists, there are some new social practices which result in an increased environmental impact; a transition from a band level of organisation to a tribal level is a possibility, resulting in a more efficient exploitation pattern and hence greater visibility.
- The original economy collapses without much warning for ecological or social reasons, with a rush to adopt new ways in order to survive and perhaps to propitiate whoever caused the collapse. Parallels might be sought with the decline of the lean-time molluscan foods of the Danish Ertbølle postulated by Blankholm (1987).

Whatever the causes, the last hunter-gatherers bequeathed to the early farmers a landscape which they would find familiar. It was a mosaic in which there were still patches of largely unmanaged forest subject primarily to natural processes of decay and renewal in which windthrow continued to open up small gaps in the canopy and in which lightning was not a significant cause of the spread of fire. Most stretches of open water in the uplands would have possessed openings, due either to management in a forest-utilisation-style model (Göransson 1986; Edwards 1993) or to the presence of beavers. Openings and depleted canopy would have marked many other areas of forest as well, and upslope the woodland gave way to a zone of hazel scrub. In and above this zone and in a limited number of places below it, patches of bog were forming: some under rushy vegetation, some under sedges, some under heather and under mosses, especially *Sphagnum*.

Agriculture might have come by trade along the networks

used to convey stone for tools (and possibly dried meat in the other direction) or might have come with an immigrant cultural-ethnic group. If the latter (an explanation not currently the most favoured), then the environment of upland EW would not have presented enormous differences from those areas of continental Europe where the new ways were well established. A major difference would, presumably, have been the temperature lapse rate; but since cereal cultivation seems to have been well established in the Bronze Age when the climate was probably worse, then its success is not surprising agronomically. The sporadic nature of the cereal finds (even given the problems surrounding the pollination and dispersal habits of the pollen of the domesticated Gramineae) suggests that for some time in the uplands the domesticated cereals of Western Asian origin (i.e. discounting for the present the possibility that native Poaceae were domesticated) were not staples. There is no indication as to their role: they might have been interesting exotica allowed in the corner of an opening once the real purpose of it had been fulfilled (but if the attraction of deer were primary function and deer liked wheat, then there might be a problem unless the deer only came after a cereal harvest); equally, they might have been crisis foods, or special-occasion foods. Or again, they might have been the concomitants of a social change rather than a piece of economic forcing. In terms of the three-stage model of Zvelebil and Rowley-Conwy (1984), the period from just before an elm decline to the establishment of a full cereal-and-plantain curve presumably includes the *availability* and at least part of the *substitution* phase. If by this horizon wild foods were no longer significant for survivals then the rest of the substitution phase has been accomplished and perhaps even some *consolidation*. The general conclusion reached by Simmons and Innes (1987), that the introduction of farming need not have been a traumatic change, seems still to hold. It might even be extended by the speculation that a culture used to attracting deer by providing grass and leaf fodder would have taken well to cattle-rearing. In essence, continuity was for some time a feature as in Eastern and Northern Europe (Zvelebil and Dolukhanov 1991). At any rate, presumably nobody was forced into agriculture by a decline in the availability of oysters as a concomitant of decreased marine salinity, as Rowley-Conwy (1984) suggested for the Danish Ertbølle.

As for the relation of the Neolithic and the elm decline, the dates for the *Ulmus* decline at North Gill, for instance, vary from 3490 ± 45 BP and 3645 ± 45 BP at profiles 6 and 8 respectively, to 5595/5690

± 45 BP at profile 9. There is no reason to doubt the validity of any of these dates, and so it is difficult to avoid the straightforward, although initially unexpected, conclusion that the decline was not synchronous over the short distances between the sites. A direct climatic cause seems unlikely because it is difficult to envisage a repeated change in a temperature and/or precipitation regime which affected only a limited number of trees each time. Disease would explain why trees died at different times, if it is accepted that Dutch elm disease was endemic and that some trees died and some survived each time there was an outbreak (cf. Peglar's (1993) and Peglar and Birks' (1993) findings at Diss Mere in lowland England). However, the incidence of disease would not explain why the elms that had died did not recover within a few decades or centuries as they have been shown to have done in more recent times, allowing the pollen frequency to return to its pre-decline values. The maintained low frequencies are better explained by assuming that every time an area of woodland was burned during a disturbance, the soil became progressively less favourable for the regeneration of elm. Burning would have modified the physical structure of the soil and thus rendered it more susceptible to erosion. Any increased grazing and browsing of the enhanced ground flora and young tree shoots would have depleted it of nutrients. In the early stages of this process, when disease attacked and killed a tree, the chances of another elm replacing it either by growing from the original rootstock or by germination from seed would have been almost as good as they had been, and so after a few decades elm-pollen production would have returned to its earlier levels leaving no trace of a decline in the record at the temporal resolution of these 1-cm-interval diagrams. But with further soil deterioration, diseased trees, once killed, would have been less easily replaced by other elms and therefore less *Ulmus* pollen produced at that spot from then on. In addition, pollarding has been shown to increase the susceptibility of elms to disease (Moe and Rackham 1992), and so any use of the branches for fodder for wild or domestic beasts would very possibly have made the trees more prone to the infection.

Such an explanation would also account for the variations in the dates. Most pollen diagrams come from deposits with large pollen catchments, and these average out fine spatial variations in elm-pollen production; any date obtained therefore represents the time at which the greatest number of elms within the region had failed to regenerate. North Gill is unusual both in having so many pollen diagrams and in each of them having such a small pollen catchment.

Though the elm decline is not of primary interest here, the incidence of disease as a product of human-led causes such as lopping and perhaps pollarding (Moe and Rackham 1992) for fodder in the Neolithic is now widely accepted (Rasmussen 1990b, 1993, following the earlier suggestion by Heybroek 1963). In Denmark, Andersen and Rasmussen (1993) found elm declines which were not always associated with evidence of early agriculture, and the implications of their careful dating and pollen analysis are that whatever caused the first elm declines was not necessarily confined to the classical Neolithic cereals-plus-domesticated-animals syndrome. It looks as if some pre-Neolithic activity has contributed to or even created conditions which under the new economy inevitably led to falls in elm-pollen production.

6. CHAPTER SUMMARY

A search of the ecological and ethnographic literatures reveals certain generalities which most likely underlie any subsistence models which are constructed.

1. These concern elements such as vegetation pattern, the seasonal and spatial patterns of food resources, population density, mobility and access to coastlines. Culture is strongly influenced by these factors but not determined by them.

2. A number of models can be made, using different combinations of terrain and population size, but a most-likely story can be selected as a better fit than the others, to the direct palaeoecological and archaeological evidence, and to analogous circumstances in time and space.

3. It postulates a largely sedentary group which spends much of the year near the coastline (near enough for sea-level change to have swallowed some of the evidence) but which moves inland up the river valleys as a unit at the end of the summer. Once out of the terrain that can be hunted over on a daily basis from the main settlement, smaller sub-groups of hunters are spun off and some of these make for upland hunting-grounds for red deer. In order to increase the chances of success, areas in the woodlands and at the forest/scrub edge have been fired in order to encourage plants known to be favoured by the deer. For summer-to-autumn hunting, grasses are more important that browse plants.

4. Fire may also act as a territorial marker; in effect it appropriates

the land to a particular group. These areas are detected as the disturbance phases of the palaeoecological data. The camp, sites are not likely to be the same exact places as the sites whose vegetation is manipulated to attract the deer, so each 'visit' spawns at least two openings and two fires. Even repeated visits to the same small area might not use the same campsites. Hence, a small hunter-gatherer population can produce a relatively large detectable environmental impact, especially in ecotonal vegetation.

5. One challenge is to determine what happens in lowland areas. Did they have separate bands, or were they part of a seasonal cycle? Was it different if there was no access to the coast or to its resources?

CHAPTER SIX

A Wider Context

In this final chapter, an attempt will be made to put the knowledge and interpretations into the wider framework of both prehistory and our own times. To do this will require consideration not only of the information which has been compiled but also of the role of that information in today's social context.

1. THE MESOLITHIC AND THE LANDSCAPE

This section will discuss three matters: the comparative environmental impact of the later Mesolithic, looked at in the light of a further 5000 years of history; the case then to be made for that period as part of any attempts to formulate landscape archaeologies; and the signalling of the later Mesolithic as a very early stage in the land-use history of a part of Britain. In all cases, judgements and choices have to be made in the face of either inadequate evidence or conflicting attitudes: those put forward here are those of the present author at the time of writing.

Comparative Environmental Impact

After a detailed investigation of one period in history, there is always the danger that it fills the mind to the point of thinking it all-important. Here, it is essential to be reminded that the later Mesolithic was only one stage in the evolution of landscape, ecology and land use of the entire Holocene. Indeed, as a former of lasting elements in the landscape and ecology of the various regions of upland EW, it was almost certainly one of the less important: Table 6.1 attempts to summarise the main phases in landscape/land-use change and to categorise them in terms of relative environmental impact. Where the later Mesolithic was important in these terms was in providing the take-off conditions for areas of ombrogenous peat which became the foci for larger areas of blanket peat which are still there today, albeit in mostly degraded form.

If these values are accepted, then the Later Mesolithic, while not

TABLE 6.1 Relative historical changes in the uplands.

Period	Impact	Category
Early Mesolithic	Apparently transient, but hints of local severity on woodland, soils	1
Later Mesolithic	Widespread management of woodlands and their edges; consequent paludification	2
Agricultural prehistory	Loss of woodland, introduction and expansion of field systems temporary and permanent, domestic cattle etc.; expanded population's need for wood. Paludification	5
Roman	Demands for corn, road-building	3
Medieval	Permanent parcelling of landscape: common lands and grazing management systems emplaced; monasteries add to grazing, ironworking; also remove some settlements. Some evidence for continued paludification	6
Early modern	Steady state with cumulative effects of grazing and metal extraction; sheep progressively replace cattle	4
Nineteenth century	Industrialisation, especially of extractive processes; moor management for sport in east. Much vegetation acidified from rain-out	10
Twentieth century	Collapse of some industries; forestry and recreation gain in importance; sheep grazing progressively on economic knife-edge; expansion of bracken very rapid	7

Column 3 is a comparative scale from 0–10 where 0 = no detectable alteration at all and 10 = the heaviest impacts that can be envisaged.

insignificant, does not rank alongside some of the later periods in the intensity of environmental change wrought by human communities. This is probably no surprise to any reader but should not be taken as indicative of an entire lack of significance. There two reasons why the later Mesolithic might carry a weight greater than Table 6.1 might seem to assign to it 2.

First it was the time when a key element of the continuing landscape was fixed in place: that of human-created openness. To that date, open landscapes were probably the result of entirely natural processes except in vary small peri-settlement zones. The later Mesolithic saw the creation and maintenance of human-induced open areas at a landscape scale. But probably not everywhere in the uplands: Tipping (1992) argues that the short time-period of 4650–4200 cal. BP, when clearing and tilling took place, was the time of the 'first significant human impact on the Cheviots', though some Mesolithic evidence (8500–7000 BP) is adduced by Innes and Shennan (1991).

It was the first time when it can definitely be inferred that there existed purposive human behaviour towards environmental manipulation; the evidence for earlier periods is still too thin, though there is a good chance that the later Mesolithic cultures were continuations of earlier patterns rather than innovations: consider the data from WFF and Tarn Moss, or the evidence presented for different parts of Yorkshire by Jones (1976) and Bush (1988). Nevertheless, in terms of today's knowledge, this is a pivotal moment comparable with the discovery of the full potential of steam power, for example: the redirection of the energy-flow patterns of the Earth in terms of human-defined, i.e. cultural, desires.

Landscape Archaeology: Implications

The last thirty years have seen a desire to interpret archaeological monuments in their entire contexts, so that both the professional and the public may see them as enmeshed in ecological, economic and social webs; to some extent, visible remains are but symbols or markers of whole landscape systems. To stretch an image, they are like the tips of icebergs, the rest of which can be reconstructed by scholars using the full gamut of modern techniques but which may well not be actually visible in the view as seen. But it needs to be emphasised for the later Mesolithic that whatever the actual environmental impact of the people, the landscape was probably fully humanised in terms of being invested with meaning by its human inhabitants. As Nelson (1983) says in his study of the Koyukon hunters of interior Alaska, the flow of the land becomes also a flow of the mind.

THE LATER MESOLITHIC: IMMORTAL PERHAPS, BUT CERTAINLY INVISIBLE

In the acid environments of the uplands, not much is preserved for very long. Thus there is very little visible evidence which is available to casual inspection; both the non-specialist and the general public have to take more on trust than usual with archaeology. A TV programme about prehistoric deforestation, for example, can only show a few bits of flint, wood, charcoal and peat *in situ*, usually along with men in funny hats; all else has to be in the laboratory, usually along with women in white coats. Spreads of charcoal and flint waste at the interface of shallow soil profiles and eroding peat are not in the same landscape league as Salisbury Plain or the Dartmoor reaves. So the materials of the landscape have to be woven into a story which relies on the written or spoken word and accompanying graphics. The choice of terms, of analogies and parallels, and eventual judgements becomes even more important than with cultures where there is something tangible for the recipients of the information to use in forming their own opinions.

Perhaps no landscape archaeology can work without accompanying commentary; but, since there is virtually nothing to experience without a prior text, the nature of that text and the type of explanations and interpretations which it gives assume a high degree of importance. This meshes with the ideas of post-processual archaeology (see above) in which the experiencing person is not seen, as in the natural sciences, as being a detached and unfeeling observer of objects and processes which have been delimited by scholarly work. The telling of a story, then, is an important phase in the imparting of this attempt to 'illumine the past for its own sake and simultaneously, to enrich our appreciation, of our present condition' (Fowler 1991).

OTHER PERIODS IN THE UPLANDS

The archaeological evidence suggests that in a number of sites in the uplands, there is a continuity of lithic material: in unstratified contexts, Mesolithic implements are found along with Neolithic material and occasionally Bronze Age tools as well. This confirms that many remains of the Mesolithic period have been overlaid by later materials and that any landscape ecology can only be seen as part of a palimpsest in which it becomes progressively more difficult to see a landscape as 'mesolithic' (as distinct from e.g. 'Bronze Age') and thus to manage it, for instance, in order to display those webs of relationships which landscape archaeology aims to inculcate. The landscape can thus be envisaged as a text whose meaning is layered and where the deeper (= older) layers can only be explained with expert help. (The parallel with poetry is suggestive.) The expert's role is therefore much more critical than in many 'heritage' situations where there can be some immediate experiential response to a monument or landscape which is evoked by the relevant objects to which attention is being drawn.

Land Use

The later Mesolithic is a turning point in another respect. It marks the full human occupation of the mixed deciduous forest which was spatially the most important element of the vegetation cover of EW during the Holocene. As such, it was the beginning of the differentiation of a series of land uses out of the matrix of the forest; each environmental impact (see Table 6.1) was the result of another economic valuation of the resources of the land and its flows of energy, water and living materials and the diversion of these flows to human purposes and societies. So, from a single land use in, say, 6000 BP, there has been a progression to many and multiple land uses (Simmons 1990).

Where the higher and unenclosed lands are concerned, their present state contrasts with that of the later Mesolithic period. Where there was a self-replicating forest with a diverse fauna and flora, there is now a moorland dominated by only a few species of grass, rush and sedge; deep areas of peat are often eroding quite quickly, and, where there is a heather monoculture over a shallow peat layer, then erosion of the mineral soil is frequent. Fire now causes the loss of a significant part of the nutrient capital of the ecosystem as well as increasing the area subject to sheet and gulley erosion, which takes considerable time to be recolonised by higher plants. The dominant plants have close relatives in tundra vegetation, and indeed that is the closest analogue in terms of biological productivity, although the term 'wet desert' is sometimes applied in the semi-popular literature.

Yet these terrains have achieved a high ranking in cultural terms. Any attempt to change the frontiers of moorland and enclosed land (a shifting boundary for several centuries at least) meets with concerted opposition, as do attempts at reforestation with fast-growing and acid-tolerant conifers. Although common-land status does not confer *de jure* rights of public access away from the rights of way, organised trespasses still attempt to reclaim the uplands for unrestricted passage of walkers and other recreationists. And several of the uplands discussed in this book form the core of a National Park, which is the highest appellation in the quasi-national ('quasi' because of differences in Scotland and Northern Ireland) system of protected landscapes, in which development control is more severe than elsewhere.

So, the interesting fact is that the later Mesolithic was a turning point in the sense that it was then that the slide to an ecologically downgraded condition began and that this state is, paradoxically, recognised by the nation as the best landscapes which it has to offer its citizens and visitors. (The reasons for this are historically conditioned, as are the economic circumstances that led to it: there seems little point in making moral judgements about people doing something 'wrong'.) Where this impinges upon the story as told here is that a landscape archaeology which attempts to preserve the concatenation of field system, monument, open pasture and blanket bog is contributing to the maintenance of an ecologically degraded landscape and should, presumably, be done with a consciousness of that actuality. In practical terms, however, there seems no movement to reclaim the uplands for deciduous woodland, and so *de facto* conflict is at present unlikely on these grounds. If European Union sheep subsidies fall yet more and the uplands become yet more marginal to productive agriculture then this could possibly become a live question.

2. THE MESOLITHIC AND THE SCHOLAR

So far, this enquiry and synthesis have been conducted in the language of positivist discourse: a body of realist phenomena is deemed to be external to the investigator. She or he then subjects this corpus to interrogation with the aim of producing findings which would have been the same had any other investigator been involved: they are not subjective to any individual. But archaeologists have, as might be expected, taken part in the re-evaluations of epistemology which have swept through the world of learning (and especially through the humanities and social sciences) in the last thirty-odd years. One result has been the identification of schools of approaches to archaeological data which focus upon rather different concerns and which may put the foregoing sections into a different perspective.

Processual Archaeology and the Need for Evidence

Within the positivist tradition, processual archaeology is concerned to find a structural matrix for all the 'objects' (construed in the widest sense) that it finds. This it does in the form of trying to get at the social relationships which result in the patterns of material finds that are the everyday stuff of the scholar in this field. In the present context, for example, the extrapolation by Petersen (1984) from Danish axe-types to differentiated 'tribal' groups, and the gathering of all the evidence for European mesolithic populations into a three-fold social structure by Newell and Constandse-Westermann (1984), are both of this type. Apart from attempts to delineate territories on a large scale for England, few attempts have been made to push the readings of the scanty evidence (compared with continental Europe in terms of human skeletal material or remains of settlement, for instance) into such compartments; hence some of the vaguenesses that accompany much of the modelling in Chapter 5. So, cliché though it is, there is nevertheless a need for more evidence, in which priority ought to be given to settlement sites and associated economic information, wherever they occur. Given the distribution of preserving conditions in Britain, wetlands are an obvious place for precedence.

Post-processual Archaeology

The epistemological awareness that is gathered under this title is not perhaps a unity. Indeed, Patterson (1990) identifies three 'postprocessual archaeologies' which are 'conceptually distinct but related, with significant areas of overlap and divergence'. Since it is not the purpose here other than to indicate that there is such a way of looking at the present work, no detail on these various discourses will be relayed. It will have to suffice to say that the three approaches have in common certain themes. For example:

- The archaeological record exists outside its knowing subjects (i.e. it is 'real' in philosophical terms); some of it is unobservable, but this may generate the observable and is no less real.
- Different segments of today's society have different concepts of the past and create different representations of it; further, it is possible that discourse on the past reflects the relations of power and authority among the participants.
- It is essential to have a self-conscious approach to analytical categories and types of claims of knowledge, since archaeology reveals the historical specificity of many analytical frameworks.
- The transmission agent of the discourse is mostly that of reading, which is thus the instrument of transfer of all the meaning, knowledge, power and ideology which may reside in the enquiry whose results are being presented. If an entrenched social order deploys political or intellectual hegemony, then it may be possible to use a self-aware piece of work to empower a counter-hegemony (Hodder 1985).

It is not difficult to see how some of these considerations might apply in academia. At one time in the 1960s, for example, the notion that Mesolithic cultures might be responsible for the recession of forest was unacceptable to some members of the Quaternary Ecology community, and various methods, it was alleged, were deployed in order to prevent the evidence from being published in high-profile journals. Now, the conventional wisdom is different. It is, though, less of a career risk to publish speculative material either when in a tenured senior position or outside one's nominal subject area.

By contrast, it is not easy to see how to harm members of a culture who have been dead some thousands of years, though not difficult to emplace a particular slant on their reputation. Consider, for example, the resonances of the word 'camp' often (indeed, usually) employed to describe the remains of mesolithic settlements. In their listings of usages, dictionaries stress the nature of impermanence inherent in the word. So, the coloration given to the Mesolithic people is often of a band of a rather impoverished culture who cannot manage anything better than 'camps'. The evidence may well suggest the relatively simple material culture characteristic of most human groups who need to move fairly frequently, but equally it requires acceptance of the notion of a high degree of environmental awareness and 'tuning' which allowed the successful adaptation of a technologically restricted group to the rapidly-changing climatic and ecological conditions of the eighth millennium BP. 'Camp' may be the appropriate word for some phases of an annual cycle, but its unthinking use might with advantage be replaced. We need at least to think beyond the impoverished material evidence of the British Mesolithic to a rich culture, sensitive to nature, sustained by myths and embedded in 'owned' landscapes: Tilley (1994) sets us on our way.

Neither is it simple to see how this kind of knowledge can be used to deploy power over others outside the academic sphere, except perhaps in the fields of landscape archaeology and planning discussed above, where it can be an element which forms part of the knowledge flows that accompany (although sometimes in a separate compartment) decision-making. Knowing about the role of Mesolithic folk in the initiation of today's moorland landscapes *could* revolutionise public attitudes to these regions, and to that extent the knowledge is potentially hegemonic. But it seems a trifle unlikely that its dissemination (and the present author has tried, in various contexts) will provoke a rush to the barricades in favour of ecological diversity. However, a knowledge of landscape and environmental history cannot but improve environmental awareness on a broad basis (Macinnes and Whickham-Jones 1992).

Given that Mesolithic people are safely dead and indeed have no living representatives to demand that their few remains are restored to sacred places, they are however a potential vehicle to carry some of our cultural constructions. On the one hand, for example, since it is not now permissible to refer to simpler, pre-industrial cultures of today and the near-recent past in pejorative terms (like 'primitive' or even 'savages'), then groups like the Mesolithic (and even more their predecessors, no doubt) can safely be given that kind of label. Since many societies feel happiest with hierarchies in which the labellers are nearer the top than the bottom, then it may be deemed useful to have such a group to occupy the lower places in the league. On the other hand, the emergence of 'green' ideas has emplaced such concepts as the environmental tenderness of hunter-gatherers (especially the aboriginal North Americans) and the way in which the Neolithic Revolutions allowed rapid population increases and thus, it is argued, set humanity on a course which is bound to end in eco-environmental disaster. Deep Ecologists thus view as iconic any decentralised, non-industrial societies with low levels of material goods. The Mesolithic might thus be appropriated as a Golden Age with lessons for today's environmentalists. (This may well be true, though probably in a more complicated fashion that involves openness to change and adaptation rather than contented consumers of the usufruct of a benign Nature.)

So the demands of post-processual archaeology are not irrelevant to this kind of investigation and its conclusions. It is, however, comforting to read that its protagonists believe in the reality of a record outside the knowing subject, however partial the results may be of any interrogation of that register. Provided that it is not totally destroyed (always a challenge for archaeology), then the questions can be posed yet again when the observers' tools of interrogation are sharper and a new generation of scholars is free from some of the perceptual shackles of their past.

Bibliography

Aaby, B. (1983), 'Forest development, soil genesis and human activity illustrated by pollen and hypha analysis of two neighbouring podzols in Draved Forest, Denmark', *Danmarks Geologiske Undersøgelse* II Række Nr 114, 1–116.

Andersen, S. Th. (1988), 'Changes in agricultural practices in the Holocene indicated in a pollen diagram from a small hollow in Denmark', in H. H. Birks, H. J. B. Birks, P. E. Kaland and D. Moe (eds), *The Cultural Landscape – Past, Present and Future*, Cambridge University Press, 395–407.

Andersen, S. Th. and Rasmussen, K. L. (1993), 'Radiocarbon wiggle-dating of elm declines in northwest Denmark and their significance', *Vegetation History and Archaeobotany* 2, 125–35.

Anell, B. (1969), 'Running down and driving of game in North America', *Studia Ethnographica Upsaliensia* 30, Uppsala, 129pp.

Atherden, M. A. (1979), 'Late Quaternary vegetational history of the North York Moors. VII. Pollen diagrams from the eastern-central area', *J. Biogeogr.* 6, 63–83.

Atherden, M. A. (1992), *Upland Britain. A Natural History*, Manchester University Press.

Austad, I. (1988), 'Tree pollarding in western Norway', in H. H. Birks, H. J. B. Birks, P. E. Kaland and D. Moe (eds), *The Cultural Landscape – Past, Present and Future*, Cambridge University Press, 11–29.

Balaam, N. D., Bell, M., David, A., Levitan, B., MacPhail, R., Robinson, M. and Scaife, R. (1987), 'Prehistoric and Romano-British sites at Westward Ho! Devon. Archaeological and palaeoenvironmental surveys 1983 and 1984', in N. D. Balaam, B. Levitan and V. Straker (eds), *Studies in Palaeoeconomy and Environment in South West England*, Oxford: British Archaeological Reports British Series 181, 163–264.

Barden, L. S. (1981), 'Forest development in canopy gaps of a diverse hardwood forest of the southern Appalachian Mountains', *Oikos* 37, 205–9.

Barden, L. S. and Woods, F. W. (1974), 'Characteristics of lightning fires in Southern Appalachian forests', *Proc. Ann. Tall Timbers Fire Ecology Conf.* 13, 345–61.

Barnes, B. (1982), *Man and the Changing Landscape. A Study of Occupation and Palaeo Environment [sic] in the Central Pennines*, Merseyside County Museums Work Notes 3.

Bartley, D. D. (1960), 'Rhosgoch Common, Radnorshire: stratigraphy and pollen analysis', *New Phytol.* 59, 238–62.

Bartley, D. D., Jones, I. P. and Smith, R. T. (1990), 'Studies in the Flandrian vegetational history of the Craven district of Yorkshire: the lowlands', *J. Ecol.* 78, 611–32.

Bay-Petersen, J. L. (1978), 'Animal exploitation in Mesolithic Denmark', in P. A. Mellars (ed.), *The Early Postglacial Settlement of Northern Europe. An Ecological Perspective*, London: Duckworth, 115–45.

Beckett, S. C. (1981), 'The Shaugh Moor project: environmental background', *Proc. Prehist. Soc.* 47, 247–53.

Bell, M. and Walker, M. J. C. (1992), *Late Quaternary Environmental Change. Physical and Human Perspectives*, London: Longmans.

Bennett, K. D. and Birks, H. J. B. (1990), 'Post-glacial history of alder (Alnus glutinosa (L.) Gaertn.) in the British Isles', *J. Quaternary Sci.* 5, 123–33.

Bennett, K. D., Simonson, W. D. and Peglar, S. (1990), 'Fire and man in post-glacial woodlands', *J. Archaeol. Sci.* 17, 635–42.

Bettinger, R. L. (1991), *Hunter-gatherers: Archaeological and Evolutionary Theory*, New York: Plenum Press.

Binford, L. R. (1980), 'Willow smoke and dogs' tails: hunter-gatherer settlement systems and site formation', *American Antiquity* 45, 4–20.

Birks, H. J. B. (1988), 'Long-term ecological change in the British uplands', in M. B. Usher and D. B. A. Thompson (eds), *Ecological Change in the Uplands*, Oxford: Blackwell Scientific Publications; British Ecological Society Special Publication no. 7, 37–56.

Birks, H. J. B. (1989), 'Holocene isochrone maps and patterns of tree-spreading in the British Isles', *J. Biogeogr.* 16, 503–40.

Blankholm, H. P. (1987), 'Late Mesolithic hunter-gatherers and the transition to farming in southern Scandinavia', in P. Rowley-Conwy, M. Zvelebil and H. P. Blankholm (eds), *Mesolithic Northwest Europe: Recent Trends*, University of Sheffield Department of Archaeology and Prehistory Recent Trends Series vol. 2, 155–68.

Bogucki, P. (1987), 'The establishment of agrarian communities on the North European plain', *Current Anthropology* 28, 1–24.

Bokelmann, K. (1986), 'Rast unter Bäumen. Ein ephemerer Mesolithischer Lagerplatz aus dem Duvenseer Moor', *Offa* 43, 149–63.

Bonsall, C. (1981), 'The coastal factor in the Mesolithic settlement of North-west England', in B. Gramsch (ed.), *Mesolithikum in Europa*, 2nd International Symposium, Potsdam, 3–8 April 1978: Veröffentlichungen des Museums für Ur- und Frühgeschichte Potsdam 14/15, 451–72.

Bonsall, C. (ed.) (1989), *The Mesolithic in Europe*, Edinburgh: John Donald.

Bonsall, C., Sutherland, D., Tipping, R. and Cherry, J. (1989), 'The Eskmeals project: late Mesolithic settlement and environment in North-West England', in C. Bonsall (ed.), *The Mesolithic in Europe*, Edinburgh: John Donald, 175–205.

Bormann, F. H. and Likens, G. E. (1979), 'Catastrophic disturbance and the steady state in northern hardwood forests', *American Scientist* 67, 660–9.

Borowski, S. and Kossak, S. (1972), 'The natural food preferences of the European bison in seasons free of snow cover', *Acta Theriologica* 17 (13), 151–69.

Borowski, S. and Kossak, S. (1975), 'The food habits of deer in the Białowieza primeval forest', *Acta Theriologica* 20, 463–506.

Bostock, J. L. (1980), 'The history of the vegetation of the Berwyn mountains, North Wales, with emphasis on the development of the blanket mires' 2 vols, Ph.D. thesis, University of Manchester.

Bradshaw, R. H. W. (1981), 'Modern pollen-representation factors for woods in south-east England', *J. Ecol.* 69, 45–70.

Bradshaw, R. H. W. and Hannon, G. (1992), 'Climatic change, human influences and disturbance regime in the control of vegetation dynamics within Fiby Forest, Sweden', *J. Ecol.* 80, 625–32.

Braun, D. P. (1974), 'Explanatory models for the evolution of coastal adaptation in prehistoric New England', *American Antiquity* 39, 582–96.

Bridge, M. C., Haggart, B. A. and Lowe, J. J. (1990), 'The history and palaeoclimatic significance of subfossil remains of Pinus sylvestris in blanket peats from Scotland', *J. Ecol.* 78, 77–99.

Broadbent, N. (1979), *Coastal Resources and Settlement Stability*, Uppsala: Uppsala Studies in North European Archaeology 3.

Brown, A. P. (1977), 'Late-Devensian and Flandrian vegetational history of Bodmin Moor, Cornwall', *Phil. Trans. Roy. Soc. Lond.* B 276, 251–320.

Buckland, P. C. and Edwards, K. J. (1984), 'The longevity of pastoral episodes of clearance activity in pollen diagrams: the role of post-occupation grazing', *J. Biogeogr.* 11, 243–9.

Bush, M. B. (1988), 'Early Mesolithic disturbance: a force on the landscape', *J. Archaeol. Sci.* 15, 453–62.

Caseldine, C. J. (1980), 'Environmental change in Cornwall during the last 13,000 years', *Cornish Archaeology* 19, 2–16.

Caseldine, C. J. and Hatton, J. (1993), 'The development of high moorland on Dartmoor: fire and the influence of Mesolithic activity on vegetation change', in F. M. Chambers (ed.), *Climate Change and Human Impact on the Landscape*, London: Chapman and Hall, 119–31.

Caseldine, C. J. and Maguire, D. J. (1986), 'Late glacial/early

Flandrian vegetation change on northern Dartmoor, south-west England', *J. Biogeogr.* 13, 255–64.

Chambers, C. (1978), 'A radiocarbon-dated pollen diagram from Valley Bog, on the Moor House National Nature Reserve', *New Phytol.* 80, 273–80.

Chambers, F. M. (1982a), 'Environmental history of Cefn Gwernffrwd, near Rhandirmwyn, mid-Wales', *New Phytol.* 92, 607–15.

Chambers, F. M. (1982b), 'Two radiocarbon-dated pollen diagrams from high-altitude blanket peats in South Wales', *J. Ecol.* 70, 445–59.

Chambers, F. M. (1983), 'Three radiocarbon-dated pollen diagrams from upland peats north-west of Merthyr Tydfil, South Wales', *J. Ecol.* 71, 475–87.

Chambers, F. M. (1988), 'Archaeology and the flora of the British Isles: the moorland experience', in M. Jones (ed.), *Archaeology and the Flora of the British Isles. Human Influence upon the Evolution of Plant Communities*, Oxford University Committee for Archaeology Monograph no. 14; BSBL Conference Report no. 19, 107–15.

Chambers, F. M. and Elliott, L. (1989), 'Spread and expansion of *Alnus* Mill. in the British Isles: timing, agencies and possible vectors', *J. Biogeogr.* 16, 541–50.

Chambers, F. M., Kelley, R. S. and Price, S.-M. (1988), 'Development of the Late-Prehistoric cultural landscape in upland Ardudwy, North-west Wales', in H. H. Birks, H. J. B. Birks, P. E. Kalund and D. Moe (eds), *The Cultural Landscape – Past, Present and Future*, Cambridge University Press, 333–48.

Chambers, F. M. and Price, S.-M. (1988), 'The environmental setting of Erw-wen and Moel y Gerddi: prehistoric enclosures in upland Ardudwy, North Wales', *Proc. Prehist. Soc.* 54, 93–100.

Chandler, C., Cheney, P., Thomas, P., Traband, L. and Williams, D. (eds) (1983), 'Fire as a natural process in forests', in idem, *Fire in Forestry*, vol. I, *Forest Fire Behavior and Effects*, New York: Wiley, 293–393.

Cherry, J. and Cherry, P. J. (1987), *Prehistoric Habitation Sites on the Limestone Uplands of Eastern Cumbria*, Kendal: Cumbria and Westmorland Antiquarian and Archaeological Society Research Series vol. II.

Clark, D. (1973), 'Peat Moss. A North Riding Mesolithic workshop', *The Brigantian*, 9–14.

Clark, J. G. D. (1972), *Star Carr: A Case Study in Bioarchaeology*, Reading, MA: Addison-Wesley Modules in Anthropology no. 10.

Clark, J. G. D. (1983), 'Coastal settlement in European prehistory, with special reference to Fennoscandia', in E. Z. Vogt and R. M. Leventhal (eds), *Prehistoric Settlement Patterns: Essays in Honor of Gordon R. Wiley*, Albuquerque: University of New Mexico Press, 295–317.

Clark, J. S., Merkt, J. and Muller, H. (1989), 'Post-glacial fire, vegetation and human history on the northern Alpine forelands, south-western Germany', *J. Ecol.* 77, 897–925.

Clarke, D. L. (1976), 'Mesolithic Europe: the economic basis', in G. de G. Sieveking, I. H. Longworth and K. E. Wilson (eds), *Problems in Economic and Social Archaeology*, London: Duckworth, 449–81.

Clutton-Brock, J. and Noe-Nygaard, N. (1990), 'New osteological and C-isotope evidence on Mesolithic dogs: companions to hunters and fishers at Star Carr, Seamer Carr and Kongemøse', *J. Archaeol. Sci.* 17, 643–53.

Coggins, D. (1986), *Upper Teesdale. The Archaeology of a North Pennine Valley*, Oxford: British Archaeological Reports British Series 150.

Coles, B. (1992), 'Further thoughts on the impact of beaver on temperate landscapes', in S. Needham and M. C. Macklin (eds), *Alluvial Archaeology in Britain*, Oxford: Oxbow Monographs 27, 93–9.

Coles, J. M. and Orme, B. J. (1983), 'Homo sapiens or Castor fiber?', *Antiquity* 57, 95–102.

Collins, B. S., Dunne, K.P. and Pickett, S. T. A. (1985), 'Response of forest herbs to canopy gaps', in S. T. A. Pickett and P. S. White (eds), *The Ecology of Natural Disturbance and Patch Dynamics*, Orlando, FL: Academic Press, 218–34.

Collins, B. S., and Pickett, S. T. A. (1988), 'Demographic responses of herb layer species to experimental canopy gaps in a Northern hardwoods forest', *J. Ecol.* 76, 437–50.

Constandse-Westermann, T. S. and Newell, R. R. (1989), 'Social and biological aspects of the West European Mesolithic population structure: a comparison with the demography of North American Indians', in C. Bonsall (ed.), *The Mesolithic in Europe*, Edinburgh: John Donald, 106–15.

Coulson, J. C. and Butterfield, J. (1978), 'An investigation of the biotic factors determining the rates of plant decomposition on blanket bog', *J. Ecol.* 66, 631–50.

Cowell, R. W. and Innes, J. B. (1994), *The Wetlands of Merseyside*, Oxford: Oxbow Books for Lancaster Imprints; North West Wetlands Survey 1.

Cox, B. (ed.) (1973), *Cultural Ecology*, Toronto: McClelland and Stewart.

Coy, J. (1982), 'Woodland mammals in Wessex – the archaeological evidence', in M. Bell and S. J. Limbrey (eds), *Archaeological Aspects of Woodland Ecology*, Oxford: British Archaeological Reports International Series 146, 287–96.

Cromertie, George, Earl of (1711), 'An account of the mosses in Scotland', *Phil. Trans. Roy. Soc. Lond.* XXVII, 296–301.

Cronon, W. (1983), *Changes in the Land. Indians, Colonists and the Ecology of New England*, New York: Hill and Wang.

Cundill, P. R. (1988), 'Limitations of soil pollen analysis – an example from Mauley Cross, a mesolithic site on the North York Moors', *Circaea* 6 (1), 43–7.

David, N. (1989), 'Some aspects of the human presence in West Wales during the Mesolithic', in C. Bonsall (ed.), *The Mesolithic in Europe*, Edinburgh: John Donald, 241–53.

Davies, G. and Turner, J. (1979), 'Pollen diagrams from Northumberland', *New Phytol.* 82, 783–804.

Davies, J. (1963), 'A Mesolithic site on Blubberhouses Moor, Wharfedale, West Riding of Yorkshire', *Yorks. Archaeol. J.* 41, 61–70.

Dimbleby, G. W. (1961), 'Soil pollen analysis', *J. Soil. Sci.* 12, 1–11.

Dimbleby, G. W. (1962), 'The development of British heathlands and their soils', *Oxford Forestry Memoirs* 23.

Dincauze, D. F. (1981), 'Paleoenvironmental reconstructions in the northeast: the art of multidisciplinary science', in D. R. Snow (eds), *Foundations in Northeast Archaeology*, New York: Academic Press, 51–96.

Dubois, A. D. and Ferguson, D. K. (1985), 'The climatic history of pine in the Cairngorms based on radiocarbon dates and stable isotope analysis, with an account of the events leading up to its colonization', *Rev. Palaeobot. and Palynol.* 46, 55–80.

Dumont, J. V. (1987), 'Mesolithic microwear research in Northwest Europe', in P. Rowley-Conwy, M. Zvelebil and H. P. Blankholm (eds), *Mesolithic Northwest Europe: Recent Trends*, University of Sheffield Department of Archaeology and Prehistory Recent Trends Series vol. 2, 82–9.

Dunbar, R. (1992), 'Why gossip is good for you', *New Scientist* 136 (Issue 1,848, 21 November 1992), 28–31.

Dzięciołowski, R. (1979), 'Structure and spatial organisation of deer populations', *Acta Theriologlca* 24, 3–21.

Edwards, K. J. (1979), 'Palynological and temporal inference in the context of prehistory, with special reference to the evidence from lake and peat deposits', *J. Archaeol. Sci.* 6, 255–70.

Edwards, K. J. (1982), 'Man, space and the woodland edge: speculations on the detection of human impact in pollen profiles', in M. Bell and S. J. Limbrey (eds), *Archaeological Aspects of Woodland Ecology*, Oxford: British Archaeological Reports International Series 146, 5–22.

Edwards, K. J. (1983), 'Quaternary palynology: multiple profile studies and pollen variability', *Progr. Phys. Geogr.* 7, 587–609.

Edwards, K. J. (1985), 'The anthropogenic factor in vegetational history', in K. J. Edwards and W. P. Warren (eds), *The Quaternary History of Ireland*, London: Academic Press, 187–220.

Edwards, K. J. (1988), 'The hunter-gatherer/agricultural transition and the pollen record in the British Isles', in H. H. Birks, H. J. B.

Birks, P. E. Kaland and D. Moe (eds), *The Cultural Landscape – Past, Present and Future*, Cambridge University Press, 255–66.

Edwards, K. J. (1989), 'The cereal pollen record and early agriculture', in A. Milles, D. Williams and N. Gardner (eds), *The Beginnings of Agriculture*, Oxford: British Archaeological Reports International Series 496, 113–35.

Edwards, K. J. (1990), 'Fire and the Scottish Mesolithic: evidence from microscopic charcoal', in P. M. Vermeersch and P. van Peer (eds), *Contributions to the Mesolithic in Europe*, Leuven University Press, 71–9.

Edwards, K. J. (1993), 'Models of mid-Holocene forest farming for north-west Europe', in F. M. Chambers (ed.), *Climate Change and Human Impact on the Landscape*, London: Chapman and Hall, 133–45.

Edwards, K. J., Ansell, M. and Carter, B. A. (1983), 'New Mesolithic sites in south-west Scotland and their importance as indicators of inland penetration', *Trans. Dumfriesshire and Galloway Natural History and Antiquarian Society* 58, 9–15.

Edwards, K. J. and Hirons, K. R. (1984), 'Cereal pollen grains in pre-Elm decline deposits: implications for the earliest agriculture in Britain and Ireland', *J. Archaeol. Sci.* 11, 71–80.

Edwards, K. J., Whittington, G. and Hirons, K. R. (1995), 'The relationship between fire and long-term wet heath development in South Uist, Outer Hebrides, Scotland', in D. B. A. Thompson, A. J. Hester and M. B. Usher (eds), *Heaths and Moorland: Cultural Landscapes*, Edinburgh: HMSO for Scottish Natural Heritage, 240–8.

Erdtman, G. (1927), 'Peat deposits of the Cleveland Hills', *Naturalist*, 39–46 [not made into volumes].

Evans, A. and Moore, P. D. (1985), 'Surface studies of *Calluna vulgaris* (L.) Hull and their relevance to the interpretation of bog and moorland pollen diagrams', *Circaea* 3, 173–8.

Fahey, T. J. and Reiners, W. A. (1981), 'Fire in the forests of Maine and New Hampshire', *Bulletin of the Torrey Botanical Club*, 108, 362–73.

Falinski, J. B. (1986), *Vegetation Dynamics in Temperate Lowland Primeval Forests. Ecological Studies in Białowieza Forest*, Dordrecht: Junk. Geobotany 8.

Falinski, J. B. (1988), 'Succession, regeneration and fluctuation in the Białowieza Forest (NE Poland)', *Vegetatio* 77, 115–28.

Faull, M. L. and Moorhouse, S. A. (eds) (1981), *West Yorkshire: An Archaeological Survey to AD 1500. Vol I. Sources. Environment and the County to AD 1066*, Wakefield: West Yorks Metropolitan County Council.

Fitzhugh, W. (1975), 'A comparative approach to Northern maritime adaptations', in idem (ed.), *Prehistoric Adaptations of the Circumpolar Zone*, The Hague and Paris: Mouton, 339–86.

Foster, D. R. (1988), 'Disturbance history, community organization and vegetation dynamics of the old-growth Pisgah Forest, south-western New Hampshire, U.S.A.', *J. Ecol.* 76, 105–34.

Fowler P. (1991), 'Dorset in depth', *Antiquity* 65, 988–92.

Francis, P. D. and Slater, D. S. (1990), 'A record of vegetational and land use change from upland peat deposits on Exmoor. Part 2. Hoar Moor', *Somerset Archaeology and Natural History* 134, 1–26.

Fraser, D. and Reardon, E. (1980), 'Attraction of wild ungulates to mineral-rich springs in central Canada', *Holarctic Ecology* 3, 36–40.

Frelich, L. E. and Lorimer, C. G. (1991), 'Natural disturbance regimes in hemlock and hardwood forests of the Upper Great Lakes region', *Ecol. Monog.* 61, 145–64.

Friis-Hansen, J. (1990), 'Mesolithic cutting arrows: functional analysis of arrows used in the hunting of large game', *Antiquity* 64, 494–504.

Gadacz, R. R. (1975), 'Montagnais hunting dynamics in historicoecological perspective', *Anthropologica* 17, 149–67.

Gaudreau, D. C. (1988), 'The distribution of Late Quaternary forest regions in the Northeast: pollen data, physiography, and the prehistoric record', in G. P. Nicholas (ed.), *Holocene Human Ecology in Northeastern North America*, London and New York: Plenum Books, 215–56.

Gębczyńska, Z. (1980), 'Food of the roe deer and red deer in the Białowieza primeval forest', *Acta Theriologica* 25, 487–500.

Gendel, P. A. (1984), *Mesolithic Social Territories in Northwestern Europe*, Oxford: British Archaeological Reports International Series 218.

Gimingham, C. H. (1989) 'Heather and heathlands', *Bot. J. Linn. Soc.* 101, 263–68.

Goddard, A. (1971), 'Studies of the vegetational changes associated with the initiation of blanket peat accumulation in Northern Ireland', Ph.D. thesis, Queen's University of Belfast.

Göransson, H. (1986), 'Man and the forests of nemoral broad-leafed trees during the Stone Age', *Striae* 24, 143–52.

Göransson, H. (1988), 'Can exchange during Mesolithic time be evidenced by pollen analysis?', *Acta Archaeologia Lundensia* 16 (Trade and Exchange in Prehistory: Studies in Honour of Berta Sternquist), 33–40.

Green, D. G. (1983), 'The ecological interpretation of fine resolution pollen records', *New Phytol.* 94, 459–77.

Green, S. W. and Zvelebil, M. (1990), 'The Mesolithic colonization and agricultural transition of south-east Ireland', *Proc. Prehist. Soc.* 56, 57–88.

Grigson, C. (1989), 'Bird-foraging patterns in the Mesolithic', in C. Bonsall (ed.), *The Mesolithic in Europe*, Edinburgh: John Donald, 60–72.

Grigson, C. and Clutton-Brock J. (eds) (1989), *Animals and Archaeology: 4. Husbandry in Europe*, Oxford: British Archaeological Reports International Series 227.

Harris, D. R. (1990), *Settling Down and Breaking Ground: Rethinking the Neolithic Revolution*, Amsterdam: Netherlands Museum of Anthropology and Prehistory.

Hayden, B. (1981), 'Subsistence and ecological adaptations of modern hunter-gatherers', in R. S. O. Harding and G. Teleki (eds), *Omnivorous Primates, Gathering and Hunting in Human Evolution*, New York: Columbia University Press, 344–421.

Heinselman, M. L. (1981), 'Fire and succession in the conifer forests of Northern North America', in D. C. West, H. H. Shugart and D. B. Botkin (eds), *Forest Succession Concepts and Application*, New York: Springer-Verlag, 374–405.

Heybroek, H. M. (1963), 'Diseases and lopping for fodder as possible causes of a prehistoric decline of Ulmus', *Acta Botanica Neerlandica* 12, 1–11.

Hiatt, B. (1967), 'The food quest and the economy of the Tasmanian aborigines', *Oceania* 38, 190–219.

Hicks, S. P. (1972), 'Impact of man on the East Moor of Derbyshire from Mesolithic time', *Archaeol. J.* 129, 1–21.

Hirons, K. R. and Edwards, K. J. (1990), 'Pollen and related studies at Kinloch, Isle of Rhum, Scotland, with particular reference to possible early human impacts on vegetation', *New Phytol.* 116, 715–27.

Hodder, I. (1985), 'Postprocessual archaeology', *Adv. in Archaeol. Method and Theory* 8, 1–26.

Holstener-Jorgensen, H. (1967), 'Influences of forest management and drainage on ground-water fluctuations', in W. E. Sopper and H. W. Lull (eds), *Forest Hydrology*, Oxford: Pergamon Press, 325–33.

Holtmeier, F.-K. (1993), 'Timberlines as indicators of climatic changes: problems and research needs', *Paläoklimaforschung* 9, 211–22.

Honeyman, A. (1985), 'Studies in the holocene vegetation history of Wensleydale', Ph.D. thesis, University of Leeds.

Huntley, B. (1988), 'European post-glacial forests: compositional changes in response to climatic change', *J. Vegetation Sci.* 1, 507–18.

Huntley, B. (1990), 'European vegetation history: palaeovegetation maps from pollen data 13,000 yr BP to present', *J. Quaternary Sci.* 5, 103–22.

Huntley, B. (1993), 'Rapid early-Holocene migration and high abundance of hazel (*Corylus avellana* L.): alternative hypotheses', in F. M. Chambers (ed.), *Climate Change and Human Impact on the Landscape*, London: Chapman and Hall, 205–16.

Innes, J. B. (1981), 'Environmental alteration by Mesolithic communities in the North York Moors', M.Phil. thesis, University of Durham.

Innes, J. B. (1989), 'Fine resolution pollen analysis of late Flandrian II peat at North Gill, North York Moors', 2 vols, Ph.D. thesis, University of Durham.

Innes, J. B. and Shennan, I. (1991), 'Palynology of archaeological and mire sediments from Dod, Borders Region, Scotland', *Archaeol. J.* 148, 1–45.

Innes, J. B. and Simmons, I. G. (1988), 'Disturbance and diversity: floristic changes associated with pre-elm decline woodland recession in north-east Yorkshire', in M. Jones (ed.), *Archaeology and the Flora of the British Isles. Human Influence upon the Evolution of Plant Communities*, Oxford University Committee for Archaeology Monograph no. 14; BSBI Conference Report no. 19, 7–20.

Jacobi, R. M. (1976); 'Britain inside and outside Mesolithic Europe', *Proc. Prehist. Soc.* 42, 67–84.

Jacobi, R. M. (1978), 'Northern England in the eighth millennium bc: an essay', in P. A. Mellars (ed.), *The Early Postglacial Settlement of Northern Europe. An Ecological Perspective*, London: Duckworth, 295–332.

Jacobi, R. M. (1980), 'The early Holocene settlement of Wales', in J. A. Taylor (ed.), *Culture and Environment in Prehistoric Wales*, Oxford: British Archaeological Reports British Series 76, 131–206.

Jacobi, R. M., Tallis, J. H. and Mellars, P. A. (1976), 'The southern Pennine Mesolithic and the ecological record', *J. Archaeol. Sci.* 3, 307–20.

Jacobsen, G. L. and Bradshaw, R. H. W. (1981), 'The selection of sites for palaeoeological studies', *Quaternary Research* 15, 80–96.

Jahn, G. (1991), 'Temperate deciduous forests of Europe', in E. Rohrig and B. Ulrich (eds), *Temperate Deciduous Forests*, Amsterdam: Elsevier, 377–502.

Jamrozy, G. (1980), 'Winter food resources and food preferences of red deer in Carpathian forests', *Acta Theriologica* 25, 221–38.

Jarman, M. R. (1972), 'European deer economies and the advent of the Neolithic', in E. S. Higgs (ed.), *Papers in Economic Prehistory*, Cambridge University Press, 125–45.

Jochim, M. A. (1976) *Hunter-Gatherer Subsistence and Settlement: A Predictive Model*, New York: Academic Press.

Jochim, M. A. (1979), 'Breaking down the system: recent ecological approaches in archaeology', *Advances in Archaeological Method and Theory* 2, 77–117.

Johnson, E. A. (1992), *Fire and Vegetation Dynamics: Studies from the North American Boreal Forest*, Cambridge University Press.

Johnson, G. A. L. and Dunham, K. C. (1963), *The Geology of Moor House*, London: HMSO, Monographs of the Nature Conservancy no. 2.

Johnson, N. and Rose, P. (1994), *Bodmin Moor. An Archaeological Survey. Vol I: The Human Landscape to 1800*, London: English Heritage Archaeological Report no. 24.

Jones, R. L. (1976), 'The activities of Mesolithic man: further palaeobotanical evidence from north-east Yorkshire', in D. A. Davidson and M. L. Shackley (eds), *Geoarchaeology. Earth Science and the Past*, London: Duckworth, 355–67.

Jones, R. L. (1977), 'Late Quaternary vegetational history of the North York Moors. V. The Cleveland dales', *J. Biogeogr.* 4, 353–62.

Jones, R. L. (1978), 'Late Quaternary vegetational history of the North York Moors. VI. The Cleveland Moors', *J. Biogeogr.* 5, 81–92.

Jones, R. L. (1988), 'The impact of early man in coastal plant communities in the British Isles', in M. Jones (ed.), *Archaeology and the Flora of the British Isles. Human Influence upon the Evolution of Plant Communities*, Oxford University Committee for Archaeology Monograph no. 14; BSBI Conference Report no. 19, 96–106.

Keeley, H. C. M. (ed.) (1984), *Environmental Archaeology. A Regional Review*, DoE Directorate of Ancient Monuments and Historic Buildings, Occasional papers 6.

Keene, A. S. (1981), *Prehistoric Foraging in a Temperate Forest. A Linear Programming Model*, New York: Academic Press.

Larsson, L. (1988), 'A construction for ceremonial activities from the Late Mesolithic', *Meddelanden från Lunds Universitets Historiska Museum* 1989–90 new series 7, 5–18.

Laurie, T. C. (1985), 'Early land division and settlement in Swaledale and on the eastern approaches to Stainmore Pass over the North Pennines', in D. A. Spratt and C. Burgess (eds), *Upland Settlement in Britain. The Second Millennium BC and after*, British Archaeological Reports British Series 143, 135–62.

Layton, R., Foley, R. and Williams, E. (1991), 'The transition between hunting and gathering and the specialized husbandry of resources. A socio-ecological approach', *Current Anthropology* 32, 255–74.

Lewis, H. T. (1977), 'Maskuta: the ecology of Indian fire in Northern Alberta', *Western Canadian J. Anthropol.* 1, 15–52.

Lewis, H. T (1982), 'Fire technology and resource management in aboriginal North America and Australia', in N. M. Williams and E. S. Hunn (eds), *Resource Managers: North American and Australian Hunter-gatherers*, Boulder, CO: Westview Press, 45–67.

Lewis, H. T. and Ferguson, T. A. (1988), 'Yards, corridors and mosaics: how to burn a Boreal forest', *Human Ecology* 16, 57–77.

Lorimer, C. G. (1989), 'Relative effects of small and large disturbances on temperate hardwood forest structure', *Ecology* 70, 565–7.

Lowe, J. J. (1991), 'Integration of pollen and other proxy data: the Holocene palaeoclimate of the British Isles and adjacent parts of Europe', *Paläoklimaforschung* 6, 37–50.

Lynch, F. (1993), *Excavations in the Brenig Valley. A Mesolithic and Bronze Age Landscape in North Wales*, Bangor: Cambrian Archaeological Association, Cambrian Archaeological Monographs no. 5.

Macinnes, L. and Whickham-Jones, C. R. (1992), *All Natural Things: Archaeology and the Green Debate*, Oxford: Oxbow Monographs 21.

Mallik, A. U., Gimingham, C. H. and Rahman, A. A. (1984), 'Ecological effects of heather burning. I. Water infiltration, moisture retention and porosity of surface soil', *J. Ecol.* 72, 767–76.

Matlack, G. R. (1994), 'Vegetation dynamics of the forest edge – trends in space and successional time', *J. Ecol.* 82, 113–23.

Mátrai, K. and Kabai, P. (1989), 'Winter plant selection by red and roe deer in a forest habitat in Hungary', *Acta Theriologica* 34, 227–34.

Maxwell, H. (1910), 'The use and abuse of forests by the Virginia Indians', *William and Mary Quarterly* 19 (1st series), 73–104.

Mellars, P. A. (1976a), 'Settlement patterns and industrial variability in the British Mesolithic', in G. de G. Sieveking, I. H. Longworth and K. E. Wilson (eds), *Problems in Economic and Social Archaeology*, London: Duckworth, 375–99.

Mellars, P. A. (1976b), 'Fire ecology, animal populations and man: a study of some ecological relationships in prehistory', *Proc. Prehist. Soc.* 42, 15–45.

Mellars, P. A. (ed.) (1978), *The Early Postglacial Settlement of Northern Europe, An Ecological Perspective*, London: Duckworth.

Mellars, P. A. (1986), 'Palaeolithic and Mesolithic', in T. Darvill (ed.), *The Archaeology of the Uplands: A Rapid Assessment of Archaeological Knowledge and Practice*, London: RCHM/CBA, 22–4.

Mellars, P. A. (1987), *Excavations on Oronsay, Prehistoric Human Ecology of a Small Island*, Edinburgh University Press.

Mellars, P. A. (1990), 'A major "plateau" in the radiocarbon timescale at c. 9650 BP: the evidence from Star Carr', *Antiquity* 64, 836–40.

Mikkelsen, E. (1978), 'Seasonality and Mesolithic adaptation in Norway', *Studies in Scandinavian Prehistory and Early History* 1, 79–119.

Mitchell, F. J. G. (1988), 'The vegetational history of the Killarney oakwoods, SW Ireland: evidence from fine spatial resolution pollen analysis', *J. Ecol.* 76, 415–36.

Mithen, S. J. (1987), 'Prehistoric red deer hunting strategies: a cost-risk-benefit analysis with reference to Upper Palaeolithic northern Spain and Mesolithic Denmark', in P. Rowley-Conwy, M. Zvelebil and H. P. Blankholm (eds), *Mesolithic Northwest Europe: Recent Trends*, University of Sheffield Department of

Archaeology and Prehistory Recent Trends Series vol. 2, 93–108.

Moe, D. and Rackham, O. (1992), 'Pollarding and a possible explanation of the neolithic elm fall', *Vegetation History and Archaeobotany* 1, 63–8.

Moore, P. D. (1972), 'Studies in the vegetational history of mid-Wales. III. Early Flandrian pollen data from west Cardiganshire', *New Phytol.* 71, 947–59.

Moore, P. D. (1973), 'The influence of prehistoric cultures upon the initiation and spread of blanket bog in upland Wales', *Nature* 241, 350–3.

Moore, P. D. (1975), 'Origin of blanket mires', *Nature* 256, 267–70.

Moore, P. D. (1986), 'Hydrological changes in mires', in B. E. Berglund (ed.), *Handbook of Holocene Palaeoecology and Paleohydrology*, Chichester: Wiley, 91–107.

Moore, P. D. (1988), 'The development of moorlands and upland mires', in M. Jones (ed.), *Archaeology and the Flora of the British Isles. Human Influence upon the Evolution of Plant Communities*, Oxford University Committee for Archaeology Monograph no. 14; BSBI Conference Report no. 19, 116–22.

Moore, P. D. (1991), 'Holocene paludification and hydrological changes as climate proxy data in Europe', *Paläoklimaforschung* 6, 255–70.

Moore, P. D. (1993), 'The origin of blanket mire, revisited', in F. M. Chambers (ed.), *Climate Change and Human Impact on the Landscape*, London: Chapman and Hall, 217–24.

Moore, P. D., Evans, A. T. and Chater, M. (1986), 'Palynological and stratigraphic evidence for hydrological changes in mires associated with human activity', in K. E. Behre (ed.), *Anthropogenic Indicators in Pollen Diagrams*, Rotterdam and Boston, MA: Balkema, 209–20.

Morrison, A. and Bonsall, C. (1989), 'The early post-glacial settlement of Scotland: a review', in C. Bonsall (ed.), *The Mesolithic in Europe*, Edinburgh: John Donald, 134–42.

Moss, R. (1989), 'Management of heather for game and livestock', *Bot. J. Linn. Soc.* 101, 301–6.

Mulholland, H. (1970), 'The Mesolithic industries of the Tweed valley', *Trans. Dumfriesshire and Galloway Natural History and Antiquarian Society* 47, 81–110.

Mulholland, M. T. (1988), 'Territoriality and horticulture. A perspective for prehistoric Southern New England, in G. P. Nicholas (ed.), *Holocene Human Ecology in Northeastern North America*, London and New York: Plenum Books, 137–66.

Myers, A. (1987), 'All shot to pieces? Inter-assemblage variability, lithic analysis and Mesolithic assemblage types; some preliminary observations', in A. G. Brown and M. R. Edmunds (eds), *Lithic Analysis and Later British Prehistory. Some Problems and Approaches*, Oxford: British Archaeological Reports British Series 162, 137–53.

Myers, A. (1989), 'Reliable and maintainable technological strategies in the Mesolithic of mainland Britain', in R. Torrence (ed.), *Time, Energy and Stone Tools*, Cambridge University Press, New Directions in Archaeology series, 78–91.

Myers, R. L. and Perni, P. A. (1983), 'Approaches to determining aboriginal fire use and its impact on vegetation', *Bull. Ecological Soc. America* 64, 217–18.

Nelson, R. (1983), *Make Prayers to the Raven*, Chicago University Press.

Newell, R. R. and Constandse-Westermann, T. S. (1984), 'Population growth, density and technology in the western European Mesolithic: lessons from analogous historical contexts', *Paleohistoria* 26, 1–18.

Niering, W. A., Goodwin, R. H. and Taylor, S. (1970), 'Prescribed burning in southern New England: introduction to long-range studies', *Proc. Ann. Tall Timbers Fire Ecology Conf.* 10, 267–86.

Odgaard, B. V. (1992), 'The fire history of Danish heathland areas as reflected in pollen and charred particles in lake sediments', *The Holocene* 2, 218–26.

Oliver, C. D. (1981), 'Forest development in North America following major disturbances', *Forest Ecology and Management* 3, 153–68.

Oliver, C. D. and Stephens, E. P. (1977), 'Reconstruction of a mixed-species forest in central New England', *Ecology* 58, 562–72.

Paludan-Müller, C. (1978), 'High Atlantic food gathering in Northwestern Zealand, ecological conditions and spatial representation', *Studies in Scandinavian Prehistory* 1, 120–57.

Pardoe, C. (1988), 'The cemetery as symbol. The distribution of prehistoric Aboriginal burial grounds in southeastern Australia', *Archaeology in Oceania* 23, 1–16.

Patterson, T. C. (1990), 'Some theoretical tensions within and between the processual and postprocessual archaeologies', *J. Anth. Archaeol.* 9, 189–200.

Patterson, W. A. and Sassaman, K. E. (1988), 'Indian fires in the prehistory of New England', in G. P. Nicholas (ed.), *Holocene Human Ecology in Northeastern North America*, London and New York: Plenum Books, 107–35.

Peglar, S. (1993), 'The mid-Holocene *Ulmus* decline at Diss Mere, Norfolk, UK: a year-by-year pollen stratigraphy from annual laminations', *The Holocene* 3, 1–13.

Peglar, S. and Birks, H. J. B. (1993), 'The mid-Holocene *Ulmus* fall at Diss Mere, South-East England disease and human impact?', *Vegetation History and Archaeobotany* 2, 61–8.

Peterken, G. F. (1996), *Natural Woodland. Ecology and Conservation in Northern Temperate Regions*, Cambridge University Press.

Petersen, P. V. (1984), 'Chronological and regional variation in the Late Mesolithic of Eastern Denmark', *J. Danish Archaeol.* 3, 7–18.

Pickett, S. T. A. and White, P. S. (eds) (1985), *The Ecology of Natural Disturbance and Patch Dynamics*, Orlando, FL: Academic Press.

Piggott, C. D. and Piggott, M. E. (1963), 'Late-glacial and post-glacial deposits at Malham, Yorkshire', *New Phytol.* 62, 317–34.

Pott, R. (1989), 'The effects of wood pasture on vegetation', *Plants Today* (September–October issue), 170–5.

Prentice, I. C. (1985), 'Pollen representation, source area and basin size: toward a unified theory of pollen analysis', *Quaternary Research* 23, 76–86.

Price, M. D. R. and Moore, P. D. (1984), 'Pollen dispersion in the hills of Wales: a pollen shed hypothesis', *Pollen et Spores* 26, 127–36.

Price, T. D. (1978), 'Mesolithic settlement systems in the Netherlands', in P. A. Mellars (ed.) *The Early Postglacial Settlement of Northern Europe. An Ecological perspective*, London: Duckworth, 81–113.

Price, T. D. (1981), 'Regional approaches to human adaptation in the Mesolithic of the North European Plain', in B. Gramsch (ed.), *Mesolithikum in Europa*, 2nd International Symposium, Potsdam, 3–8 April 1978: Veröffentlichungen des Museums für Ur- und Frühgeschichte Potsdam 14/15, 217–34.

Price, T. D. (1989), 'The reconstruction of Mesolithic diets' in C. Bonsall (ed.), *The Mesolithic in Europe*, Edinburgh: John Donald, 48–59.

Rackham, O. (1988), 'Trees and woodland in a crowded landscape the cultural landscape of the British Isles', in H. H. Birks, H. J. B. Birks, P. E. Kaland and D. Moe (eds), *The Cultural Landscape – Past, Present and Future*, Cambridge University Press, 53–77.

Radley, J. and Marshall, G. (1963), 'Mesolithic sites in South-west Yorkshire', *Yorks. Arch. J.* 41, 81–97.

Radley, J. and Mellars, P. A. (1964), 'A Mesolithic structure at Deepcar, Yorkshire, England, and the affinities of its associated flint industries', *Proc. Prehist. Soc.* 30, 1–24.

Radley, J., Tallis, J. H. and Switsur, V. R. (1974), 'The excavation of three "narrow blade" Mesolithic sites in the Southern Pennines, England', *Proc. Prehist. Soc.* 40, 1–19.

Rajala, E. and Westergren, E. (1990), 'Tingby – a Mesolithic site with the remains of a house, to the west of Kalmar, in the province of Småland', *Meddelanden från Lunds Universitets Historiska Museum* 1989–90 new series 8, 5–30.

Ralska-Jasiewiczowa, M. and van Geel, B. (1992), 'Early disturbance of the natural environment recorded in annually laminated sediments of Lake Gościąż', *Vegetation History and Archaeobotany* 1, 33–42.

Rasmussen, P. (1989), 'Leaf-foddering of livestock in the Neolithic:

archaeobotanical evidence from Weier, Switzerland', *J. Danish Archaeol.* 8, 51–71.

Rasmussen, P. (1990a), 'Pollarding of trees in the Neolithic: often presumed – difficult to prove', in D. E. Robinson (ed.), *Experimentation and Reconstruction in Environmental Archaeology*, Oxford: Oxbow Books, 77–99.

Rasmussen, P. (1990b), 'Leaf-foddering in the earliest Neolithic agriculture. Evidence from Switzerland and Denmark', *Acta Archaeologia* 60, 71–86.

Rasmussen, P. (1993), 'Analysis of goat/sheep faeces from Egolzwil 3, Switzerland: evidence for branch and twig foddering in the Neolithic', *J. Archaeol Sci.* 20, 479–502.

Renouf, M. A. P. (1984), 'Northern coastal hunter-fishers. An archaeological model', *World Archaeology* 16, 18–2.

Richards, K. S. (1981), 'Evidence of Flandrian valley alluviation in Staindale, North York Moors', *Earth Surface Processes and Landforms* 6, 183–6.

Richards, K. S., Peters, N. R., Robertson-Rintoul, M. S. E. and Switsur, V. R. (1987), 'Recent valley sediments in the North York Moors: evidence and interpretation', in V. Gardner (ed.), *International Geomorphology 1986, Part I*, Chichester: Wiley, 869–83.

Riches, D. (1982), *Northern Nomadic Hunter-Gatherers. A Humanistic Approach*, London: Academic Press.

Roberts, N. (1989), *The Holocene. An Environmental History*, Oxford: Blackwell.

Rodwell, J. S. (ed.) (1991a), *British Plant Communities*, vol. 1, *Woodlands and Scrub*, Cambridge University Press.

Rodwell, J. S. (ed.) (1991b), *British Plant Communities*, vol. 2, *Mires and Heaths*, Cambridge University Press.

Rowley-Conwy, P. (1983), 'Sedentary hunters: the Ertbølle example', in G. Bailey (ed.), *Hunter-Gatherer Economy in Prehistory. A European Perspective*, Cambridge University Press, 111–26.

Rowley-Conwy, P. (1984), 'The laziness of the short-distance hunter: the origins of agriculture in Western Denmark', *J. Anth. Archaeol.* 3, 300–24.

Rowley-Conwy, P. (1993), 'Season and reason: the case for a regional interpretation of Mesolithic settlement patterns', in G. L. Peterkin, H. Bricker and P. Mellars (eds), *Hunting and Animal Exploitation in the Later Palaeolithic and Mesolithic of Eurasia*, Archaeological Papers of the American Anthropological Association 4, 179–88.

Rowley-Conwy, P. (1995), 'Making first farmers younger: the West European evidence', *Current Anthropology* 36, 346–53.

Rozoy, J. G. (1978), *Les Deniers Chasseurs*, Rheims: Soc. Archaeol. Champenoise, 3 vols.

Runkle, J. R. (1985), 'Disturbance regimes in temperate forests', in S. T. A. Pickett and P. S. White (eds), *The Ecology of Natural Disturbance and Patch Dynamics*, Orlando, FL: Academic Press, 17–33.

Russell, E. W. S. (1983), 'Indian-set fires in the forests of the
     northeastern United States', *Ecology* 64, 78–88.

Sakellaridis, M. (1979), *The Mesolithic and Neolithic of the Swiss Area*,
     Oxford: British Archaeological Reports International Series 67.
Shaw, T. (1969), 'Tree felling by fire', *Antiquity* 43, 52.
Simmons, I. G. (1964), 'Pollen diagrams from Dartmoor', *New
     Phytol.* 53, 164–80.
Simmons, I. G. (1969), 'Pollen diagrams from the North York
     Moors', *New Phytol.* 68, 807–27.
Simmons, I. G. (1990), 'The mid-Holocene ecological history of
     the moorlands of England and Wales and its significance for
     conservation', *Environmental Conservation* 17, 61–9.
Simmons, I. G. (1995), 'The evolution of the early human environment',
     in B. Vyner (ed.), *Moorland Monuments: Studies in the Archaeology
     of North-east Yorkshire in Honour of Raymond Hayes and Don Spratt*,
     London: CBA Research Report 101, 5–15.
Simmons, I. G., Atherden, M. A., Cundill, P. R. and Jones, R. L.
     (1975), 'Inorganic inwash layers in the soligenous mires of the
     North York Moors', *J. Biogeogr.* 2, 47–56.
Simmons, I. G. and Cundill, P. R. (1974), 'Late Quaternary vegetational
     history of the North York Moors. II. Pollen analyses of landslip
     bogs', *J. Biogeogr.* 1, 253–61.
Simmons, I. G., Cundill, P. R. and Jones, R. L. (1979), 'Archaeology
     and palaeobotany on the North York Moors and their environs',
     Yorks. Archaeol. J. 51, 15–22.
Simmons, I. G. and Innes, J. B. (1981), 'Tree remains in a North
     York Moors peat profile', *Nature*, 294, 191–3.
Simmons, I. G. and Innes, J. B. (1987), 'Mid-Holocene adaptations
     and later Mesolithic disturbance in northern England', *J. Archaeol.
     Sci.* 14, 1–20.
Simmons, I. G. and Innes, J. B. (1988a), 'Late Quaternary vegetational
     history of the North York Moors. VIII. Correlation of Flandrian
     II litho- and pollen stratigraphy at North Gill, Glaisdale Moor',
     J. Biogeogr. 15, 249–72.
Simmons, I. G. and Innes, J. B. (1988b), 'Late Quaternary vegetational
     history of the North York Moors. X. Investigations on EastBilsdale
     Moor', *J. Biogeogr.* 15, 299–324.
Simmons, I. G. and Innes, J. B. (1988c), 'The later Mesolithic period
     (6000–5000 bp) on Glaisdale Moor, North Yorkshire', *Archaeol.
     J.* 145, 1–12.
Simmons, I. G. and Innes, J. B. (1996a), 'Disturbance phases in peat
     profiles at North Gill, North York Moors: form and process', *J.
     Archaeol. Sci.* 23, 183–91.
Simmons, I. G. and Innes, J. B. (1996b), 'Prehistoric charcoal in peat
     profiles at North Gill, North Yorkshire, England', *J. Archaeol. Sci.*
     23, 193–7.

Simmons, I. G. and Innes, J. B. (1996c), 'An episode of prehistoric canopy manipulation at North Gill, North Yorkshire, England', *J. Archaeol. Sci.* 23, 337–41.

Simmons, I. G., Rand, J. I. and Crabtree, K. (1983), 'A further pollen analytical study of the Blacklane peat section on Dartmoor, England', *New Phytol.* 94, 655–67.

Simmons, I. G., Rand, J. I. and Crabtree, K. (1987), 'Dozmary Pool, Bodmin Moor, Cornwall: a new radiocarbon dated pollen profile', in N. D. Balaam, B. Levitan and V. Straker (eds), *Studies in Palaeoeconomy and Environment in South West England*, Oxford: British Archaeological Reports British Series 181, 125–33.

Simmons, I. G., Turner, J. and Innes, J. B. (1989), 'An application of fine-resolution pollen analysis to later Mesolithic peats of an English upland', in C. Bonsall (ed.), *The Mesolithic in Europe*, Edinburgh: John Donald, 206–17.

Smith, A. G. (1970), 'The influence of Mesolithic and Neolithic man on British vegetation', in D. Walker and R. G. West (eds), *Studies in the Vegetational History of the British Isles*, Cambridge University Press, 81–96.

Smith, A. G. (1984), 'Newferry and the Boreal-Atlantic transition', *New Phytol.* 98, 35–55.

Smith, A. G. and Cloutman, E. W. (1988), 'Reconstruction of Holocene vegetation history in three dimensions at Waun-Fignen-Felen, an upland site in South Wales', *Phil. Trans. Roy. Soc. Lond.* B 322, 159–219.

Smith, A. G., Whittle, A., Cloutman, E. W. and Morgan, L. A. (1989), 'Mesolithic and Neolithic activity and environmental impact on the South-east fen-edge in Cambridgeshire', *Proc. Prehist. Soc.* 55, 207–49.

Smith, C. (1992a), *Late Stone Age Hunters of the British Isles*, London and New York: Routledge.

Smith, C. (1992b), 'The population of Late Upper Palaeolithic and Mesolithic Britain', *Proc. Prehist. Soc.* 58, 37–40.

Smith, K., Coppen, J., Wainwright, G. J. and Beckett, S. (1981), 'The Shaugh Moor project: third report – settlement and environmental investigations', *Proc. Prehist. Soc.* 47, 205–74.

Smith, R. T. (1986), 'Aspects of the soil and vegetation history of the Craven District of Yorkshire', in T. G. Manby and P. Turnbull (eds), *Archaeology in the Pennines*, Oxford: British Archaeological Reports British Series 158, 3–28.

Smith, R. T. and Taylor, J. A. (1989), 'Biopedological processes in the inception of peat formation', *International Peat J.* 3, 1–24.

Spratt, D. A. (ed.) (1993), *Prehistoric and Roman Archaeology of North-East Yorkshire*, London: CBA Research Report no. 87.

Spratt, D. A., Goddard, R. E. and Brown, D. R. (1976), 'Mesolithic settlement sites at Upleatham, Cleveland', *Yorks. Archaeol. J.* 48, 19–26.

Spratt, D. A. and Simmons, I. G. (1976), 'Prehistoric activity and environment on the North York Moors', *J. Archaeol. Sci.* 3, 193–210.

Squires, R. H. (1970), 'A contribution to the vegetational history of Upper Teesdale', Ph.D. thesis, University of Durham.

Squires, R. H. (1971), 'Flandrian history of the Teesdale rarities', *Nature* 229, 43–4.

Squires, R. H. (1978), 'Conservation in Upper Teesdale: contributions from the palaeoecological record', *Trans. Inst. Brit. Geogr.* (new series) 3, 129–50.

Stockmarr, J. (1975), 'Retrogressive forest development, as reflected in a mor pollen diagram from Mantingerbos, Drenthe, the Netherlands', *Palaeohistoria* 17, 37–51.

Stonehouse, P. B. (1987/88), 'Mesolithic sites on the Pennine watershed', *Greater Manchester Archaeol. J.* 3, 5–17.

Stonehouse, P. B. (1990), 'Some Mesolithic sites in the central Pennines: comments on 23 years of field work', *Manchester Archaeol. Bull.* 5, 58–64.

Stonehouse, P. B. (1992), 'Two early Mesolithic sites in the central Pennines', *Yorks Archaeol. J.* 64, 1–15.

Straus, L. G. (1981), 'On the habitat and diet of *Cervus elaphus*', *Munibe* 33, 175–82.

Stuiver, M. and Reimer, P. J. (1993), 'Extended C-14 data-base and revised Calib 3.0 calibration program'; *Radiocarbon* 35, 215–30.

Switsur, V. R. and Jacobi, R. (1979), 'A radiocarbon chronology for the early postglacial stone industries of England and Wales', in R. Berger and H. E. Suess (eds), *Radiocarbon Dating*, Berkeley and Los Angeles: University of California Press, 41–68.

Tallis, J. H. (1975), 'Tree remains in southern Pennine peats', *Nature* 256, 482–4.

Tallis, J. H. (1991), 'Forest and moorland in the South Pennine uplands in the mid-Flandrian period. III. The spread of moorland – local, regional and national', *J. Ecol.* 79, 401–15.

Tallis, J. H. and Switsur, V. R. (1983), 'Forest and moorland in the south Pennine uplands in the mid-Flandrian period. I. Macrofossil evidence of the former forest cover', *J. Ecol.* 71, 585–600.

Tallis, J. H. and Switsur, V. R. (1990); 'Forest and moorland in the south Pennine uplands in the mid-Flandrian period. II. The hillslope forests', *J. Ecol.* 78, 857–83.

Tauber, H. (1977), 'Investigations of aerial pollen transport in a forested area', *Dansk Botanisk Archiv* 32 (1), 1–121.

Taylor, J. A. (1975); 'The role of climatic factors in environmental and cultural changes in prehistoric times', in J. G. Evans, S. J. Limbrey and H. Cleere (eds), *The Effect of Man on the Landscape: The Highland Zone*, London: CBA Research Report no. 11 6–19.

Taylor, J. A. (1980), 'Environmental changes in Wales during the Holocene period', in idem (ed.), *Culture and Environment in*

Prehistoric Wales, Oxford: British Archaeological Reports British Series 76, 101–30.

Taylor, J. A. and Smith, R. T. (1980), 'The role of pedogenic factors in the initiation of peat formation, and in the classification of mires', *Proc. 6th Int. Peat Congress*, Duluth, 109–17.

Thompson, D. A. (1971), 'Lightning fires in Galloway, June 1970', *Scottish Forestry* 25, 51–2.

Thompson, D. Q. and Smith, R. H. (1977), 'The forest primeval in the northeast – a great myth?', *Proc. Ann. Tall Timbers Fire Ecology Conf.* 10, 255–65.

Tilley, C. Y. (1979), *Post-Glacial Communities in the Cambridge Region*, Oxford: British Archaeological Reports British Series 66.

Tilley, C. Y. (1994), *A Phenomenology of Landscape*, Oxford and Providence, RI: Berg Press.

Tinsley, H. M. (1975), 'The former woodland of the Nidderdale Moors (Yorkshire) and the role of early man in its decline', *J. Ecol.* 63, 1–26.

Tinsley, H. M. and Smith, R. T. (1974), 'Surface pollen studies across a woodland/heath transition and their application to the interpretation of pollen diagrams', *New Phytol.* 73, 547–65.

Tipping, R. (1992), 'The determination of cause in the generation of major valley fills in the Cheviot Hills, Anglo-Scottish border', in S. Needham and M. C. Macklin (eds), *Alluvial Archaeology in Britain*, Oxford: Oxbow Monographs 27, 111–21.

Tooley, M. J. (1978), *Sea-Level Changes in North-West England during the Flandrian Stage*, Oxford: Clarendon Press.

Turner, C. (1970a), 'Der Einschluß großer Mammalier auf die interglaciale Vegetation', *Quartärpaläontologie* 1, 13–19.

Turner, C. (1970b), 'The Middle Pleistocene deposits at Mark's Tey, Essex', *Phil. Trans. Roy. Soc. Lond.* B 257, 373–437.

Turner, J. (1984), 'Pollen diagrams from Cross Fell and their implication for former tree-lines', in E. Y. Haworth and J. W. G. Lund (eds) *Lake Sediments and Environmental History*, Leicester: Leicester University Press, 317–57.

Turner, J., Hewetson, V., Hibbert, F. A., Lowry, K. H. and Chambers, C. (1973), 'The history of the vegetation and flora of Widdybank Fell and the Cow Green reservoir basin, Upper Teesdale', *Phil. Trans. Roy. Soc. Lond.* B 265, 327–408.

Turner, J. and Hodgson, J. (1979), 'Studies in the vegetational history of the Northern Pennines. I. Variations in the composition of the early Flandrian forests', *J. Ecol.* 67, 629–46.

Turner, J. and Hodgson, J. (1983), 'Studies in the vegetational history of the northern Pennines. III. Variations in the composition of the mid-Flandrian forests', *J. Ecol.* 71, 95–118.

Turner, J., Innes, J. B. and Simmons, I. G. (1993), 'Spatial diversity in the vegetation history of North Gill, North Yorkshire', *New Phytol.* 123, 599–647.

Turner, J., Simmons, I. G. and Innes, J. B. (1989), 'Two pollen diagrams from the same site', *New Phytol.* 113, 409–16.

van Wijngaarden-Bakker, L. H. (1989), 'Faunal remains and the Irish mesolithic', in C. Bonsall (ed.), *The Mesolithic in Europe*, Edinburgh: John Donald, 125–33.

Vermeersch, P. M. and van Peer, P. (eds) (1990), *Contributions to the Mesolithic in Europe*, Leuven/Louvain: Leuven University Press.

Walker, D. (1956), 'A site at Stump Cross, near Grassington, Yorkshire, and the age of the Pennine microlithic industry', *Proc. Prehist. Soc.* 22, 23–8.

Walker, M. J. C. (1982), 'Early and mid-Flandrian environmental history of the Brecon Beacons, South Wales', *New Phytol.* 91, 147–65.

Walker, M. J. C. and Austin, D. (1985), 'Redhill Marsh: a site of possible Mesolithic activity on Bodmin Moor, Cornwall', *Cornish Archaeology* 24, 15–21.

Walker, R. (1978), 'Diatom and pollen studies of a sediment profile from Melynllyn, a mountain tarn in Snowdonia, North Wales', *New Phytol.* 81, 791–804.

Watanabe, H. (1972), 'The Ainu', in M. G. Bicchieri (ed.), *Hunters and Gatherers Today*, New York: Holt, Rinehart and Winston, 448–84.

Wein, R. M., Burzynski, M. P., Sreenivasa, B. A. and Tolonen, K. (1987), 'Bog profile evidence of fire and vegetation dynamics since 3000 years BP in the Acadian forest', *Canadian J. Botany* 65/66, 1, 180–6.

Welinder, S. (1989), 'Mesolithic forest clearance in Scandinavia', in C. Bonsall (ed.), *The Mesolithic in Europe*, Edinburgh: John Donald, 362–6.

White, R. (1989), 'Husbandry and herd control in the Upper Palaeolithic', *Current Anthropology* 30, 609–32.

Williams, C. T. (1985), *Mesolithic Exploitations in the Central Pennines. A Palynological Study of Soyland Moor*, British Archaeological Reports British Series 139.

Williams, D. J., Richardson, J. A. and Richardson, R. S. (1987), 'Mesolithic sites at Malham Tarn and Great Close Mire, North Yorkshire', *Proc. Prehist. Soc.* 53, 362–83.

Williams, E. (1987), 'Complex hunter-gatherers: a view from Australia', *Antiquity* 81, 310–21.

Williams, E. (1989), 'Dating the introduction of food production into Britain and Ireland', *Antiquity* 63, 510–21.

Wilson, P. R. (ed.) (1988), *North-East Yorkshire Studies: Archaeological papers by Raymond H. Hayes* MBE FSA, Leeds: Yorkshire Archaeological Society, 1–27.

Wiltshire, P. E. J. and Edwards, K. J. (1993), 'Mesolithic, early

Neolithic and later prehistoric impacts on vegetation at a riverine site in Derbyshire, England', in F. M. Chambers (ed.), *Climate Change and Human Impact on the Landscape*, London: Chapman and Hall, 157–68.

Wiltshire, P. E. J. and Moore, P. D. (1983), 'Palaeovegetation and palaeohydrology in upland Britain', in K. J. Gregory (ed.), *Background to Palaeohydrology. A Perspective*, Chichester: Wiley, 433–51.

Wobst, H. M. (1974), 'Boundary conditions for paleolithic social systems', *American Antiquity* 39, 147–78.

Woodman, P. C. (1985), *Excavations at Mt Sandel 1973–77*, Archaeological Research Monographs No. 2, Belfast.

Woodman, P. C. and Andersen, E. (1990), 'The Irish Later Mesolithic: a partial picture', in P. M. Vermeersch and P. van Peer (eds), *Contributions to the Mesolithic in Europe*, Leuven University Press, 377–87.

Yesner, D. R. (1980), 'Maritime hunter-gatherers: ecology and prehistory', *Current Anthropology* 21, 727–50.

Young, R. (1987), *Lithics and Subsistence in North-Eastern England. Aspects of the Prehistoric Archaeology of the Wear Valley. Co Durham, from the Mesolithic to the Bronze Age*, Oxford: British Archaeological Reports British Series 161.

Zvelebil, M. (1994), 'Plant use in the Mesolithic and its role in the transition to farming', *Proc. Prehist. Soc.* 60, 35–74.

Zvelebil, M. and Dolukhanov, P. (1991), 'The transition to farming in Eastern and Northern Europe', *J. World Prehistory* 5, 233–78.

Zvelebil, M. and Rowley-Conwy, P. (1984), 'Transition to farming in Northern Europe: a hunter-gatherer perspective', *Norwegian Archaeological Review* 17, 104–28.

COMPILATIONS OF SPECIAL INTEREST

The following books and edited collections each contain a particular density of material germane to the themes of the present work.

Atherden, M. A. (1992), *Upland Britain. A Natural History*, Manchester University Press.

Bailey, G. (ed.) (1983), *Hunter-Gatherer Economy in Prehistory. A European Perspective*, Cambridge University Press.

Bell, M. and Limbrey, S. J. (eds) (1982), *Archaeological Aspects of Woodland Ecology*, Oxford: British Archaeological Reports International Series 146.

Bonsall, C. (ed.) (1989), *The Mesolithic in Europe*, Edinburgh: John Donald.

Chambers, F. M. (ed.) (1993), *Climate Change and Human Impact on the Landscape*, London: Chapman and Hall.

DARVILL, T. (ED.) (1986), *The Archaeology of the Uplands: A Rapid Assessment of Archaeological Knowledge and Practice*, London: RCHM/CBA.

Evans, J. G., Limbrey, S. and Cleere, H. (eds) (1975), *The Effect of Man on the Landscape: The Highland Zone*, London: CBA Research Report no. 11.

Falinski, J. B. (1986), *Vegetation Dynamics in Temperate Lowland Primeval Forests. Ecological Studies in Białowieza Forest*, Dordrecht: Junk. Geobotany 8.

Jones, M. (ed.) (1988), *Archaeology and the Flora of the British Isles. Human Influence upon the Evolution of Plant Communities*, Oxford University Committee for Archaeology Monograph no. 14; BSBI Conference Report no. 19.

Mellars, P. A. (ed.) (1978), *The Early Postglacial Settlement of Northern Europe. An Ecological Perspective*, London: Duckworth.

Nicholas, G. P. (ed.) (1988), *Holocene Human Ecology in Northeastern North America*, London and New York: Plenum Books.

Price, T. D. and Brown, J. A. (eds) (1985), *Prehistoric Hunter-Gatherers. The Emergence of Cultural Complexity*, New York: Academic Press.

Rowley-Conwy, P., Zvelebil, M. and Blankholm, H. P. (eds) (1987), *Mesolithic Northwest Europe: Recent Trends*, University of Sheffield Department of Archaeology and Prehistory Recent Trends Series vol. 2.

Smith, C. (1992), *Late Stone Age Hunters of the British Isles*, London and New York: Routledge.

Usher, M. B. and Thompson, D. B. A. (eds) (1988), *Ecological Change in the Uplands*, Oxford: Blackwell Scientific Publications; British Ecological Society Special Publication no. 7.

Index

Note: Authors' names are indexed where their work is described or discussed but not where they are merely cited in the text without comment. The names of individual sites are indexed thoroughly throughout, but not their palaeoecology: subject entries are largely confined to general statements and conclusions. Animal and plant species appear if singled out for special mention in the text. Page references in *italics* relate to tables, figures and plates.